Community Counseling

Judith A. Lewis
Michael D. Lewis

Governors State University

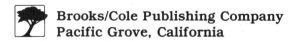 Brooks/Cole Publishing Company
Pacific Grove, California

Brooks/Cole Publishing Company
A Division of Wadsworth, Inc.

Printed in the United States of America

10 9 8 7 6 5 4 3 2 1

Library of Congress Cataloging-in-Publication Data

Lewis, Judith A.
    Community counseling.

    Includes bibliographies and index.
    1. Mental health services.   2. Counseling.   I. Lewis,
Michael D.   II. Title.
RA790.5.L478   362.2′2   89-15787
ISBN 0-534-10248-4

Sponsoring Editor: *Claire Verduin*
Marketing Representative: *Thomas L. Braden*
Editorial Assistant: *Gay C. Bond*
Production Editor: *Penelope Sky*
Manuscript Editor: *Lynne Y. Fletcher*
Permissions Editor: *Carline Haga*
Interior and Cover Design: *Roy R. Neuhaus*
Cover Photo: *Norman Prince*
Cover Photo Research: *Sue C. Howard*
Art Coordinator: *Lisa Torri*
Interior Illustration: *Lisa Torri*
Typesetting: *Bookends, Ashland, Oregon*
Cover Printing: *Phoenix Color Corporation, Long Island City, New York*
Printing and Binding: *Arcata Graphics, Fairfield, Pennsylvania*

To Keith M. Lewis

Preface

People who are involved in the work of helping others have begun to sense a need for change. Increasingly, counselors have come to realize that they have a role to play, not just in helping individuals, but in affecting whole communities. They have become aware that the kinds of services they offer must meet the unique needs of both their clients and their communities. They have learned that the best kind of help is self-help derived from the strengths inherent in each individual and in each community.

We first coined the term "community counseling" well over a decade ago. At that time, we developed a multifaceted approach that focused on prevention and encouraged counselors to use a combination of direct services and environmental interventions to meet community needs. Today, community counseling remains innovative, but it is far from untried. More and more counselors have implemented real-life programs that reflect the multifaceted model that we describe in this book. Thus, we have been able to include within these covers both general guidelines for community counseling and numerous examples of effective practice.

In Chapter 1 we provide an overview of the community counseling model and describe several programs that share the same multifaceted orientation despite their widely varying settings and clientele. Next, we focus on direct services to clients and communities, describing broadly based programs of preventive education in Chapter 2, the special needs of vulnerable client populations in Chapter 3, and the implications of the community counseling model for direct, one-to-one counseling in Chapter 4. Then we examine environmental approaches, presenting a case for intervention in social policy issues in Chapter 5, and delineating the counselor's role in client advocacy in Chapter 6. Finally, in Chapter 7 we show counselors how to apply the multifaceted model in diverse settings, and in Chapter 8 we recommend ways of planning and managing their programs most effectively. We hope that counselors and other human service professionals who read this book will use it as a basis for their own work. It is their creativity and that of their communities that will bring their programs to life.

Many people have already succeeded in developing and implementing effective community counseling programs. We appreciate the effort and generosity of the community counselors who allowed us to describe their exemplary programs here. We also appreciate the thoughtful and constructive suggestions made by Richard Hayes, Bradley University; Richard J. Malnati, Temple University; and Robert Newbrough, Vanderbilt University, who reviewed drafts of this text. Brad Gumbert and David Kleist, graduate assistants at Governors State University, were very helpful in the final stages of production. As always, the staff at Brooks/Cole was talented and professional. Special thanks go to Claire Verduin for her encouragement of this project, and to Penelope Sky for her incredible patience, consistency, and support.

Judith A. Lewis
Michael D. Lewis

Contents

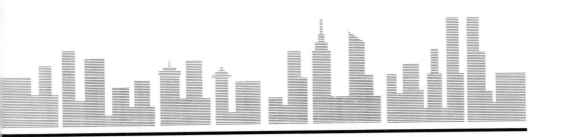

Community Counseling

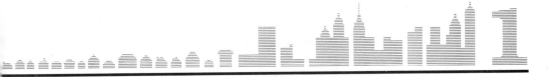

The Community Counseling Model: An Introduction

At a Midwest mental health center, participants in popular workshops learn to cope with unemployment, manage chronic stress, adjust to change, or beat the holiday blues.

At a suburban youth counseling center, young people study community issues, explore their rights and responsibilities as students, and learn to monitor and influence legislation that concerns them.

On a New England college campus, students benefit from a substance-abuse program that supplements counseling services with such preventive measures as the "Late Night Local," a free transportation service between the university and the city.

In a Western City, disabled people run a community-based agency formed to help themselves and other disabled community members live independently.

At a center designed specifically to meet their needs, Vietnam veterans confront the interpersonal, emotional, and vocational problems brought on by the stressors of war.

Though the focus, setting, and clientele of each of these programs vary widely, each exemplifies the principles and values on which the community counseling model is based. Although community counselors may work in a wide variety of settings, they have a great deal in common. They share an awareness of the effects of the social environment on every community member. They share a perception of clients as whole persons with strengths and resources as well as deficits. They share a desire to prevent the debilitating problems they see before them every day. Above all, they share an understanding that individuals and communities alike can be helped most effectively by giving them the skills they need to help themselves.

Basic Assumptions

Though community counselors provide many types of services, underlying and shaping all their activities is a coherent set of assumptions:

1. People's environments may either nurture or limit them.
2. A multifaceted approach to helping is more efficient than a single-service approach.
3. Prevention is more efficient than remediation.
4. The community counseling model can be applied in any human service setting.

The Effect of the Environment

People interact with their surroundings constantly, in ways that may help them or harm them. As people grow and develop, they rely on the environment as a source of learning and support, meeting their individual needs chiefly through interaction with others. But the environment can also be a negative force, stunting growth and limiting development.

Because the environment affects people so significantly, community counselors know that trying to help people without also dealing with their social systems is ineffective. Rather, efforts to help individuals directly must constantly be supplemented by efforts to change the community in which they live.

Recognizing this, community counselors avoid making the *fundamental attribution error,* a common tendency to underestimate the influence of situational factors on human behavior and overestimate that of personal attributes.

Racial, economic, and social injustice force particular roles and circumstances on people, and problems which derive from these roles and circumstances are all too often regarded and treated as psychological in nature, emanating from mental deficits within the individual. The very phrase "mental illness" connotes a disease which must be treated by focusing one's ameliorative efforts on the individual. Psychologists, who have traditionally attributed the causes of mental disorders to the personal dispositions of their clients, have no doubt been unwitting perpetrators of the fundamental attribution error." (Strickland & Janoff-Bulman, 1980, pp. 105–106)

Environmental factors clearly contribute to the development of almost any kind of problem a client may face. Sometimes the connection is overt and definable: the adult denied vocational options because of racism or sexism, the child victimized by a destructive family environment, the ex-offender or chronically ill client denied free entry into the mainstream community. Just as often, however, problems that have their source in environmental factors have become so much a part of the person that their cause cannot be clearly attributed. In such cases, the individual may feel powerless or lack a sense of purpose, be unable to recognize alternatives and make decisions, feel trapped in highly restrictive roles and unrewarding interpersonal relationships, be unclear about his or her personal values, or feel that the community is hostile to his or her development. In fact, our modern environment may be hostile: the characteristics described above have reached epidemic proportions; we all share some of these uncomfortable feelings.

Yet, if the environment can work against an individual's growth, it can just as surely aid personal development. For example: people vary in their ability to cope with stressful events and situations, and at least some of this variation is due to differences in the degree and type of social support that is available (Cohen & Wills, 1985; Lin, Woelfel, & Light, 1985; Wethington & Kessler, 1986). An actively supportive social environment can therefore foster development by helping people cope more effectively with stress.

Because the environment affects people in so many ways, recognizing the impact of environmental factors such as social support is, for the community counselor, only a first step. As Cowen (1985a) has noted, "Social environments can either facilitate or restrict people's competence development and adaptation. . . . The de facto choice is either to accept such effects as they fall randomly or to develop and apply bodies of knowledge designed to promote psychologically facilitative microenvironments" (p. 38). The community counselor chooses the latter, working to make the community as a whole a psychologically safe and nurturing environment.

In discussing system-level approaches to the prevention of mental health problems, Cowen (1985a, 1985b) distinguished between *macrosocial reform,* which addresses the widespread social injustices at the root of many individual problems, and *microsocial change,* which addresses specific environments that directly shape the lives of their inhabitants. Community counselors involve themselves at both levels, exerting influence on broad-based social policies that affect the lives of their clients while working to change directly the organizations and institutions that are the microenvironments of the people they aim to serve.

A Multifaceted Approach to Helping

The community counselor uses a number of methods to help people, never relying on just one type of service. In contrast, conventional counselors have traditionally depended on one-to-one interaction with clients as their sole method of treatment. More and more, this model is being called into question.

Aubrey and Lewis (1983), for instance, described the failure of traditional counseling approaches to meet the needs of clients affected by the rapid social change that began in the 1960s.

> The perspective was myopic, concentrating on intrapsychic functioning to the exclusion of environmental influences. In turn, applications focused on individual self-discovery and insight when, for many, this process failed to alleviate the presenting condition. What seemed called for, therefore, was both a broadening of perspective and a wider array of intervention techniques. (p. 2)

Counselors responded to what was in fact a crisis in professional development by spending more time on group interventions and on education. Yet, many of the counselors taking this "evolutionary leap" seem to have kept one foot on the ground.

> Counselors have learned to feel comfortable dealing with groups, as well as with individuals. They have come to regard training as a natural ally of counseling. They have ventured into new settings and dealt with new audiences. Despite this increase in the number and focus of interventions, however, the basic perspective of counselors has not changed to the extent one might expect. Counselors still tend to overlook the impact of environmental factors on individual functioning, to distrust the efficacy of preventive interventions, and to narrow the scope of their attention to the individual psyche. (Aubrey & Lewis, 1983, p. 10)

To redress this problem, community counselors emphasize the variety of approaches that are appropriate to counseling work.

Furthermore, they highlight the efficacy of preventive efforts by making prevention a central component of the community counseling model.

Logic tells us that clients of one-to-one counseling come for assistance because of some immediate need. A counselor may be able to help such individuals, but, if one-to-one counseling is the only option offered, there is no way to reach people before the onset of problems. Such a narrow focus wastes human resources: to reach a large number of individuals, a small number of helpers must present the same kinds of services again and again. As the population that needs services grows, so does the need to consider programs that can reach large numbers of people, expand the pool of resources, share skills as widely as possible, and bring about changes in the social environment. Counselors need to use what D'Andrea (1984) calls "a multi-method framework wherein the counselor becomes a sort of architect. As an architect, in this sense, the counselor consciously designs and structures various experiences in ways aimed at maximizing the client's opportunity to develop psychologically, emotionally, cognitively, morally, and physically" (p. 7).

Emphasis on Prevention

The goal of prevention is to lower the incidence of a problem among the members of the population being served. Mental health professionals have borrowed from public health terminology to differentiate among *primary, secondary,* and *tertiary prevention.*

> Primary prevention . . . focuses on lowering the incidence of emotional problems and on promoting positive mental health among people not identified as having any special difficulty. It can be distinguished from secondary prevention, which aims toward early identification and prompt treatment of problems, and from tertiary prevention, which attempts to decrease the long-term effects of disabilities. In essence, primary prevention involves activities designed to reduce environmental stressors or to build people's competencies and life skills. (Lewis & Lewis, 1981, p. 173)

Primary prevention is central to the work of the community counselor. In community counseling, as in mental health, a preventive focus means developing programs that reach healthy persons and their communities. These programs are *proactive;* that is, they are the result of organizers taking forceful independent steps to initiate them. The President's Commission on Mental Health (1978) has listed the characteristics of primary prevention as follows:

1. Most fundamentally, primary prevention is proactive in that it seeks to build adaptive strengths, coping resources, and health in people; not to reduce or contain already manifest deficit.
2. Primary prevention is concerned about total populations, especially including groups at high risk; it is less oriented to individuals and to the provision of services on a case-by-case basis.
3. Primary prevention's main tools and models are those of education and social engineering, not therapy or rehabilitation, although some insights for its models and programs grow out of the wisdom derived from clinical experience.
4. Primary prevention assumes that equipping people with personal and environmental resources for coping is the best of all ways to ward off maladaptive problems, not trying to deal (however skillfully) with problems that have already germinated and flowered. (p. 1833)

If one examines human services planning in long-range terms, it becomes apparent that preventing problems allows helpers to reallocate resources according to logical priorities. Instead of basing their objectives on current crises, community counselors and their communities can outline goals and then develop the resources and methods most appropriate for accomplishing them.

Fortunately, the knowledge base on which preventive programs can be built is growing at a steady pace (Conyne, 1987; Cowen, 1983; Felner, Jason, Moritsugu, & Farber, 1983; Price, Bader, & Ketterer, 1980).

> The knowledge base for prevention comes from insights of clinicians, prevention research, epidemiological and biomedical research, and the behavioral sciences. To prevent mental-emotional disabilities, attention must be given to organic and biological factors, the development of competence and coping skills, social support, the relationship of stressors to the development of disorders and the context and interrelationships of these factors. . . . The guiding principles for developing preventive interventions are the reduction of undue stressors and the development of competencies and support. (National Mental Health Association [NMHA] Commission on the Prevention of Mental-Emotional Disabilities, 1986, p. 1)

Preventive programs may involve *direct* services, offering individuals opportunities to participate in competency-building experiences. Services may also be *indirect;* that is, they may focus on changing the social surroundings that affect people's lives. No matter which approach is used, if a program is meant to serve a population that has not been identified as having developed a specific problem or dysfunction, it is preventive, rather than remedial. Community counselors can combine direct and indirect services to meet the needs of the population being served, regardless of the setting in which they work. And they should: "The human and financial burden of mental-emotional disabilities makes prevention imperative. The growing knowledge base makes prevention efforts feasible" (NMHA Commission on the Prevention of Mental-Emotional Disabilities, 1986, p. 7).

The Applicability of the Community Counseling Model

Anyone offering psychological, social, educational, or vocational services to individuals or groups has a responsibility to some community. This is obvious to a worker in a community mental health center, whose clients reside within a geographically defined area and who has a clear mandate to identify community needs. It is less obvious where the nature of the community is not well defined. School counselors who emphasize the interplay between the individual and the environment, for instance, are, in effect, community counselors.

In a complex and highly mobile society, to think of community solely in geographical terms may be obsolete. For the purpose of this book, we define *community* as a system of interdependent persons, groups, and organizations that (1) meets the individual's primary needs, (2) affects the individual's daily life, and (3) mediates between the individual and society as a whole.

That the community is a *system* means that it has unity and continuity. Members can therefore learn to predict its responses. That the individuals, groups, and organizations making up a community are *interdependent* means that they are all linked, both affecting and being affected by one another. The community also links individuals with society as a whole. Thus, the community serves as a medium through which individuals can act on the world and through which society as a whole transmits its norms—that is, its behavioral expectations—to the individual.

Under this working definition, a neighborhood can be a community, as can a school, a hospital, or a corporation. Accordingly, an individual may be a member of more than one community at a time. In any case, the presence and power of community is such that anyone working with individuals as a helper must, at some point, examine the effects of a community on clients' behavior and the impact of individuals on their environment.

The Role of the Community Counselor

The assumptions on which the community counseling model is based require practitioners to find new ways of operating. Each assumption implies some change in the counselor's attitudes and actions. Each requires the counselor to develop new ways of organizing services. Each calls for the counselor to take on roles that may extend beyond what professional helpers have traditionally been trained to do.

The Individual and the Environment

Accepting that the social environment affects every individual, either enhancing or stunting personal and social development, alters both counselors' activities and their view of themselves as service providers.

For example, assessing the relationship between the client and his or her social system adds new dimension to the interaction between the counselor and the individual client. In traditional, one-to-one counseling relationships, counselors help clients examine their behavior, take responsibility for their actions, and change that which can most easily be changed: themselves. Community counselors take these activities a step further, seeing the environment not as a static reality to which adjustment must be made but as a dynamic structure that—like the client—can be changed. The counselor and the client together explore the following questions:

1. To what extent is the individual capable of resolving the issue through personal change?
2. What resources in the environment are available to help the individual grow?
3. To what extent does the solution depend on changing the environment, rather than on changing the individual?
4. How can the counselor, the client, or both bring about necessary changes in the environment?

The counselor also considers these questions in collective terms, examining the interaction between the community and all of its members. With practice, the counselor can learn to recognize factors that might limit the growth of a number of current or potential clients. Becoming aware of these forces is easy when a number of clients present problems exacerbated by a common set of environmental factors. More difficult, but just as important, is sensing the potential for such problems before they arise, being so attuned to what is going on within a community that action can be taken before casualties begin to appear.

Working to bring about positive change in the community is a key part of the community counselor's role. Because this task also involves discovering and cultivating positive forces in the environment, the community counselor needs, in addition to the strength and the skill to confront that which is limiting, the sensitivity to recognize and foster that which holds the promise of health.

The Multifaceted Approach

The multifaceted approach taken in community counseling challenges practitioners to develop new skills. The community counselor must learn to deal with large groups as well as individuals, to become an educator as well as a counselor, and to deal with the environment as well as the affected person. Letting go of the familiar is not always easy, however.

> [There is] a tendency for human service deliverers to concentrate more on the nature of the services being delivered than on the ultimate purposes of these services. Familiar methods are often used long after changes in community needs or agency mission should have dictated changes in professional services. (Lewis & Lewis, 1983, p. 21)

Carver (1979) put it more strongly: "It certainly is not an overstatement to observe that clinicians are primadonnas who . . . fervently believe that their method of training and legitimacy are their products, not the degree to which they are effective in producing results" (p. 3).

Community counselors recognize that they need to have a variety of resources and techniques available to them. To meet the needs of their clientele, they must develop expertise in areas that go beyond their formal training. They become perpetual learners, developing new skills in consultation, advocacy, and planning to meet needs as they arise.

If that which counselors know best how to do—helping individual clients gain insight—could be counted on to meet the real needs of the community, the task would be much easier. Because such is not the case, however, counselors must continually evolve and change. Such growth should be tempered by an awareness of individual limitations. As community counselors expand their skills in new areas, they must also learn to recognize expertise in other people—professional or non-professional. Instead of counting on themselves to be super-persons, they can develop and work in interdependent teams, leading when it is necessary, following when it is not.

Emphasis on Prevention

Community counseling's emphasis on healthy development and on the prevention of problems calls for a continually fresh perspective on problems and their potential solutions. Community counselors must see beyond the problems themselves to perceive the factors that contribute to their cause. Though a more traditional approach might treat dysfunctions as belonging to individuals and though community counselors certainly work with individuals in trouble, a preventive model like that of community counseling evaluates dysfunctions in the context of a larger system. Prevention implies bringing about changes in the community, rather than concentrating on the victims of the system—who can be helped only if the right remedy can be found.

This emphasis on prevention makes community counseling highly active. There can be no passive waiting for the next task, the next problem, the next crisis to appear. Instead, practitioners continually watch for situations in which they can be of help, planning and initiating new programs to meet specific needs.

From Model Concept to Model Program

Having examined the assumptions underlying community counseling and their implications for the role of the counselor, we can begin to define the model in more specific and concrete terms. *Community counseling* can be defined as a multifaceted approach combining direct and indirect services to help community members live more effectively and to prevent the problems most frequently faced by those who use the services.

Although community counselors clearly need to be creative and flexible in their approach, they do not lack guidelines for action. The activities that make up a comprehensive community counseling program fall into clear and distinct categories.

First, as noted earlier in the chapter, we can distinguish between *direct* and *indirect* services. Direct services provide community members opportunities to learn new skills or develop fresh understanding that can help them live more effectively and independently. Indirect programs address the settings that affect people's well-being. The community counselor intervenes, or enters into a situation, in order to bring about change that will make the environment more suitable for individual growth. Thus, direct programs focus on specific target populations; indirect programs, on the environment.

Second, we can distinguish between *community* services and *client* services. Community services are available to each member of the general community or target population. They are aimed at large numbers of people who have not been identified as having specific dysfunctions. Client services, in contrast, are more concentrated. They are aimed at people who have been identified as needing more active assistance.

Combining these categories, we find that the community counseling approach has, in practice, four distinct facets:

1. *Direct community services (preventive education):* Communitywide educational programs that provide direct experience and are made available to the population as a whole.
2. *Direct client services (outreach):* Programs that provide direct assistance to clients or potential clients who might be at risk for developing mental health problems.
3. *Indirect community services (influencing public policy):* Efforts to make the social environment more responsive to the needs of the population as a whole.
4. *Indirect client services (advocacy):* Programs that intervene in the environment of specific individuals or groups, allowing their special needs to be met.

Each facet of the comprehensive community counseling program is associated with specific modes of service, as shown in Table 1.1.

To provide a truly comprehensive program, the community counselor must ensure that services in all four quadrants of the table are offered.

Table 1.1 The Four Facets of Community Counseling and Their Service Modes

	Community services	*Client services*
Direct	Preventive education	Counseling
		Outreach to vulnerable clients
Indirect	Influencing public policy	Client advocacy
		Consultation

Direct Community Services: Preventive Education

Counselors providing direct community services work to educate or train the population at large. The purpose of their interventions is to share psychological knowledge and skills and thus lessen the need for professional helpers. Ideally, through participating in these experiences, community members gain the skills to help themselves.

Voluntary educational programs provide individuals and groups opportunities to increase their awareness and develop skills that can help them live more effectively and deal with their problems more competently. Such programs may run the gamut from value clarification seminars to assertiveness training, from courses in decision making and life planning to workshops in cross-cultural understanding, from relaxation training for adults to training in interpersonal skills for children.

The possibilities are endless. For each of the foregoing programs, as for numerous others, techniques, concepts, and even course outlines have already been developed. All that needs doing is to make them available to people, as broad a range of people as possible. Through preventive educational programs like these, community counselors can help people experience their own competence and come to recognize that effective life skills can prevent a variety of problems.

Direct Client Services: Counseling and Outreach to Vulnerable Populations

Though the principles and values of community counseling lend a slightly different perspective to the counseling process—as we will examine in detail in Chapter 4—counseling remains an important tool in the community counselor's repertoire. Counseling remains necessary for a simple reason: not all problems can be prevented.

Many problems can, however, and, as we have already seen, community counselors concentrate their efforts on these. By identifying stressful situations that make some individuals susceptible to developing dysfunctions, counselors can reach people who might be especially vulnerable at particular times— and intervene before problems develop.

> Instead of searching for a specific underlying precondition associated with a particular pattern of maladaptive behavior, researchers have begun to focus their interests much more directly on stressful life events which appear to be capable of triggering patterns of maladaptive behavior in a proportion of the population

that experiences those events. Thus, researchers have begun to shift their attention from "high risk populations" to "high risk situations" and events. (Price et al., 1980, p. 11)

Stressful situations can trigger a variety of physical, psychological, and social dysfunctions, though the stress reaction, in itself, is transient. "What follows after the immediate, transient stress reaction depends on the mediation of situational and psychological factors that define the context in which this reaction occurs" (Dohrenwend, 1978, p. 4). Whether individuals are able to withstand a high degree of stress depends, at least in part, on factors that can serve as buffers to protect the individual's sense of well-being. Such buffers include social support systems (Gottlieb, 1981; Holahan & Moos, 1982; Wilcox, 1981), a sense of control over events (Bandura, 1982; Johnson & Sarason, 1979), and cognitive problem-solving skills (Shure & Spivack, 1982). Further, people can develop what Kobasa (1979) terms *hardiness,* the strength to withstand stressful situations.

We know that people facing difficult situations need to develop new and practical problem-solving strategies and approaches to everyday living. We also know that such people need close contact with others, links to human beings who can provide support and encouragement. Community counselors can provide for these needs by making intensive help available to people facing either volatile life changes or chronic, ongoing stressors that strain their ability to cope.

Indirect Community Services: Influencing Public Policy

In addition to helping individuals, the community counselor often must intervene in the environment. This happens when conditions in the community are seen as limiting instead of facilitating the growth and competence of community members.

As community counselors and other helping professionals endeavor to respond to the needs of their communities, the desirability of change becomes apparent. Their work brings them face to face with the victims of poverty, racism, sexism, and stigmatization; of political, economic, and social systems that leave individuals feeling powerless; of governing bodies that deny the need for responsiveness; of social norms that encourage isolation. In the face of these realities, counselors' only choices are to seek change or blame the victims. Counselors get involved in community action and work to influence public policy because there is often no other way to prevent serious mental or physical health problems among their clientele.

> Most mental conditions are not identifiable by objective tests, and most have not been shown to be real organic diseases. Rather, epidemiological studies find clear correlations between most forms of psychopathology and one or more of the following: (a) emotionally damaging infant and childhood experiences; (b) poverty and degrading life experiences; (c) powerlessness and low self-esteem; and (d) loneliness, social isolation, and social marginality. (Albee, 1986, p. 891)

Given the impact of the environment on the well-being of individual clients, counselors need to address social and political systems by recognizing the problems common to their clients, supporting movement toward healthful change, influencing policy makers, and encouraging positive community action. As Joffe and Albee (1981) have pointed out, "To prevent psychopathology, we should not alleviate feelings of powerlessness by altering perceptions but by altering reality" (p. 323).

Indirect Client Services: Client Advocacy and Consultation

The impact of the environment becomes especially clear when the counselor works with individuals and groups who have special needs. To help such clients get their needs met, counselors must become advocates, speaking up on their clients' behalf, intervening actively in the surroundings of the individual or group.

Client advocacy begins with the identification of groups of people who might benefit from increasing their own strength, for example, "socially devalued populations," people who, because of some disability or past behavior, have been downgraded by the community at large. Their worth as people is not fully appreciated by others, and they have become separated from the mainstream community.

To prevent further difficulty, the community counselor works to empower such people. The counselor encourages such clients to help themselves, tries to boost their sense of independence and effectiveness, and helps them use whatever community resources might be available.

One important resource is the "helping network," consisting of the persons and agencies available to provide assistance when it is needed. Community counselors can inform individuals about potential helping resources. Counselors may also act as consultants, helping other professionals deal with specific issues more effectively.

Sometimes, more active support is needed. When inequities exist, when rigid rules or attitudes impinge on the individual's right to grow, or when rights are being violated, the community counselor may step in to act as a personal advocate. Suppose, for example, that a teenage single mother has been barred from public school. A traditional counselor might help her find private tutoring or plan a career in a field requiring few academic qualifications. The community counselor would battle the policy of exclusion, both for the sake of the individual and for the sake of others to come.

There are, in fact, countless situations in which client advocacy can make a difference to large segments of the population. When a group having difficulties has been identified, services to that group can be complemented with efforts to make the community a help instead of a hindrance. Seeking an alternative to the corrections system for adolescent offenders or striving to bring the physically handicapped into the mainstream of community life are both examples of indirect client services.

Unified Approach

The four facets of community counseling combine in practice into a unified whole that can be implemented in any agency or educational setting. Community counselors do not need to choose between helping individuals or acting as agents of social change. Instead, they can take an ecological perspective:

> An ecological perspective lies somewhere at the nexus of system and person change. The ecological perspective views people and environments as being in reciprocal transaction, each mutually influencing the other in subtle and obvious ways. Thus, understanding, growth, and change would emanate from and within the relevant ecological transaction. (Conyne, 1985, p. 1)

The skills involved in facilitating individual development and influencing environments are complementary. Although an individual counselor cannot effect a multifaceted program alone, he or she can be aware of the multiplicity of human needs and work toward developing a combination of programs offering an appropriate array of services.

The idea of providing multifaceted, preventive services strikes some traditional caregivers as idealistic. In fact, however, more and more agencies and institutions are finding that it is possible to implement programs that exemplify the community counseling model. Aunt Martha's Youth Service Center, the University of Maine's Substance Abuse Services, and the Community Mental Health Center at Piscataway, New Jersey, demonstrate how.

Community Counseling in Action: Aunt Martha's Youth Service Center

In 1986, the board of trustees of Park Forest, Illinois, where Aunt Martha's Youth Service Center is located, considered making drastic cuts in the funding allocated for the center's programs. Within days, an outpouring of public support for the agency compelled the board to reconsider. Typical of the community's response was a petition signed by fifteen local clergymen:

> We the undersigned clergymen of Park Forest are painfully aware of the growing needs Aunt Martha's has been fulfilling in our community. We are, therefore, most alarmed that recent draft budgets could even contemplate the idea of decreased funding for our youth services agency. We strongly urge that there be no decrease in allocation, and that instead the village trustees search for ways to restore the Aunt Martha's allocation to what it was three years ago. ("Clergy Asks," 1986)

Similar sentiments were expressed by a broad range of individuals, groups, and organizations throughout the area served by Aunt Martha's. As a result, while many agencies are floundering in an era of financial cutbacks, this center is flourishing, maintaining an impressive level of community support and growing at a steady pace. This success can be attributed largely to the agency's close ties to the community, its efforts to provide a welcoming environment for young people, its responsiveness to the real needs of its clientele, and the comprehensiveness of its services. In short, Aunt Martha's is a healthy agency, as well as an effective one, because it embodies the community counseling concept.

The founders' own words express the agency's philosophy most clearly:[1]

> "You've Got a Friend" is the theme of Aunt Martha's Youth Service Center, Inc., a community-based youth-serving organization which offers comprehensive programs to meet the needs of young people and families residing in a fifteen-township region of metropolitan Chicago. Established in 1972, Aunt Martha's offers a range of services for young people and their families and has created innovative programs which enable young people to participate as positive contributing members of their communities. The initial community commission which led to the creation of Aunt Martha's was composed of both young people and

[1]From *You've Got a Friend* by E. Mazer and C. G. Leofanti, 1980, Park Forest, IL: Aunt Martha's Youth Service Center. Copyright 1980 by Aunt Martha's Youth Service Center. Reprinted by permission.

adults. The name *Aunt Martha's* was chosen to reflect the quality of warmth and concern one would find in the home of a close relative and which the community hoped young people would find at Aunt Martha's Youth Service Center. Since its beginning, Aunt Martha's has grown from a simple counseling center to a complex, highly structured agency serving a wide geographic area through a dozen programs, a staff of 89 and over 250 community volunteers. Aunt Martha's serves a richly varied population, including both suburban and rural residents, as well as ethnic, racial, and economic groups. The service area also encompasses industrial areas with many of the characteristics of an urban setting. . . .

Aunt Martha's founding principles strongly advocated community participation at all levels, particularly with regard to the involvement of young people in the planning and operations of programs. Additionally, every effort was made to ensure that services were accessible to all young people in the community and that the bulk of service delivery was to be accomplished by community volunteers. These principles have been followed in the development of Aunt Martha's programs. Youth and adult volunteers are the heart of Aunt Martha's service delivery system. . . . Thus, Aunt Martha's offers the community, especially youth, the opportunity to give as well as to receive help and to advocate on their own behalf [*sic*].

Community and youth participation assure programs which are responsive to young people and to the community. Volunteers are involved at all levels of the agency's operations—service delivery, program planning and policy making. Most of the staff are long-time residents of the communities they serve; many were previously volunteers. Volunteer training and supervision are crucial aspects of Aunt Martha's programs. . . .

Aunt Martha's Youth Service's commitment to youth participation both within the organization and throughout the community is based on the belief that the majority of youth problems which communities experience are caused by alienation and the perceived lack of access to meaningful social roles on the part of young people. Thus, Aunt Martha's comprehensive approach not only offers assistance to those who are experiencing problems but also seeks to provide vehicles through which young people may experience the senses of competence, usefulness, belonging, and potency needed to develop as healthy, productive adults who are integrated members of the community.

Aunt Martha's demonstrates how effectively the community counseling model can be put into practice. The agency provides programs utilizing each of the service modes that make up a comprehensive program: (1) preventive education, (2) counseling and outreach to vulnerable populations, (3) influencing public policy, and (4) client advocacy and consultation.

Preventive Education

Aunt Martha's has traditionally offered a number of programs aimed at preventing problems that young people are likely to encounter. These programs have in common a focus on building competency and an emphasis on youth participation at all stages of problem identification, planning, and implementation.

In Project Listen, for instance, young people use dramatic presentations to encourage youths and adults to communicate about issues that are important to them. *Changes,* for example, a play written by teenagers, deals with having choices and making decisions in regard to sexuality, addressing such issues as birth control, teen pregnancy, homosexuality, and taking responsibility for one's actions. *Different People, Different Times* focuses on youth participation and is aimed at increasing the community's awareness of young people's talents and potential. *Who Needs It* is a series of skits and improvisations designed to elicit audience participation in a discussion of alcohol and other drugs. Project Listen performances are designed not just to provide information but to encourage frank discussions among young people and between parents and children.

Students Involved in Pregnancy Prevention, also developed by young people, has high school students making presentations to area middle schools. A four-session program designed for seventh graders deals with social and peer pressures and problem solving. In each session, a combination of learning tools, including brainstorming, discussions, audiovisuals, role playing, and work sheets, is used to teach relevant skills.

These and other activities foster the participation of young people who come to Aunt Martha's not because they have problems but because they enjoy feeling involved. Because the agency attracts such a broad range of people, individuals need not feel stigmatized when they seek help through the center's more intensive programs.

Counseling and Outreach to Vulnerable Populations

Aunt Martha's offers highly accessible counseling services, training community volunteers to serve as counselors in addition to the staff members. Services include general counseling, drop-in counseling, substance-abuse treatment, and twenty-four-hour crisis intervention.

The agency also attempts to recognize and help populations likely to develop problems. Pregnant teenagers, for instance, are assisted through a prenatal clinic that provides medical attention, childbirth classes, nutritional information, and referrals for postnatal care. Pregnant teens can also apply for public aid through an office located at Aunt Martha's.

Project New Chance helps teens who have already become parents, providing educational and vocational assessment and life-skills training to help them gain independence from public assistance as rapidly as possible. This project represents a joint effort of Program PLUS, a Parents Too Soon initiative, and the agency's ongoing employment and educational services for disadvantaged youths. A Head Start program at the agency has enabled it to serve the children of these teenage parents as well.

Among other programs designed to meet the needs of specific client groups are EDGE (Employment-Direction-Growth-Experience), an employment and training program for economically disadvantaged youths; Project Truck Stop, an outreach program aimed at interstate runaways; and Transition to Independence, which provides shelter for homeless youths.

Influencing Public Policy

In addition to offering innovative direct services, Aunt Martha's works with other youth-serving systems, increasing the access young people have to those systems and demonstrating their right to be involved in community affairs.

The Center for Student Citizenship, Rights, and Responsibilities (CSCRR) is a youth leadership, involvement, and advocacy program sponsored by Aunt Martha's and designed to promote the development of leadership skills among young people. The activities of the CSCRR include:

- Publication of a book designed to raise consciousness about issues affecting young people
- Publication of a newsletter to increase awareness of the program's advocacy efforts
- Seminars on educational issues, including alternatives to suspension from school
- Educational forums on issues selected by participants
- School-based study groups that deal with such issues as student rights and responsibilities, school attendance policies, student representation on school boards, and gang activities
- Training programs in skills such as negotiation, conflict resolution, or public speaking
- Formation of a legislative committee to identify issues of concern to young people and learn how to monitor related legislation (Committee members sometimes help

organize young people to write to legislators, testify at hearings, visit legislators, or draft legislation.)

The center was also responsible for a survey of high school dropouts that resulted in a report and recommendations to help school districts prevent dropouts and better meet the needs of young people experiencing problems. Other efforts related to school policies and practices include training parent-student teams to monitor legislation related to educational reform. Although Aunt Martha's participated in setting up hearings on educational excellence, the agency maintains a concern that reforms brought about through the excellence movement be fair to all students. Participation in the Illinois Fair Schools Coalition, which protects student rights and oversees educational reform, is one of the avenues leading toward this end.

Client Advocacy and Consultation

Most of the young people who make up Aunt Martha's clientele are affected by school policies. A smaller number of the agency's clients need more active, more specific advocacy efforts. Sometimes, this advocacy is provided on an individual, case-by-case basis; legal services, for example, are provided by volunteer attorneys who offer their initial advice free of charge. Frequently, however, Aunt Martha's and other youth-serving agencies must join together to ensure that young people with special needs are treated equitably and to protect the quality and availability of youth services. Thus, the administration, staff, and volunteers of Aunt Martha's play an active role in the work of such organizations as the American Youth Work Center, the Youth Network Council, the Illinois Collaboration on Youth, and the Children's Defense Fund Youth Lobby. Aunt Martha's director has chaired the Illinois Governor's Task Force on Youth Employment, as well as a number of other advocacy-related committees and commissions.

When Aunt Martha's staff members recognize that a problem exists, they join with other concerned systems to take action. They are actively involved in consultation with other agencies and with the many systems that affect young people. In Aunt Martha's service area, for example, troubled young people who could not be reunited with their families were once served only through the court system. The fact that they now have a community-based alternative attests to this agency's effectiveness, not just as a service provider but as an advocate for disenfranchised youth and as a consulting resource for the community.

Unified Approach

The separate facets of a community counseling agency's efforts form a unified whole, with direct and indirect and community-wide and client-focused services complementing one another. As the director of Aunt Martha's has pointed out,

> services must be guaranteed to the most seriously troubled youth residing within the jurisdiction of the youth agency. Youth agencies must develop the resources needed to reach the most troubled and reduce the number of young people who become subject to large non-community-based institutions. Services to this group provide the youth agency with firsthand information regarding the failings of community institutions and a base to propose community change. (Leofanti, 1981, p. 25)

Thus, agencies like Aunt Martha's recognize the importance of combining direct services to individuals in need with indirect methods that focus on public policy. What community counselors learn from their clients has direct implications for their work with the community at large.

Table 1.2 shows the comprehensiveness of Aunt Martha's services.

Table 1.2   The Four Facets of Community Counseling: Aunt Martha's Youth Service Center

	Community services	*Client services*
Direct	Project Listen	Counseling
	Students Involved in Pregnancy Prevention	Substance-abuse treatment
		Crisis intervention
		Project New Chance
		Head Start
		EDGE
		Project Truck Stop
		Transition to Independence
Indirect	Center for Student Citizenship, Rights, & Responsibilities	Legal advocacy
		Affiliations with the American Youth Work Center, Youth Network Council, Illinois Collaboration on Youth, and Children's Defense Fund Youth Lobby
	Participation in the Illinois Fair Schools Coalition	
		Juvenile justice alternatives

As Table 1.2 makes clear, Aunt Martha's exemplifies the multifaceted community counseling model. While directly helping young people at risk or in trouble, the staff and volunteers of the agency continue to work to prevent serious problems from developing, both by improving the problem-solving skills of young people and by actively advocating their cause.

Community Counseling in Action: The University of Maine's Substance Abuse Services

The community counseling model can also be applied to very specific issues. The Substance Abuse Services program of the University of Maine at Orono serves as a clear example of this. Although this program was developed to address a single identified problem—substance abuse—its approach is comprehensive: services are aimed at all segments of the campus community, include preventive programming, and promote change in the environment within which substance abuse develops. The substance abuse coordinator described the program in a letter sent to professors, residence hall directors, and other members of the university community:

> Substance abuse is a complex and multiply determined behavior that frequently disrupts the academic environment and adversely affects educational outcomes and experiences for students. In an effort to address these and other realities the University Substance Abuse Services were created in August of 1985. . . . This program provides comprehensive substance abuse services for the entire university community. These services include, but are not limited to, preventive programming; student, staff, and faculty training; consultation; referral; assessment; treatment; public speaking; and academic lecturing. The Substance Abuse Services Office is very actively involved with individuals who use/abuse all types of substances such as nicotine, caffeine, food, drugs, and alcohol. This service is also engaged in ongoing college-age-related research concerning determinants of substance abuse, incidence of substance use and abuse, programming efficacy and strategic prevention and intervention strategies.
>
> The Substance Abuse Services staff advises the University's Boost Alcohol Consciousness Concerning the Health of University Students (BACCHUS) chapter and a Students Against Driving Drunk (SADD) chapter. Also, the "Late Night Local," a student-run safe transportation service between campus, Orono, and Old Town, is provided, free of charge, through this office to all students.

Additionally, this office provides community consultation and information sessions to schools, medical centers, civic organizations, newspapers, radio, and television stations. The Substance Abuse Services staff is also involved at the state level in prevention programming and service provision for substance abusing individuals.

Clearly, the program offers services in each of the modes characteristic of the community counseling model.

Preventive Education

One of the most important aspects of this program is its emphasis on prevention. Instead of focusing solely on individuals already identified as having drug- or alcohol-related problems, the Substance Abuse Services office endeavors to have an impact on the campus as a whole. The office's many educational efforts include providing accurate drug and alcohol information for the university community at large and training individuals and groups who, because of their key social roles, can be expected to influence others.

Drug and alcohol information is disseminated to the general student population in many forms, through films, posters, dormitory discussions, newspaper columns and letters, displays, and radio public service announcements. In addition, the substance-abuse coordinator presents frequent open lectures and training sessions. The many topics that have been addressed through this format include:

- The scope and nature of alcoholism
- Substance use and abuse among college students
- The effects of alcohol on behavior
- Drinking during pregnancy
- Responsible drinking skills
- Substance abuse and sexuality
- Synergism between drugs and alcohol
- Alternatives to alcohol
- The dangers of cocaine

Training sessions designed for those in key social roles also enhance primary prevention. Among the many groups who have participated in such training sessions are peer educators, residence hall directors and assistants, fraternity and sorority groups, and athletic teams. Special training sessions are scheduled for student orientations to familiarize new students with the university's alcohol and drug policies and to discuss ways of coping with peer pressures in the university setting.

In addition, a number of students participate in BACCHUS or SADD, both of which encourage and plan alcohol-free social activities.

Counseling and Outreach to Vulnerable Clients

Substance Abuse Services provides direct treatment, at appropriate levels of intensity, for substance abusing clients. Students coming to the health center for an alcohol or drug concern are assessed by the substance abuse coordinator, acting as a consultant, and then either seen for a one-time educational session or referred for more intensive group education, individual treatment, group treatment, or further evaluation, depending on the nature and severity of their problems.

Proactive outreach services help to identify students at risk for developing problems related to substance abuse, making early intervention possible. Students who have violated drug- or alcohol-related conduct codes, for example, are referred to the Substance Abuse Services office. A university conduct officer determines what, if any, disciplinary measures will be taken, but the referral to Substance Abuse Services provides a valuable opportunity to educate the offender. On a first offense, students are required to participate in a special class. After a second offense, students must attend more intensive small-group meetings that include training in coping skills, assertion, relaxation, communication, problem solving, and identifying alternatives to drug and alcohol use. Further offenses call for still more intensive evaluation and treatment.

For other students who might need more intensive help than that offered the community at large, Substance Abuse Services offers such services as group meetings for adult children of alcoholics and peer-led drop-in groups for recovering alcohol abusers. Of course, the training provided key university personnel and student leaders results in a greater number of referrals, increasing the opportunities for early intervention.

Influencing Public Policy

Although direct services to students are important, their effectiveness depends in part on the nature of the environment within which the substance use occurs. In the field of substance abuse, indirect community services focus on fostering environments that discourage the misuse of alcohol and drugs and encourage the development of personal responsibility. An important aspect of the substance abuse prevention effort at the University of Maine is the existence of appropriate social policies. The Alcoholic Beverage Policies, for instance, represent a thoughtful attempt to develop reasonable and enforceable guidelines. Included in the policy statement, which was developed through consultation with the Substance Abuse Services coordinator, are the following sections:

A. *Philosophy:* States that those who use alcohol on the campus are expected to do so responsibly and appropriately and that alcohol should never be the primary focus of any activity.

B. *Basic Principles:* States that consumption of alcoholic beverages is limited to people 21 or older, that individuals are expected to assume responsibility for their own behavior, and that a variety of nonalcoholic beverages, served in containers resembling those of the alcoholic beverages, and sufficient food to last the entire event must be available whenever alcohol is served.

C. *General Guidelines:* Spells out restrictions on the delivery of alcoholic beverages to the campus and on the settings where people can drink and encourages limits on consumption to decrease the likelihood of intoxication.

D. *Maine State Law:* Reviews state age restrictions and licensing laws and states that the university cannot provide immunity from prosecution.

E. *State Alcoholic Beverage Control Commission/ State Liquor Inspectors:* Reiterates the university's policy of cooperation with this authority.

F. *Alcohol Awareness Education:* Expresses the university's support for alcohol education and mandates such specific efforts as Alcohol Awareness Month, workshops on alcohol in residence halls, an alcohol education series for fraternity and sorority pledges, and education of the faculty and staff concerning alcohol-related issues.

G. *Pub Policy:* States that, in addition to complying with local, state, and federal laws, facilities licensed to serve liquor must post advertisements outlining safe levels of consumption, alternatives to alcohol consumption, and management of situations involving an intoxicated guest. Fraternities and sororities may serve alcoholic beverages only through the university's catering service, with sales limited to designated guests and times.

H. *Residence Halls:* Provides guidelines for private functions where alcoholic beverages are available, calling for designated hosts and attendants who are to ensure that liquor is not given to minors. In addition, the guidelines limit the use of common-source containers of alcohol such as kegs.

I. *Alcoholic Beverage Marketing and Promotion Policy:* Limits the promotion and advertising of alcohol and requires that any advertising that is accepted avoid demeaning portrayals of individuals; discourage alcohol misuse; subscribe to the philosophy of responsible and legal use; and avoid associating alcoholic beverages with sexual prowess, athletic ability, or the performance of skilled tasks.

J. *Coerced/Forced Consumption of Alcohol:* Calls for immediate and strict sanctions against students who force others to consume alcohol or who fail to take direct action to stop such incidents.

K. *University's Relationship to Students:* States that students are responsible for their own behavior while acknowledging the university's responsibility for providing education and services that will reduce alcohol misuse, as well as enforcing its alcohol-related policies.

In addition to shaping the general policies regarding alcoholic beverages, the Substance Abuse Services office makes recommendations and acts as needed to encourage a safe environment. To reduce the incidence of drunk driving, for example, Substance Abuse Services recommended that during football games tailgate-party areas be closed after halftime and picnic areas where alcohol use is prohibited be opened instead. A more ongoing, highly effective effort has been the "Late Night Local," a bus service sponsored by the Substance Abuse Services that transports about 150 students per weekend between town and campus.

Client Advocacy and Consultation

In the substance abuse field, client advocacy generally means making the network of potential helpers more aware of and knowledgeable about alcohol and drug problems and thus able to intervene more effectively. To make the University of Maine's Orono Campus more responsive to the needs of students with substance abuse problems, Substance Abuse Services has provided special training for the counseling center staff, the University Ambulance Corps, the health center staff, the student affairs staff, the conduct office, and the police. This training increases the likelihood that substance abuse problems will be recognized early and that those students affected will be served appropriately. Substance Abuse Services staff members also act as consultants whenever needed.

Unified Approach

The substance abuse program that has been implemented at the University of Maine at Orono is holistic in its attempts to combine prevention with intervention and services focused on the individual with those focused on the campus environment. Table 1.3 summarizes the services and activities of the Substance Abuse Services program, which clearly adheres to the community counseling model.

As indicated in Table 1.3, each of the four facets of the community counseling model plays a strong role in the university's substance abuse programming.

Table 1.3   The Four Facets of Community Counseling: Substance Abuse Services at the University of Maine, Orono

	Community services	Client services
Direct	Drug and alcohol education for the campus at large	Assessment and treatment of substance abusers
	Training for individuals and groups in key social roles	Education for alcohol-/drug-code violators
	Sponsorship of BACCHUS and SADD chapters	Groups for children of alcoholics and recovering substance abusers
Indirect	Development of Alcoholic Beverage Policies	Consultation and training for members of the university helping network
	"Late Night Local" and other drunk-driving prevention measures	

Community Counseling in Action: University of Medicine and Dentistry of New Jersey, Community Mental Health Center at Piscataway

The consultation and education program of the UMDNJ Community Mental Health Center at Piscataway also exemplifies the preventive, multifaceted approach that characterizes the community counseling model. Community mental health centers, like that at Piscataway, generally offer comprehensive programs with services including crisis intervention, outpatient therapy, inpatient psychiatric treatment, day hospital programs, rehabilitation services, substance abuse referral and treatment, and family counseling, in addition to consultation and education. Such agencies usually emphasize direct services to clients at risk, however. What makes the Piscataway center exceptional is the degree to which it goes beyond traditional, direct treatment. The center's consultation and education program delivers services of such broad scope that all four facets of the community counseling model are encompassed by this component alone.

Preventive Education

The Community Mental Health Center offers decentralized services, allowing staff members to develop educational programs on issues important to the specific populations being served. A 1985 summary of services showed that, during the previous year alone, the topics that had been addressed included:

> separation and divorce; suicide prevention; the stress of suicide survivors; chemical abuse; parenting skills; stress management; basic necessities of the urban poor and minorities; community health education; family life cycle education; criminal victimization; incest and child sexual abuse; family violence; teen pregnancy and parenting; AIDS; social problem-solving and decision-making skills; the stress of latchkey children; the impact of Alzheimer's disease and related disorders; urban youth stressors, including unemployment; and step-family issues.

Educational programs for the general public are offered at a variety of sites and help people deal with everyday concerns related to family life and normal development, as well as with the unexpected. Information about mental health issues is also disseminated through the mass media, through newspaper, radio, and television interviews and forums. Programs like the school-based Social Problem-Solving Project teach children and parents, as well as teachers, problem-solving and decision-making skills. The aim of these educational activities is to prevent the kinds of problems most prevalent among the members of the communities the center serves.

Outreach to Vulnerable Client Populations

Educational programs help prevent problems from arising, but some situations still put individuals at risk for developing dysfunctions. Effective programs recognize high-risk situations and attempt to strengthen the resources of those people affected by them. At the Community Mental Health Center at Piscataway, for example, Program CARRI (Children at Risk: Resources and Intervention) serves teenage parents and their children. COPSA

(Community Outreach Program for Senior Adults), another good example of outreach to populations with special needs, provides innovative programming for the families of people affected by Alzheimer's disease. The center also offers timely and accessible help to young people through programs like Phone Friend, for latchkey children; school-based student assistance programs; and the New Jersey Youth Corps, for high school dropouts. Each of these programs addresses a high-risk population or situation, providing outreach, support, and assistance to reduce the likelihood that individuals in such circumstances will develop disabling problems. Of course, the comprehensive scope of the center ensures clients' access to intensive individual, group, or family counseling.

Influencing Public Policy

The center's work in consultation and education also involves organizing and empowering the community. For instance, a youth-helping-youth program was initiated to enhance the leadership skills and the employability of urban teenagers by training them in human relations and involving them in community service projects. A community empowerment program developed under the center's New Brunswick Outreach Unit conducts community conferences on such issues as health, fair labor practices, and cultural awareness, as well as helping families obtain basic necessities. In addition, the center's staff members are actively involved in the work of the Piscataway township's Statewide Community Organization Project (SCOP) and a number of other community advocacy efforts. The center is also well represented on the statewide level, with staff members serving on task forces dealing with such issues as suicide prevention, alcoholism, and child abuse.

Client Advocacy and Consultation

Strong efforts are made on behalf of specific groups, especially the elderly and the deinstitutionalized chronically mentally ill. Advocacy for people with chronic mental health problems includes work with such groups as the New Jersey Alliance for the Mentally Ill and the Concerned Citizens for Chronic Patients Association. Similarly, the staff of COPSA complements its direct services to the elderly by providing leadership and technical assistance to such groups as the Housing Coalition of Middlesex County, the Middlesex County Adult Protective Services Coalition, and the Alzheimer's Disease Support Network.

To enhance the responsiveness of the total helping network, members of the mental health center staff provide extensive consultation and training to health and human service professionals. Examples of their activities include:

- Skill development workshops for school personnel on such topics as sexual abuse, suicide, chemical abuse, eating disorders, stepfamilies, and the problems of school-age children of alcoholics
- Seminars on Alzheimer's disease and related disorders for nursing home staff members
- Training in group counseling for the staff of Abused Women's Services
- Training in counseling skills for the staff of the student counseling center at a local college
- Workshops for court and probation officers working with troubled families
- Training for key community members and human service "gatekeepers" such as day care workers, police, clergy, family services staff, nurses, mental health professionals, corporate managers and human resources personnel, state hospital workers, and vocational counselors

Ongoing liaison efforts and participation in interagency councils and networks do even more to enhance the responsiveness of the community's helping network.

Unified Approach

The consultative and educational services provided by the Community Mental Health Center at Piscataway are truly comprehensive, encompassing prevention as well as intervention and advocacy as well as outreach. The scope of the center's consultation and education program is made clear in Table 1.4.

The Community Mental Health Center at Piscataway, like Aunt Martha's Youth Service Center and the University of Maine's Substance Abuse Services, demonstrates the applicability of the multifaceted approach to real-life settings and situations.

Summary

Community counseling is a multifaceted approach combining direct and indirect services to help community members live more effectively and prevent the problems most frequently faced by those who use the counseling services.

Table 1.4 The Four Facets of Community Counseling: The Community Mental Health Center at Piscataway, New Jersey

	Community services	Client services
Direct	Educational programs for the general public	Program CARRI
		COPSA
	Mental health education through the media	Phone Friend
		Student assistance programs
	Social Problem-Solving Project	New Jersey Youth Corps
Indirect	Community organization and empowerment	Advocacy for the chronically mentally ill, the elderly, and other groups
	Youth leadership programs	
	Community conferences	Consultation and training for human service professionals and community gatekeepers
	Policy task forces	
		Liaison with other helping agencies

Community counselors work in a wide variety of settings, but they share a common concern with prevention, an awareness of the potential effects of the social environment, and an understanding that people can be served most effectively by giving them the skills and resources they needed to help themselves. Four assumptions guide the work of the community counselor: (1) People's environments may either nurture or limit them; (2) a multifaceted approach to helping is more efficient than a single-service approach, (3) prevention is more efficient than remediation, and (4) the community counseling model can be applied in any human services setting.

The community counseling approach, when put into practice, involves four distinct facets, each carried out through specific modes of service. Direct community services provide educational experiences to the community as a whole; the mode of service through which they are implemented is preventive education. Direct client services provide for the needs of clients and potential clients, those at risk for developing mental health problems; the service modes used here are counseling and outreach to high-risk populations. Indirect community services are efforts to make the social environment more responsive to the needs of the population as a whole and are carried out primarily through influencing public policy. Indirect client services intervene in the environments of individuals or groups at risk to ensure that their special needs are met; these services primarily involve consultation and client advocacy.

More and more agencies and institutions are finding it possible to implement such comprehensive programs. Three examples of community counseling in action are Aunt Martha's Youth Service Center, the Substance Abuse Services office of the University of Maine at Orono, and the Community Mental Health Center at Piscataway, New Jersey.

Supplemental Activities

1. Visit a local community agency or counseling program, using the community counseling model as a tool to help you understand the program's aims. Think about the agency or program in these terms:

   a. What kinds of direct, communitywide services are offered?

   b. To what degree is the agency involved in efforts to change the community?

   c. What direct client services are offered? Do these services appear to take environmental factors into account?

   d. Is the agency involved in indirect client services? Does it actively work on behalf of those that use the agency's services?

   In many instances, you may find that one or more facets are missing from an agency's program. If that is the case, can you think of services that might enhance the agency's effectiveness in meeting its goals?

2. Think about a specific group or population (for example, adults with physical disabilities, survivors of child abuse, unemployed professionals, women, high school students). Consider what aspects of the social environment might affect the well-being of this group. What social, economic, political, or psychological pressures affect members of this population? Taking these factors into account, develop some ideas for appropriate services for the population you have selected. You will probably notice that direct counseling services alone are unlikely to meet the group's needs. Beginning with a clear statement of your goals, develop a hypothetical community counseling program incorporating all four facets of the model described in Chapter 1. At this point, concentrate on the general thrust of each facet, rather than

emphasizing the details of each service. Give your agency a name and begin to think of it as your own. As you become even more familiar with community counseling concepts, you will begin to think about your agency's services in more concrete terms.

Related Reading

BLOOM, B. L. (1984). *Community mental health: A general introduction* (2nd ed.). Pacific Grove, CA: Brooks/Cole.

CONYNE, R. K. (1987). *Primary preventive counseling: Empowering people and systems.* Muncie, IN: Accelerated Development.

EDELSTEIN, B. A., & MICHELSON, L., Eds. (1986). *Handbook of prevention.* New York: Plenum.

FELNER, R. D., JASON, L. A., MORITSUGU, J. N., & FARBER, S. S., Eds. (1983). *Preventive psychology: Theory, research, and practice.* New York: Pergamon Press.

GIBBS, M. S., LACHENMEYER, J. R., & SIGAL, J., Eds. (1980). *Community psychology: Theoretical and empirical approaches.* New York: Gardner Press.

JASON, L. A., HESS, R. E., FELNER, R. D., & MORITSUGU, J. N., Eds. (1987). *Prevention: Toward a multidisciplinary approach.* New York: Haworth Press.

KESSLER, M., & GOLDSTON, S. E., Eds. (1986). *A decade of progress in primary prevention.* Hanover, NH: University Press of New England.

MAGNUSSON, D., & ALLEN, V. L., Eds. (1983). *Human development: An interactional perspective.* New York: Academic Press.

NATIONAL MENTAL HEALTH ASSOCIATION COMMISSION ON THE PREVENTION OF MENTAL-EMOTIONAL DISABILITIES. (1986). *The prevention of mental-emotional disabilities: Report of the National Mental Health Association Commission on the Prevention of Mental-Emotional Disabilities.* Arlington, VA: National Mental Health Association.

O'CONNOR, W. A., & LUBIN, B., Eds. (1984). *Ecological approaches to clinical and community psychology.* New York: Wiley.

PRICE, R. H., KETTERER, R. F., BADER, B. C., & MONAHAN, J., Eds. (1980). *Prevention in mental health: Research, policy, and practice.* Beverly Hills: Sage Publications.

References

ALBEE, G. W. (1986). Toward a just society: Lessons from observations on the primary prevention of psychopathology. *American Psychologist, 41,* 891–898.

AUBREY, R. F., & LEWIS, J. A. (1983). Social issues and the counseling profession in the 1980s and 1990s. *Counseling and Human Development, 15*(10), 1–15.

BANDURA, A. (1982). Self-efficacy mechanism in human agency. *American Psychologist, 37,* 122–147.

CARVER, J. (1979, September). *Mental health administration: A management perversion.* Address to the Association of Mental Health Administrators Annual Meeting.

Clergy asks Aunt Martha's funding. (1986, June 15). *Park Forest Star,* p. A-3.

COHEN, S., & WILLS, T. A. (1985). Social support, stress, and the buffering hypothesis. *Psychological Bulletin, 98,* 310–357.

CONYNE, R. K. (1985). The counseling ecologist: Helping people and environments. *Counseling and Human Development, 18*(2), 1–12.

CONYNE, R. K. (1987). *Primary preventive counseling: Empowering people and systems.* Muncie, IN: Accelerated Development.

COWEN, E. L. (1983). Primary prevention in mental health: Past, present, and future. In R. D. Felner, L. A. Jason, J. N. Moritsugu, & S. S. Farber (Eds.), *Preventive psychology: Theory, research, and practice* (pp. 11–30). New York: Pergamon Press.

COWEN, E. L. (1985a). Person-centered approaches to primary prevention in mental health: Situation-focused and competence-enhancement. *American Journal of Community Psychology, 13,* 31–48.

COWEN, E. L. (1985b). Primary prevention in mental health. *Social Policy, 15*(4), 11–17.

D'ANDREA, M. (1984). The counselor as pacer: A model for revitalization of the counseling profession. *Counseling and Human Development, 16*(6), 1–15.

DOHRENWEND, B. S. (1978). Social stress and community psychology. *American Journal of Community Psychology, 1978,* 1–14.

FELNER, R. D., JASON, L. A., MORITSUGU, J. N., & FARBER, S. S. (1983). Preventive psychology: Education and current status. In R. D. Felner, L. A. Jason, J. N. Moritsugu, & S. S. Farber (Eds.), *Preventive psychology: Theory, research, and practice* (pp. 3–10). New York: Pergamon Press.

GOTTLIEB, B. H. (1981). *Social networks and social support.* Beverly Hills: Sage Publications.

HOLAHAN, C. J., & MOOS, R. H. (1982). Social support and adjustment. *American Journal of Community Psychology, 10,* 403–413.

JOFFE, J. M., & ALBEE, G. W. (1981). Powerlessness and psychopathology. In J. M. Joffe & G. W. Albee (Eds.), *Prevention through political action and social change.* Hanover, NH: University Press of New England.

JOHNSON, J. H., & SARASON, I. G. (1979). Moderator variables in life stress research. In I. G. Sarason & C. D. Spielberger (Eds.), *Stress and anxiety* (pp. 151–167). Washington, DC: Hemisphere.

KOBASA, S. C. (1979). Stressful life events, personality and health: An inquiry into hardiness. *Journal of Personality and Social Psychology, 37,* 1–11.

LEOFANTI, C. G. (1981). *The organization of community-based youth services: Direct service versus community action.* Unpublished manuscript.

LEWIS, J. A., & LEWIS, M. D. (1981). Educating counselors for primary prevention. *Counselor Education and Supervision, 20,* 172–181.

LEWIS, J. A., & LEWIS, M. D. (1983). *Management of human service programs.* Pacific Grove, CA: Brooks/Cole.

LIN, N., WOELFEL, M. W., & LIGHT, S. (1985). The buffering effect of social support subsequent to an important life event. *Journal of Health and Social Behavior, 26,* 247–263.

NATIONAL MENTAL HEALTH ASSOCIATION COMMISSION ON THE PREVENTION OF MENTAL-EMOTIONAL DISABILITIES. (1986). *The prevention of mental-emotional disabilities: Report of the National Mental Health Association Commission on the Prevention of Mental-Emotional Disabilities.* Arlington, VA: National Mental Health Association.

PRESIDENT'S COMMISSION ON MENTAL HEALTH. (1978). *Report of the task panel on prevention.* Washington, DC: U.S. Government Printing Office.

PRICE, R. H., BADER, B. C., & KETTERER, R. F. (1980). Prevention in community mental health: The state of the art. In R. H. Price, R. F. Ketterer, B. C. Bader, & J. Monahan (Eds.), *Prevention in mental health: Research, policy, and practice.* Beverly Hills: Sage Publications.

SHURE, M. B., & SPIVACK, G. (1982). Interpersonal problem solving in young children: A cognitive approach to prevention. *American Journal of Community Psychology, 10,* 341–356.

STRICKLAND, B. R., & JANOFF-BULMAN, R. (1980). Expectancies and attributions: Implications for community mental health. In M. S. Gibbs, J. R. Lachenmeyer, & J. Sigal (Eds.), *Community psychology: Theoretical and empirical approaches* (pp. 97–119). New York: Gardner Press.

WETHINGTON, E., & KESSLER, R. C. (1986). Perceived support, received support, and adjustment to stressful life events. *Journal of Health and Social Behavior, 27,* 78–89.

WILCOX, B. L. (1981). Social support, life stress, and psychological adjustment: A test of the buffering hypothesis. *American Journal of Community Psychology, 9,* 371–386.

Preventive Education

In any agency or institution, some clients are likely to have similar problems. Traditional helping professionals may have found this phenomenon comforting. Encountering a particular problem or issue frequently, they knew exactly how to deal with it. But though familiarity might have bred competence, it also bred redundancy. Professionals, counseling clients on a one-to-one basis, spent countless hours helping individuals solve problems that might have been avoided.

Increasingly, however, counselors are coming to recognize that they are also educators and trainers (Matthes & Dustin, 1980). Community counselors strive to identify needs that are common to many community members and to develop preventive programs that confront significant issues head on. By reaching large numbers of people before their problems become critical, community counselors can work more efficiently. They also help prevent crises and dysfunctions by training people in life skills and competencies that can help them withstand stress and maintain their mental and physical health.

> Mental health education attempts to develop important competencies within normal and at-risk groups. Such efforts, often referred to as competence training, are designed to improve the capacity of normal and at-risk populations to cope with predictable life transitions and to more effectively manage stressful situations. The premise underlying this approach is that disorders can be avoided by strengthening an individual's or group's capacity to handle environmental stress or life crises. (Ketterer, Bader, & Levy, 1980, p. 271)

Community counselors, when involved in this kind of competency training, are educators as well as clinicians. Their purpose is not just to solve problems but also to prevent them; not just to cure ills but also to enhance wellness.

> This approach uses the school as its model and instruction as the means for enhancement. The intervenor becomes a teacher, rather than a therapist. Adopting such a model allows the intervenor to be a skill trainer who teaches the client . . . life skills . . . and facilitates the retention of the skills throughout the lifespan. (Danish, 1977, p. 50)

Competency training programs are well suited to helping clients deal with issues frequently faced in particular settings. Thus, a university counseling center presents workshops on test anxiety and educational decision making; a career counseling agency offers lifework planning groups; a family service agency teaches parenting skills; a women's center provides courses in assertiveness and self-defense.

Preventive education can also help community members build general psychosocial competencies that can buffer the effects of stress and decrease their vulnerability to a variety of mental and physical health problems. These preventive programs do not have to be focused specifically on a single type of dysfunction.

> Just as a single disorder may come about as a consequence of a variety of stressful life events, any specific stress event may precipitate a variety of disorders, as a result of differing life histories and patterns of strengths and weaknesses in individuals. For example, an unanticipated death, divorce, or a job loss may increase the risk of alcoholism in one person, coronary artery disease in another, depression and suicide in a third, and a fatal automobile accident in a fourth. . . . With this acceptance comes the realization that successful efforts at the prevention of a vast array of disorders (particularly emotional disorders) can take place without a theory of disorder-specific causative mechanisms. (President's Commission on Mental Health, 1978, p. 1847)

Thus, even without knowing the unique biological, social, or psychological source of a particular problem, we may be able to prevent that problem, along with others, by strengthening the coping skills and general life competencies of people who have not yet developed dysfunctions. Examples of the many promising educational strategies that have been developed include stress management, health promotion, general life skills training, life planning, parenting education, and preventive interventions aimed at young children. Table 2.1 illustrates the place of such strategies in the community counseling model.

Stress Management[1]

To train clients to manage their reactions to stressful situations, community counselors need a clearly defined model of *stress*. Ivancevich and Matteson (1980) have defined stress as "an adaptive response, mediated by individual characteristics and/or psychological processes, that is a consequence of any external action, situation or event that places special physical and/or psychological demands upon a person" (pp. 8–9). Stress is thus a function of both external—that is, environmental—and individual factors; accordingly, stress management strategies should take into account environmental stressors, individual coping mechanisms, and personal perceptions of threat.

Table 2.1 Preventive Educational Strategies and the Community Counseling Model

		Community services	Client services
Direct	Stress management		/ / / / / / / / / / / /
	Health promotion		/ / / / / / / / / / /
	Life skills training		/ / / / / / / / / / / /
	Life planning		/ / / / / / / / / / / /
	Parenting education		/ / / / / / / / / / / /
	Primary prevention work with children		/ / / / / / / / / / /
Indirect		/ / / / / / / / / / / /	/ / / / / / / / / / / /
		/ / / / / / / / / / / /	/ / / / / / / / / / / /
		/ / / / / / / / / / / /	/ / / / / / / / / / / /

[1]The following sections are based on material from *Counseling Programs for Employees in the Workplace* by J. A. Lewis and M. D. Lewis, 1986, Pacific Grove, CA: Brooks/Cole. Copyright 1986 by Wadsworth. Adapted by permission.

The Origin of Stress-Related Problems

Stress-related problems originate in an individual's response to demands. An event or situation challenges the person's well-being, forcing him or her to adapt in some way. Few external events are, in themselves, universally stressful. The stress response depends on the individual's interpretation of the situation.

Whether someone will find a situation threatening or not depends on a number of factors: whether or not the person feels competent to handle the new demand, whether or not he or she has surmounted similar situations in the past, how much control he or she feels over events, whether or not the new demand conflicts with other needs, how high the person's standards of performance are, and how demanding the environment is with which the person is already coping. Their belief systems make some people continually vulnerable to stress, especially those who "write 'disaster' over every unwanted event at home and at work" (Veninga & Spradley, 1981, p. 20) or who insist on perfection in their own performances.

Suppose, for example, that an individual is assigned new duties at work. Though one employee might see such a change as a relief from tedium, another might find it stressful. The difference in response can, in part, be attributed to the individual's perception—accurate or inaccurate—of his or her ability to perform the new duties effectively. And this perception can, in turn, be affected by the person's current state of mind—does she already feel overworked? is he under pressure at home? does she believe the new tasks are important?—and by his or her general attitudes and beliefs—does he feel uncomfortable with change and stimulation? does she prefer work that is so familiar that it can be done perfectly? does he tend to worry obsessively about failing?

When human beings perceive an event as threatening, we react physiologically: to cope with the danger, our bodies prepare for vigorous physical activity. In the "fight-or-flight" response, the same physical changes are evoked regardless of the nature of the stressor.

> It starts in the hypothalamus, a tiny bundle of nerve cells at the center of the brain. Messages race from that command post and spread the alarm throughout the nervous system. Muscles tense. Blood vessels constrict. The tiny capillaries under the skin shut down altogether. The pituitary gland sends out two hormones that move through the bloodstream to stimulate the thyroid and adrenal glands. . . . The adrenals send some thirty additional hormones to nearly every organ in the body. This automatic stress response causes the pulse rate to shoot up; blood pressure soars.

The stomach and intestines stop all the busy activity of digestion. Hearing and smell become more acute. Hundreds of other physical changes occur without us even knowing it. (Veninga & Spradley, 1981, p. 11)

The stress response appropriately prepares us to deal with physical danger; following fight or flight, the body returns to its original equilibrium. When stressors are social or psychological rather than physical, however, the stress response builds up tension that is not released, utilizes energy that is not restored, and ultimately leads to exhaustion. Thus, in our complex, modern society, the stress response is not adaptive and tends to cause problems instead of helping us solve them.

The ongoing effects of stress are many. Individuals who are consistently under stress may find themselves troubled with physical symptoms such as respiratory problems, gastrointestinal difficulties, headaches, backaches, chronic high blood pressure, generally low energy levels, and even cardiovascular diseases. Stress is also manifested in psychological problems such as depression and anxiety.

Methods of Intervention

Since stress-related problems result from a combination of external demands, individual perceptions, and physiological responses, such problems can be lessened through intervention at any of these points. Individual clients can learn to examine the stressors in their lives, study their own responses, and make purposeful choices to reduce or manage stress. Table 2.2 lists methods of breaking the stress cycle by altering the environment, the mental processes by which the person interprets external events, or the person's physiological response to stress.

Altering the environment   One way that individuals can lower their stress levels is by learning how to better control their environments. First, clients can examine their lifestyles to identify stressors that are amenable to change. Although some stress will always be present, people can use *problem solving, time management,* and *interpersonal skills* to confront problems directly. One important means of reducing stress is developing a *support system;* not only can it make the environment less threatening, a support system also provides reinforcement for change.

Altering the mental processes   Besides trying to change external factors, people can also change the ways in which they appraise environmental demands. People can actually learn to

Table 2.2   Breaking the Stress Cycle: Methods of Intervention

External demands		*Internal processes*
Altering the environment	Altering the mental processes	Altering the physiological processes
Counseling focused on decision making and problem solving	Cognitive modification	Relaxation training
	Values clarification	Training in self-hypnosis
Time management counseling	Training in goal setting	Training in meditation
Training in interpersonal skills (assertiveness, leadership, helping)	Lifestyle assessment and counseling	Training in biofeedback
		Sensory awareness training
	Training in problem-solving skills	
Training in self-management procedures		
Support groups		

Note: Adapted from "A model of stress and counseling interventions" by J. C. Barrow and S. S. Prosen, 1981, *Personnel and Guidance Journal, 60,* p. 7. Copyright 1981 by the American Personnel and Guidance Association. Adapted by permission.

think differently in particular situations, and thus choose to avoid the stress response. Such *cognitive restructuring* involves altering the person's reaction to problematic events.

> The first phase in restructuring is recognition of certain self-appraisals that play a major role in giving the stressor potency, that is, turning an essentially neutral situation into a highly stressful one. ("Oh no, this is awful.") Second, it is suggested that the individual begin to monitor the self-appraisals to gain awareness of maladaptive ones, such as exaggeration, that tend to maintain the stressful event. (Moracco & McFadden, 1982, p. 550)

After recognizing their tendencies to perceive certain stimuli as threats, clients can purposefully substitute "self-statements" for the maladaptive appraisals or utilize other methods for changing their mental processes.

What Goldfried and Goldfried (1980) call *rational restructuring* can be applied both to stress management and to anxiety states that are unrelated to specific stressors. The process includes four basic steps: (1) helping clients recognize that cognitions mediate emotional arousal, (2) helping clients recognize the irrationality of certain beliefs, (3) helping clients understand that unrealistic cognitions mediate their own maladaptive emotions, and (4) helping clients change their unrealistic cognitions.

> Simply understanding the cause of the problem will do little to alleviate it; clients must consciously and deliberately engage in doing something differently when feeling upset. This emotional reaction must now serve as a "cue" for them to stop and think: "What am I telling myself that may be unrealistic?" They must learn to "break up" what was before an automatic reaction and replace it with a more realistic appraisal of the situation. . . . Clients eventually can totally eliminate the initial upset phase by having made the more realistic appraisal an automatic reaction. (Goldfried & Goldfried, 1980, p. 107)

Altering the physiological response   Neither environmental factors nor an individual's cognitive responses can always be controlled. Individuals also need to learn to intervene at the physiological level of the stress response. Through such techniques as *relaxation training, self-hypnosis, biofeedback,* or *meditation,* individuals can learn to substitute relaxation for the fight-or-flight response and thus avoid the long-term negative effects of stress.

Biofeedback training teaches individuals to control various aspects of their physiological functioning. Using instruments that provide immediate information—feedback—about functions that are less involuntary than was once thought, clients can learn to bring stress-related physical symptoms under control and achieve states of calm at will.

> EMG feedback, which can teach a person to relax muscle tension; GSR feedback, which can teach a person to relax autonomic nervous system arousal; temperature feedback, which can teach a person to relax vascular tension; and EEG feedback, which can teach a person to produce alpha waves associated with mental relaxation—all lead towards physiological states which are incompatible with anxiety. (Sarnoff, 1982, p. 358)

Similarly, relaxation training can help people gain control over physical tension. Clients can learn to use directed mental imagery, learning to relax by picturing scenes or states they associate with comfort and ease. Just as useful are muscle relaxation techniques, which help people distinguish between tense and relaxed muscles. Clients move systematically through the major muscle groups of the body, alternately tensing and relaxing them. Once they have learned to distinguish between the tensed and relaxed states, they can consciously control their tension.

Achieving a relaxed state is a first step in utilizing self-hypnosis. The main difference between relaxation and hypnosis is that hypnosis uses suggestions: the subject imagines that what is being suggested is actually happening.

> Doing hypnosis successfully requires the subject to shift into a literally extraordinary frame of mind. While ordinarily we direct our mental processes toward coping with the outer world as we reconstruct or define it within our self-interactions, in hypnosis you shift your attention away from the objective universe, to focus instead upon the imaginary universes you construct internally. You literally forget about the "real world" and concentrate upon the ever-shifting inner reality you are creating for yourself as you think, feel, and imagine along with the suggestions. (Straus, 1982, p. 51)

The suggestions used can relate to changing behavior, modifying attitudes and perceptions, or managing stress.

> A very important set of self-suggestions are those for absolute calmness and total relaxation. These kinds of deep-relaxation suggestions, which are typically given subvocally to oneself while alone, with eyes closed, are especially helpful for relieving stress and tension and for alleviating psychosomatic ailments. (Barber, 1982, p. v)

While counselors are, of course, familiar with the idea of using hypnosis to help clients bring about changes in their lives, they should consider the extra benefits to be gained from training them in self-hypnosis. Through self-hypnosis, individuals can learn both how to deal with specific problems in their lives and to what extent they can control their own well-being.

Individuals can also deal effectively with stress through meditation, which produces a state of consciousness best described as peaceful.

> According to the teachings of Buddha, the source of man's [sic] problems is his extreme attachment to his senses, his thoughts, and his imagination. Peace can be attained only when he frees himself from these attachments, directing his awareness inward, transcending the incessant bombardment of the consciousness so as to experience a quiet body, a subtle mind, and a unified spirit. (Girdano & Everly, 1979, p. 168)

Individuals can learn to free the mind and body of turmoil by using any one of several techniques that aid concentration. Some techniques use visual imagery or attention to breathing. A number of others, including that of the popular transcendental meditation, use oral or mental repetition of a word or sound, called a mantra, to induce the desired state of consciousness. Benson's (1975) "relaxation response," also a form of meditation, uses the word *one* as a mantra for entering a tension-free state. Regardless of the method used, through meditation, clients can improve their ability to withstand stress by attaining control over their physical and psychological responses.

The Stress Management Workshop

A workshop format facilitates the learning of stress management skills because it provides clients with opportunities for mutual support and assistance. Sparks and Ingram (1979), listed the following as goals of their stress management workshops for public school teachers:

> (a) to reduce isolation; (b) to identify sources of job-related stress (self-awareness); (c) to identify sources of job satisfaction and job-related strengths that may be drawn on to increase participants' satisfaction with their work; and (d) to formulate a tentative plan and action steps to prevent or alleviate stress. (p. 198)

Several exercises can be used to meet these goals and to introduce methods for intervening in the stress cycle.

1. *Identifying stressors:* Stress management begins with recognizing the stressors in one's life. To promote self-awareness and build mutual support, the workshop leader can divide participants into small groups and ask them to generate lists of common work, school, or social stressors. After then sharing these lists, participants can discuss commonalities and potential solutions to specific problems.

2. *Cognitive restructuring:* The workshop leader can deepen participants' self-awareness by inviting them to look for patterns in how they deal with stressful situations. Participants can be asked to list specific recent events that made them anxious. By analyzing these situations and their reactions to them, participants can discover what kinds of events they tend to perceive as threatening. A short lecture and discussion can then help them consider alternative ways of thinking about their environment and its impact on them.

3. *Stress reduction:* The workshop leader should provide an overview of the physiology of stress. Once participants understand the fight-or-flight response, they can also understand how the stress cycle can be broken. Afterward, participants usually enjoy practicing a relaxation exercise or trying self-hypnosis. Follow-up workshops or individual sessions can focus on specific methods of relieving anxiety and enhancing relaxation. Offering alternatives allows participants to explore the methods that work best

for them, whether relaxation training, self-hypnosis, meditation, or biofeedback.

4. *Identifying successful strategies:* In this exercise, participants share ways in which they have dealt successfully with stress. As they discuss the ways they manage stress, they often notice that the commonly used tactics run the gamut from environmental problem solving to changes in cognition to relaxation methods. Because it invites participants to talk about their successes rather than their problems, this exercise provides an encouraging counterpoint to the workshop's emphasis on stressors.

5. *Making stress management plans:* The long-term benefits of the workshop can be enhanced by creating personalized stress management plans. Each participant can select several stress-related issues and generate immediate steps by which to deal with them. A follow-up session can be scheduled to monitor and reinforce clients' successes in making needed lifestyle changes.

Health Promotion Programs

The nature of contemporary health problems has brought increasing recognition of the need for preventive programs designed to promote attitudes and behaviors that enhance wellness. Vast expenditures on health care have not had their expected impact on the health of the general population, at least in part because changes in the prevalence of various conditions demand new approaches. A century ago, infectious diseases were the leading causes of death. During the course of the 20th century, health patterns have changed. Because of scientific advancements, diseases like tuberculosis, measles, poliomyelitis, influenza, and pneumonia are no longer the killers they once were. As Matarazzo (1982) has pointed out, however, "Unfortunately, the reduction in these conditions has occurred along with an increase during the same years in such conditions as lung cancer, major cardiovascular disease, drug and alcohol abuse, and motorcycle and alcohol-related automobile accidents" (p. 3). Even those infectious diseases that are increasing in prevalence, such as Acquired Immune Deficiency Syndrome (AIDS), correlate highly with lifestyle variables.

Today, most deaths are caused by afflictions that can often be avoided or at least mitigated by changes in personal lifestyle. Cardiovascular disease alone accounts for half of the mortalities among Americans; cancer and accidents are also major causes of death. These problems are preventable and, in fact, do not respond well to traditional medical interventions.

> Clearly, the next health revolution must be aimed at these new killers and cripplers, and it clearly makes sense to emphasize strategies in that revolution for preventing these afflictions rather than to rely on treating them after they have already struck. . . . As much as half of all mortality in the United States is due to unhealthy behavior or lifestyle. Of the rest, 20% is due to environmental factors, 20% to human biological factors, and only 10% to inadequacies in health care. In spite of that, only a minuscule percentage of the 1982 federal budget [was] specifically identified for prevention-related activities. Yet it is clear that improvement in the health of our citizens will not be made predominantly through the treatment of disease, but rather through its prevention. (Michael, 1982, pp. 936–937)

And how can health be improved and the costs of medical care lowered? According to Michael, most Americans can improve their health and extend their life spans through "elimination of cigarette smoking, reduction of alcohol misuse, moderate dietary changes to reduce intake of excess calories and excess fats, moderate exercise, periodic screening for major disorders such as high blood pressure and certain cancers, adherence to traffic speed laws, and use of seat belts" (p. 937).

All of these behaviors constitute lifestyle changes that can be facilitated through education and support. Community counselors may address these issues through programs based in agencies, hospitals, schools, or workplaces. More important than the setting is that the program take a holistic approach to the enhancement of wellness.

For community counselors, a holistic approach to wellness means taking into account physiological, environmental, and psychological factors affecting clients' well-being.

Holistic programs benefit both clients and counselors. Martin and Martin (1982) have listed some of the many advantages of a holistic approach:

1. It teaches clients a total sense of personal responsibility.
2. Its effects are immediate and create a better sense of well-being.
3. Wellness rather than the absence of symptoms is the main goal of therapy.
4. All modalities of healing are used.
5. The client's inner capacity for change has a distinct and clear direction to better health and well-being.

6. Clients can continue patterns that are healthy and significantly decrease problem recurrence.
7. Self-discipline is learned and appreciated.
8. Disease prevention is enhanced for clients.
9. Counselors can benefit from all these aspects and be a significant model for clients. (p. 22)

In a holistic approach to health promotion, clients are encouraged to take personal responsibility for their physical and mental health, with wellness, instead of just the absence of symptoms, being the ideal outcome. The key element in this process is thus the individual's willingness and ability to take control over his or her well-being.

Health promotion programs should offer some activities focused on specific issues (for example, smoking cessation clinics, weight loss groups, exercise classes). Just as important, however, is a general orientation toward wellness. People need to understand the concept of wellness; they need to discover that they have the power to prevent illness through their own initiative and that they can take responsibility for meeting their own health needs. A sense of personal power does seem to be among the most important factors in helping people avoid chronic illness. Research by Kobasa (1979) indicates that, among people facing comparable degrees of stress, the factors distinguishing those who remained healthy from those who became ill included a vigorous attitude toward the world, strong self-commitment, a sense of meaning in life, and an internal locus of control. People who believed in themselves, who believed that they could control events through their own behavior, had a "hardiness" that protected them against illness. A central purpose of health promotion programs—and one that is highly consistent with the community counseling model—is to help clients develop hardiness along with concrete skills.

Clients working to optimize their health should begin with some form of assessment to determine what factors jeopardize their health and to establish a basis for planning. Clients can use computerized health assessments, such as Control Data's PLATO Health Risk Profile, or, if computerized assessments are not available, paper-and-pencil inventories that help to identify individual risk factors while heightening respondents' awareness of potential risks.

Assessment inventories can alert individuals to their risk of developing heart disease, for instance, since a number of risk factors that make individuals coronary-prone have been identified. Factors associated with heart disease include age, sex, elevated serum cholesterol, high intake of animal fat, elevated blood pressure, cigarette smoking, diabetes, a family history of heart disease, obesity, and lack of exercise (Gatchel & Baum, 1983, p. 110). Questionnaires can be used to identify "Type A" behavioral patterns, which are also thought to increase one's vulnerability to heart disease (Friedman & Rosenman, 1974). The Type A individual is characterized by a sense of urgency, competitiveness, aggressiveness, hostility, overinvolvement in work, and a strong need to control all situations. The characteristics of the hard-driving Type A individual can be measured through self-reports; more effective and less risky ways of coping with stress can then be substituted.

The purpose of using assessment instruments of any type is to point the way toward appropriate behavioral changes. Each client should set personal, health-related objectives that are realistic given his or her current level of fitness. Ardell and Tager (1982) have suggested the following guidelines:

1. Translate goals and behaviors into specific terms. . . .
2. Add a measurement component. . . .
3. Identify a time schedule for [the] component. . . .
4. Make sure your goal is realistic, but also challenging. . . .
5. Goals should always be in writing. . . . (p. 43)

Especially when beginning new exercise routines, clients must plan carefully. Different types of exercises meet different goals, so individuals need to choose activities that serve their purposes, whether increasing endurance, building strength, improving flexibility, or losing or gaining weight. Novices also need to be cautious in setting objectives; slight, steady increases in physical activity can be more beneficial than sudden spurts of activity that are too ambitious to be maintained.

Health promotion programs at the work site can be especially helpful. Individuals are most likely to adhere to their health plans if they have as much support for their new endeavors as they did for their former, less healthy lifestyles. Wellness training at the work site provides such support because participants tend to interact with one another regularly.

The Johnson & Johnson Live for Life Program

A good example of health promotion at the work site is the Live for Life Program, a comprehensive program designed to enhance the health of the 75,000 people employed by the highly decentralized Johnson & Johnson family of companies. The program, as described by Wilbur (1983), has as its goal "to provide the means for Johnson & Johnson employees to become among the healthiest employees in the world." Two basic assumptions underlie the program:

1. Activities that shape an individual's lifestyle, such as eating, exercise, smoking, and stress management, contribute substantially to the individual's health status.
2. Activities that support good health can be successfully promoted in the work setting.

The program works toward improving employees' health-related behaviors by focusing on general lifestyle changes, as well as on specific issues such as nutrition, weight control, stress management, fitness, and smoking cessation.

As an organization, Live for Life operates on a corporate level, providing consultation, training, core program components, professional services, promotional materials, planning, and evaluation to participating companies.

> Following a decision by a company management to accept and support the Program, voluntary employee leaders at that company are selected and trained to manage it. Working closely with Live for Life staff, these employee leaders assume primary responsibility for promoting good health practices at work among their fellow employees. Employee participation in the Program is voluntary and involves no employee financial outlay. Development of exercise facilities, improving the quality of foods offered in the company cafeteria, and establishment of a company smoking policy are examples of work site environmental changes undertaken by Live for Life Program leaders. Throughout the year the employee leaders also schedule and promote a comprehensive array of Live for Life programs and activities for all employees. Such programs include a Health Screen which allows individual employees to examine how healthy their current lifestyles are, a Lifestyle Seminar which introduces employees to the Live for Life concept in depth, and a variety of lifestyle improvement programs (e.g., Action Programs) in smoking cessation, stress management, exercise, nutrition, weight control, and general health knowledge. (Wilbur, 1983)

A key aspect of the Johnson & Johnson program is its attention to the central role of management and employees in adapting the program to meet the specific needs of the workers at each work site. Although the Live for Life staff offers guidance and expertise, how the program is implemented at each location depends on the commitment of those who work at those sites. Wellness programs of this type encourage healthy lifestyles by providing basic guidance, by helping participants develop effective plans, and by reinforcing new behaviors through ongoing support. These programs promote feelings of self-efficacy and control, which are important to the maintenance of both mental health and physical well-being.

Community-Based Heart Disease Prevention Programs

Community-based health promotion programs are also beginning to yield promising results, with several of the best-researched efforts focusing on heart disease. A good example is the Recurrent Coronary Prevention Project (Thoresen & Eagleston, 1985), which focused on altering Type A behavior patterns. The Recurrent Coronary Prevention Project worked with residents of the San Francisco Bay area who had had at least one myocardial infarction. One group received cardiological counseling, which focused on diet, exercise, medications, and other issues related to cardiovascular physiology. The second group received Type A behavioral counseling in addition to the cardiological information.

As noted earlier, Type A behavioral patterns are characterized by hostility, a sense of urgency and impatience, and excessive competitiveness. Through group discussion, modeling, relaxation training, and practice, participants in the group counseling sessions learned how to alter the specific cognitions, behaviors, and environmental and physiological factors associated with Type A behavioral patterns.

> In the cognitive area, treatment covered such topics as self-instructional training, evaluation of basic beliefs, active listening skills, and mental relaxation. Behaviorally, participants learned to alter certain speech patterns (such as interrupting others), psychomotor actions (such as excessive or abrupt emphatic gesturing), and other physical activities (such as reducing hurried walking [and] fast eating, and increasing smiling and complimentary comments). . . . The basics of social problem solving were used to help participants alter stressful environmental factors, such as revising work routines cooperatively with a supervisor or scheduling time to practice relaxation. Physiologically, participants were informed how biochemical processes appear to function in chronic stress reactions. . . . The feelings of anger, irritation, aggravation, and impatience . . . were equated with potential increases in a variety of biochemical and cardiovascular variables. (Thoresen & Eagleston, 1985, pp. 60–61)

Examination of the results of these interventions showed that, after three years, participants in the Type A behavioral group had 44% fewer recurrences of infarctions than those in either the group receiving only cardiological counseling or a control group. The participants who markedly reduced their

Type A behavior showed the best results, experiencing fewer than one-fourth of the number of recurrences experienced by subjects who changed their behavior less substantially. Thus, "results for the first three years reveal a clinically notable reduction in recurrences for postcoronary subjects who received the behavioral treatment coupled with evidence that the magnitude of reduction in the TABP [Type A Behavioral Pattern] is associated with the magnitude of reduced recurrences" (Thoresen & Eagleston, 1985, p. 62).

A much broader effort aimed at primary prevention of heart disease, the Stanford University Heart Disease Prevention Program, attempted to reduce the risk of heart disease in two California communities (Farquhar et al., 1977). In one community, a mass media campaign that focused on such risk factors as smoking, high blood pressure, and diet and nutrition tried to teach self-management principles in addition to providing information. In the second community, the same mass media campaign was supplemented with more intensive counseling for people identified as being at high risk. A third community served as a control. The encouraging results of this study—a 20% improvement in risk factors within the communities after two years—have led to an expansion of the project to include five cities.

An important aspect of all of these health promotion/ disease prevention programs is their emphasis on skill development and concrete behavioral changes. Although cognitive learning about health factors is important, information alone is unlikely to bring about lasting change unless people learn new ways to think about themselves and their environments.

Life Skills Training

In 1978, the President's Commission on Mental Health received a report from its task panel on prevention identifying "competency training emphasizing developmental approaches" as an area having a substantial-enough knowledge base to justify accelerated efforts in the future (President's Commission on Mental Health, 1978, pp. 1847–1848). Increasing recognition has been given to the notion that effective life skills, especially those related to social interaction and problem solving, can facilitate successful adjustment (Danish & D'Augelli, 1980; Danish, Galambos, & Laquatra, 1983; National Mental Health Association Commission on the Prevention of Mental-Emotional Disabilities, 1986; Spivack, 1986). Bloom (1984), asserting that personal competence, particularly in social situations, can moderate the effects of stressful life events, found support for this idea in the current research:

> Much human misery appears to be the result of a lack of competence—that is, a lack of control over one's life, a lack of effective coping strategies, and the lowered self-esteem that accompanies these deficiencies. This opinion is emerging out of an analysis of a substantial body of research from a variety of domains that appears to converge on competence building as one of the most persuasive preventive strategies for dealing with individual and social issues in many communities. (p. 279)

Although many models for psychosocial competence training have been advanced, both Bloom (1984) and Masterpasqua (1981) have suggested that competency enhancement efforts call for alliances between researchers interested in human development and those concerned with community interventions. Particularly promising is a developmental approach to life skills training.

Gazda's Life Skills Training Model

A training model designed by Gazda and others (Gazda, 1984; Gazda, Childers, & Brooks, in press) and actually called Life Skills Training successfully applies developmental theory to the task of competence building. The model emphasizes four "generic" skills: (1) interpersonal communication/human relations, (2) problem solving/decision making, (3) physical fitness/health maintenance, and (4) identity development/purpose in life. Generic life skills represent families of related skills. Gazda and his colleagues have also identified some 300 specific life skills, however, categorizing them according to their age appropriateness and the area of human development to which they relate. Underlying the Life Skills Training model are several basic assumptions, which Gazda (1984) has summarized as follows:

> 1. Within the multiple dimensions of human development [psychosocial, physical-sexual, vocational, cognitive, ego, moral, and affective development], there are stages through which all persons must progress if they are to lead effective lives. Some of these are age-related; some are not.
> 2. Satisfactory progression through the stages depends on the successful accomplishment of developmental tasks that are specific to the stages.
> 3. Accomplishment of the developmental tasks is dependent on mastery of life skills appropriate to stage and task.

4. Each person encounters many agents (parents, siblings, teachers, peers, social institutions, and so on) through which life skills may be learned.

5. There are certain age ranges during which certain life skills can be most easily learned.

6. Individuals inherit their capacity for learning, but the degree to which they are able to achieve their maximum potential is the result of their environment and/or life experiences.

7. Individuals achieve optimal functioning when they attain operational mastery of fundamental life skills.

8. Neuroses and functional psychoses result from failure to develop one's life skills. Persons experiencing such dysfunctions are usually suffering from multiple life skills deficits. Within the context of an interview-counseling group or in individual consultation with a therapist, such persons are able to identify their life skills deficits as well as the areas in which life skills mastery has been reached.

9. Life skills can be taught most effectively through the medium of the small group, provided members are developmentally ready. Therefore, the most satisfactory means of ensuring positive mental health and of remediating psychological dysfunction is through direct teaching/ training in life skills, especially if two or more areas of life skills deficits are addressed concurrently. (p. 93)

In accordance with these general principles, Life Skills Training teaches skills that have been identified by analyzing the coping behaviors appropriate to the developmental tasks of a given age or stage across the seven dimensions of human development. Gazda and his colleagues use an instructional mode in a small group setting to teach life skills appropriate to the deficits and readiness of individual participants. The same training approach is used whether the life skills training is used for prevention or for remediation. Regardless of the degree of dysfunction among clients/trainees, the goal of the sessions is to move participants up a pyramid of training from client/trainee to trainer. The four steps that make up this training pyramid include the following:

Step 1: Training in generic life skills.
1. Didactic presentation of the rationale for the model of the generic life skill to be taught— "tell."
2. Modeling or demonstration of the behavior(s) or response(s) to be mastered—"show."
3. Practice by trainees/students of the skills to be mastered—"do."

    4. Homework application of new skill to daily living—"transfer."

    5. Self-monitoring/assessment (as well as monitoring/assessment by trainer and fellow trainees) of skill level achieved—"feedback."

    6. Trainees assist one another in developing skills—"peer bonding."

Step 2: Cotraining with "master" trainer (usually staff member but may be fellow client/trainee who has "graduated" from Step 4).

Step 3: Training under supervision of "master" trainer.

Step 4: Training alone. (Gazda, 1984, p. 95)

Life Skills Training is actually a part—the heart—of a program Gazda calls Multiple Impact Training. We can see how the training works in context by examining the Multiple Impact Training program implemented by the psychiatric division of the Veterans Administration Medical Center in Augusta, Georgia. When patients enter the program, they first participate in a screening group for one hour a day, four days a week. In this screening group, they learn about the Life Skill Training options that are open to them and explore their own problem areas. The patients then choose for themselves the Life Skills Training group or groups in which they will participate. The medical center offers the following groups:

> Interpersonal Communications, Physical Fitness/Health Maintenance, Purpose in Life, Problem Solving, Vocational/Career Development, and Leisure Time. . . . [plus] Relaxation Therapy (a subgroup of Physical Fitness), Assertiveness Training (a subgroup of Interpersonal Communications), [and] Problem Drinking. (Gazda, 1984, p. 88)

In addition to the Life Skills Training, patients can choose a traditional therapy group, occupational therapy, corrective therapy, or recreational therapy. These elements are combined to form individualized plans based on each client's current skills and deficits; final responsibility for the course of training belongs to the client.

At the medical center, which is an inpatient, remedial setting, the training is intensive, with groups meeting for two hours a day, four to five days a week, for up to three weeks. But the Life Skills Training model is designed not just for remediation but for prevention. Early results of applications in school systems in both Georgia and Illinois have shown promise (Gazda, 1984) and Gazda and Brooks (1980) have suggested that Life Skills Training could serve as an organizing framework for preventive service delivery in university counseling centers and community mental health centers. Among the various training modes that can be adapted to the needs of specific populations and settings following this model are consultant-led training groups, trainer-led training groups (where consultants have trained trainers within an organization), media-assisted training groups, leaderless skill development groups, and teleconference training groups (Gazda, Childers, & Brooks, in press).

Guerney's Relationship Enhancement Training

Another example of a systematic general approach to life skills is Relationship Enhancement (RE) training (Guerney, 1977, 1984; Guerney, Coufal, & Vogelson, 1981). Like Gazda's model, Guerney's approach has been designed for prevention or remediation; further, Relationship Enhancement (RE) training has been adapted for use with individuals, families, organizations, and helping professionals. The purpose of this training is to build skills that will:

1. Help the participants to find realistic ways to achieve personal and interpersonal goals and to achieve better understanding of their self-concepts, their emotions, their conflicts, their problems, and their wishes and goals.
2. Help them to better elicit help and cooperation from others that will enable them to deepen their understanding and meet their personal and vocational goals.
3. Help them to become more personally appealing to other persons who are important to them.
4. Help them to better understand others' self-concepts, emotions, conflicts, problems, desires, and goals.
5. Help them to be more effective in helping others by promoting others' self-understanding; by showing others compassionate appreciation of their needs; by offering to others, in appropriate ways and at appropriate times, insights and suggestions for constructive change.
6. Help participants to understand and resolve problems between themselves and others in a constructive and enduring way—a way that takes all realities, including emotional ones, into account and a way that comes closest to satisfying all parties.
7. Increase participants' ability to enrich their relationships with those who are important to them in love, work, and play—that is, enable them to discover more ways to increase the enjoyment and productivity they experience in such relationships.

8. Help participants to increase their ability to generalize and to transfer these skills (and other desired skills) into their daily life and to maintain them over time.
9. Help participants to increase their ability to teach significant others the skills necessary to accomplish the above. (Guerney, 1984, pp. 173–174)

RE training is based on the notion that effective living depends on an individual's abilities both to give understanding and to receive it, to empathize with others and to generate their empathy in return. The training therefore teaches people how to respond more effectively to others. Cognitive and behavioral instruction are systematically combined to teach participants (1) *expressive skills* (self-understanding and the ability to communicate this understanding effectively), (2) *empathic skills* (seeing the world as others see it, emotionally identifying with the feelings of others, and showing respect and compassion), (3) *mode switching* (using expressive and empathic skills appropriately), (4) *interpersonal conflict and problem resolution,* (5) *facilitation* (eliciting reactions from others that will enrich relationships and foster personal growth), and (6) *generalization and maintenance* (making the newly learned behaviors an integral part of one's life).

Although many of these attitudes and behaviors can be fostered through counseling or therapy, Guerney emphasizes the importance of basing the skill training on a mass educational model rather than a clinical or medical model. The role of the trainer is to

(1) motivate, (2) explain, (3) demonstrate, (4) model/prompt, (5) supervise skill practice within the training sessions, (6) prepare the learner to be successful with homework, (7) supervise homework, (8) prepare the learner to use the skills spontaneously in everyday living, (9) supervise the transfer of skills into everyday living, and (10) supervise the acquisition of maintenance skills. (Guerney, 1984, pp. 186–187)

The trainer thus facilitates the learning process; the client, however, maintains responsibility for mastering and maintaining selected goals.

The Structured Learning Model

Still another example of a skill training model designed to respond to the needs of participants is Structured Learning Therapy (Goldstein, 1981; Goldstein, Gershaw, & Sprafkin, 1984). Its creators, recognizing that traditional therapies tend to succeed primarily with middle- or upper-class patients, designed

Structured Learning Therapy to meet the needs of lower-class patients, developing a treatment that is "brief, concrete, behavioral, actional, and authoritatively administered and which require[s] imitation of specific, overt examples, [teaches] role-taking skills, and provide[s] early, continuing, and frequent reinforcement for enactment of seldom-used but adaptive skill behaviors" (Goldstein, Gershaw, & Sprafkin, 1984, p. 73).

This model is unusual both in the specific skill areas it addresses and in the training methods it uses. Fifty-nine specific skills are taught, as listed below:[2]

Basic Skills

Series I   Conversations: Beginning Skills
1. Starting a conversation
2. Carrying on a conversation
3. Ending a conversation
4. Listening

Series II   Conversations: Expressing Oneself
5. Expressing a compliment
6. Expressing appreciation
7. Expressing encouragement
8. Asking for help
9. Giving instructions
10. Expressing affection
11. Expressing a complaint
12. Persuading others
13. Expressing anger

Series III   Conversations: Responding to Others
14. Responding to praise
15. Responding to the feelings of others (empathy)
16. Apologizing
17. Following instructions
18. Responding to persuasion
19. Responding to failure
20. Responding to contradictory messages
21. Responding to a complaint
22. Responding to anger

Series IV   Planning Skills
23. Setting a goal
24. Gathering information

[2]Adapted from "Structured Learning Therapy: Background, Procedures, and Evaluation" by A. P. Goldstein, N. J. Gershaw, and R. P. Sprafkin, 1984. In D. L. Larson (Ed.), *Teaching Psychological Skills: Models for Giving Psychology Away* (pp. 76–77), Pacific Grove, CA: Brooks/Cole. Copyright © 1984 by Wadsworth, Inc. Adapted by permission.

25. Concentrating on a task
26. Evaluating your abilities
27. Preparing for a stressful conversation
28. Setting problem priorities
29. Decision making

Series V Alternatives to Aggression
30. Identifying and labeling your emotions
31. Determining responsibility
32. Making requests
33. Relaxation
34. Self-control
35. Negotiation
36. Helping others
37. Assertiveness

Application Skills
38. Finding a place to live
39. Moving in (typical)
40. Moving in (difficult)
41. Managing money
42. Neighboring
43. Job seeking (typical)
44. Job seeking (difficult)
45. Job keeping (average day's work)
46. Job keeping (strict boss)
47. Receiving telephone calls (difficult)
48. Restaurant eating
49. Organizing time
50. Using leisure time (learning something new)
51. Using leisure time (interpersonal activity)
52. Social (party)
53. Social (church supper)
54. Marital (positive interaction)
55. Marital (negative interaction)
56. Using community resources (seeking money)
57. Using community resources (avoiding red tape)
58. Dealing with crises (transition from inpatient to nonpatient)
59. Dealing with crises (loss)

The methods used to train participants in these skills include modeling, role playing, and performance feedback, as well as strategies to ensure that participants transfer what they learn to real life. Trainees, working in groups with others who share the same skill deficiencies, first listen to audiocassettes on which actors model the skill to be learned in a variety of situations. (A library of 59 tapes, each focused on a single skill, has been developed for the training.) The trainees then discuss what they have heard, use role playing to practice the skill, receive feedback on their role playing, practice some more, and receive reinforcement for performing the skills in real-life situations.

Structural Learning Therapy is appropriate for individuals with major needs, including deinstitutionalized patients, but the model is clearly adaptable to preventive intervention as well. A separate set of structured learning skills has been developed for adolescents, and Goldstein (1981) has suggested that future variations might focus on children, premarital adults, parents, retirement planners, or others who could profit from learning developmental skills.

Life Planning

Counselors in all settings are likely to encounter individuals grappling with decisions affecting their personal or career plans. Although these kinds of issues can be resolved effectively through individual counseling, they also lend themselves well to educational workshops.

Life Planning Workshops

Workshops such as Life Work Planning (Kirn & Kirn, 1978) are likely to appeal to the general population and can be conducted with or without a leader for any number of small groups working simultaneously. Participants in the groups use a number of exercises, all described in detail in Life Work Planning workbooks, to examine their current work situations, their past experiences, their values, their preferences, and their personalities. Participants are encouraged to fantasize their ideal future, as well as to make practical assessments about the constraints in their lives. On the basis of the self-awareness gained through the exercises, participants develop specific plans, acquiring skills in program planning and decision making. Ideally, each participant emerges from the workshop with some kind of concrete plan for immediate action. More important, however, the participants have acquired life planning skills that they can use whenever necessary.

Any approach to life planning is likely to include three components: (1) self-assessment procedures, (2) goal-setting activities, and (3) strategy formulation (Lewis & Lewis, 1986).

Counselors offering life planning workshops to community members frequently use standardized assessment instruments to begin the decision-making process. The *Career Maturity Inventory* (New York: McGraw-Hill) is especially useful for developmentally oriented career counseling, measuring two aspects of career maturity: attitudes and competence. The attitudes measured include involvement, independence, orientation, decisiveness, and compromise—all important in the decision-making process. The competence scale measures career-related cognitive areas such as self-appraisal, occupational information, goal selection, planning, and problem solving. Participants' interests can be clarified through the *Strong-Campbell Interest Inventory* (Palo Alto, CA: Stanford University Press) or the *Kuder Preference Records and Interest Surveys* (Chicago: Science Research Associates). Holland's *Self-Directed Search* (Palo Alto, CA: Consulting Psychologists Press), a self-administered, self-scoring workbook, lets clients determine their personality types and the kinds of work environments likely to suit them. The *Vocational Preference Inventory* (Palo Alto, CA: Consulting Psychologists Press), based on a list of job titles, also uses Holland's categories to identify individual vocational types: realistic, investigative, artistic, social, enterprising, and conventional.

A workshop or group session can also begin with less formal self-awareness exercises, with participants using open-ended questions or nonstandardized checklists to identify their values, interests, and attitudes. Members can write down and share fantasies, maintain calendars to depict their work history and career plans, describe peak work experiences, analyze their hobbies, or compile lists of satisfying achievements or things that make them happy. Each exercise encourages group interaction and, at the same time, lays the groundwork for setting goals.

Once participants have clarified their interests through the self-assessment process, they can begin to formulate immediate and long-range goals. On the basis of their self-assessments, participants can now establish clear goals in relation to their careers or lifestyle. With the counselor's support, group members can help one another devise objectives that are concrete, realistic, and consistent with their interests and skills.

Realistic goals make possible the formulation of concrete, practical strategies. Participants begin developing a practical plan of action by generating alternatives. They then weigh the costs and benefits of each option to end up with a list of goal-oriented activities. All participants should emerge from the life planning workshop with a set of concrete steps they can take immediately.

> The real purpose of self-exploration is to provide a foundation from which individuals can clarify directions for future growth and development and initiate plans to achieve their goals. And the more specific and thoughtful the action plans, the greater the likelihood that the goals will be reached. (Fisher & Walz, 1982, p. 65)

The process can thus be considered successful if participants emerge with a program of action that is likely to lead to the successful attainment of each goal.

Career Transition Workshops

Workshops and seminars can also be used to assist community members dealing with career-related transitions. These clients, too, need to go through the steps of self-assessment, goal setting, and strategy formulation. They might, however, also need information and support to help them deal with the specific life change they are contemplating. For this reason, community counselors frequently provide focused experiences for groups of people undergoing similar transitions. For example, counselors working with adult clients might develop workshops for community members preparing for retirement.

Retirement from the work world is a difficult transition because many life factors are affected simultaneously.

> The economic impact of retirement is almost universal; even if retirement benefits are good, the individual's income will probably decrease. But social and psychological factors can be equally important to the retiree. If the individual's needs for social status, human relationships, and a sense of being valued have been met primarily through his or her work, these social purposes must be met in some other way after retirement. If an employee has used his or her job to maintain self-esteem, identity, and feelings of competence, his or her psychological well-being can be jeopardized by feeling that a valued career is over. . . . Retirees need to come to grips with a sense of loss, develop new support systems, and plan for an adjustment to a new lifestyle and environment. (Lewis & Lewis, 1986, p. 186)

Because the retirement transition is so psychologically demanding, personal support is important. A group format both gives members an opportunity to help one another and offers an efficient means for disseminating information. In the group, participants can develop retirement strategies based on careful self-assessment and accurate information. Among the factors that can be discussed are finances, health enhancement, lifestyle issues, social systems outside of work, and retirement stresses. Planning can make retirement—or any important life transition—a positive event: "The sensible person doesn't really retire. He or she changes activities or occupations. One who retires to do something else, to live life in a positive new way, is still in command. One who has 'been retired' is a victim" (Downs & Roll, 1981, p. 2).

Retirement planning, like all of the educational interventions provided by community counselors, is meant to enhance participants' personal control over their own lives and to give them the tools they will need for effective living at any age.

Parent Education

Of all of the life skills that have been identified as affecting individual well-being, parenting is clearly among the most important. Furthermore, as Weissbourd (1986) has pointed out, parenthood involves not just a set of behaviors or the application of a skill but a developmental stage.

> Being a parent involves not only interconnectedness and interaction with a child but recognition that being a parent is a developmental state of adulthood. After many years of focusing upon the development of the child and looking at parents primarily as vehicles through which that development could proceed, emphasis has shifted toward examining parents as developing persons and understanding the interactional qualities and effects of parent-child relationships upon parents, children, and families. (Weissbourd, 1986, p. 44)

Understanding parenthood as a time of intense adult development brings with it a change in the focus of parent education. There is increased recognition now that parents need support as well as information, and opportunities to grow as well as means to foster their children's growth. In response, many agencies have developed family support programs designed to build parents' confidence, coping skills, and knowledge. Weissbourd's 1986 definitions of the types of programs now being offered by the many organizations that make up the Family Resource Coalition include the following:

- *Adolescent parenting programs:* Comprehensive services offered to adolescent mothers and fathers
- *Day care/Head Start parent programs:* Programs designed to support the child rearing roles of parents whose children are being served in day care centers
- *Community-based drop-in centers:* Centers offering supportive services such as parent groups and parent-child activities

- *Home visitor programs:* Services provided to high-risk parents in their homes
- *Parent support groups:* Parent education and support groups in which parents, especially single or working parents, can share experiences, concerns, and feelings
- *Parent support networks:* Networks run by parents and providing activities such as discussion groups, socials, classes, and information and referral services
- *Warm-lines:* Telephone consultation services providing support and information to help parents deal with everyday concerns

All these programs combine personal and social support with information dissemination. This is true of more and more programs as agencies seek to play a preventive role by acting as resources for parents rather than as service systems on which families might become dependent.

> Parent support programs represent an ecological approach to the family. They exist to offer parents opportunities to connect with others: to relieve isolation, cope with stress, absorb and integrate the information they need to be able to rear competent and healthy children, and to advocate for social policies which benefit their families. If available when couples become parents, the resources of family support programs can enable the healthy start which defines primary prevention. (Weissbourd, 1986, p. 48)

Parent education programs that have a radiating effect—that is, that facilitate the transfer of learning from the initial participants to their friends and neighbors—are especially powerful primary prevention tools. Programs that promote this kind of learning can reach larger numbers of people than could ever be reached by professionals alone. They also encourage people to take responsibility for their own learning. A community counselor can affect many individuals by training a small number of people who can in turn teach others within the community.

As early as 1959, a number of "parent study groups" had been established in conjunction with Child Guidance Centers in Chicago and Los Angeles, as well as in Iowa, New York, and Oregon (Reed, 1959). As the idea spread, groups of parents sharing their knowledge and ideas about child rearing were formed in a myriad of locations, with professionals providing only the initial impetus, materials, and study guides. Often, professionals would lead just one parent study group, training that group to lead new groups with a minimum of supervision. Books such as *Raising a Responsible Child: Practical Steps to Successful Family Relationships* (Dinkmeyer & McKay, 1973) served as reference manuals for such groups.

Packaged programs represent a variation on this approach. One particularly well-organized program is STEP (Systematic Training for Effective Parenting), a nine-session program developed by Dinkmeyer and McKay (1976). STEP, like the more recently developed STEP/Teen (Dinkmeyer & McKay, 1983), is designed to teach parents skills helpful in raising children. The package includes reading materials for each participant as well as audiotapes and guides for the trainer. Each session features exercises and discussions on topics such as understanding behavior, expressing encouragement, effective discipline, communication patterns, decision making, and family meetings.

STEP and STEP/Teen are based on a coherent theoretical framework at the core of which is the belief that parents can discipline their children most effectively if they understand the goals of their children's behavior and make youngsters responsible for the consequences of their own actions. Through these two programs, parents learn to communicate more effectively, to encourage their children, and to use family meetings to reach decisions, promote mutual support, resolve conflicts, and foster cooperation and social learning.

Another approach that has remained popular for many years is Parent Effectiveness Training, or PET (Gordon, 1971). In PET, trained instructors lead a series of discussion sessions in which:

1. Parents are taught to differentiate between those situations in which the child is making it difficult for himself to meet his own needs . . . and those situations in which the child is making it difficult for the parent to meet his own needs.
2. Parents are given skill training in . . . verbal communication. . . .
3. Parents are given skill training in those forms of verbal communication that have been shown to be most effective when one person wants to influence another person to modify behavior. . . .
4. Parents are then given skill training in specific methods of preventing conflicts between parent and child. . . .
5. Parents are taught the hazards and harmful effects of using . . . win-lose (power struggle) methods of conflict resolution. . . .
6. Parents are then given skill training in using a non-power or "no-lose" method of resolving all conflicts between parent and child. . . . (Gordon, 1971, p. 49)

A program known as SOAP (Solution Oriented Approach to Problems) takes a more eclectic approach. The assumption here is that "we should be working with parents to help them understand ways of approaching problems, rather than arriving on the scene with our solutions derived from theoretical positions" (Lamb, 1986, pp. 177–178). Accordingly, group members are asked to generate at least 10 possible solutions to each problem presented by a parent. The group leader, meanwhile, tries to ensure that the solutions suggested represent a variety of theoretical perspectives, since families vary in the degree to which any one approach may fit.

> Anyone who attempts to have a family engage in a nonfitting procedure is bound to be something less than successful. By having the target parents select from the array of solutions, after first stating something they like and something they do not like about each item in the array, we find parents selecting items or combinations of items that are compatible with their style. Such compatibility is prerequisite to the parent implementing the solution. (Lamb, 1986, pp. 178–179)

Though finding solutions is a goal of most parent education programs, in the end, the content of a particular training course may be less important than the context. The benefit parents derive from supporting and encouraging one another in the search for new ideas and skills can be as valuable as the actual information they obtain.

School-Based Programs

People concerned with primary prevention have come to recognize that programs can and should focus on the developmental needs of young children, especially in the areas of social skills and problem solving. Both the prevention task panel of the President's Commission on Mental Health (1978) and the more recently formed National Mental Health Association Commission on the Prevention of Mental-Emotional Disabilities (1986) recommended that prevention programs for the very young be given priority and that school-based programs, beginning at the preschool level, be implemented and studied. The logic of this approach is unrefutable.

> Given that (a) a large number of children suffer from poor relationships, (b) the quality of children's social relationships affects the development of current and future psychopathology, and (c) many adequately functioning children remain vulnerable to later maladaptation, social competence training to improve children's skills at relating with others appears to be a very desirable prevention strategy. (Weissberg & Allen, 1986, p. 156)

If children are an appropriate target group for primary prevention, the school is an ideal setting.

> Schools are . . . well suited as sites for interventions that are designed particularly to prevent social maladjustment and peer relationship problems. In a school setting the youngsters have multiple opportunities to discuss rationales for using social skills, practice using them, and receive feedback on their behavior. Further, classroom-based efforts to enhance social skills are desirable because most children find the group setting more attractive than relatively infrequent interactions with an unfamiliar therapist. . . . School-based prevention approaches reduce the possibility that children will be stigmatized, because youngsters receiving training need not be labeled as emotionally disturbed or mentally ill. . . . Without direct intervention to promote adaptive interpersonal behavior, the adjustment of too many children who have social relationship problems gets worse, or at best, remains unchanged, and these untreated children continue to be vulnerable to later problems. (Weissberg & Allen, 1986, p. 157)

School-based programs allow children to be reached efficiently at the ages most appropriate for learning particular skills. Even more important, because they are aimed at a broad range of young people who have not necessarily exhibited problems, school-based programs help to exemplify the focus on competency building and health promotion.

The notion of developing structured programs to enhance the social skills of school children is not a new one. In fact, several programs have been in existence for a number of years and have withstood enough rigorous evaluation to warrant their continuance (President's Commission on Mental Health, 1978). Programs that have successfully taught interpersonal cognitive problem-solving skills to young children provide a striking example.

Interpersonal cognitive problem-solving (ICPS) skills involve "the capacity to think of alternative solutions to a problem, the tendency to think of consequences before taking action, the ability to conceptualize the steps necessary in carrying out a problem-solving plan of action, and the tendency to see causes for and in human behavior" (Spivack, 1986, p. 72). The ability to perform these skills seems to distinguish healthy from maladapted groups of children.

> Those who have and use those skills effectively appear to others in interpersonal relations as well adjusted behaviorally. Those who lack or are deficient in such skills are seen as maladjusted. . . . ICPS skills can thus be thought of as mediating effective behavioral adjustment. If that is so, the challenge it presents for primary prevention is to find ways to equip children, as early

and effectively as possible, with those skills. (President's Commission on Mental Health, 1978, p. 1841)

Considerable work has been done to teach interpersonal cognitive problem-solving skills to nursery school and elementary-age children, with the benefits enduring beyond completion of the curriculum (Spivack, 1986). A number of studies (Spivack & Shure, 1974, 1982; Shure & Spivack, 1982) have attempted to measure both the effects of ICPS training on children's skills and the long-term effects of skill development on behavioral adjustment. Training groups consistently improved more than controls after participating in well-designed programs that taught basic skills, trained children to generate alternatives and anticipate consequences, and provided practice in solving real problems as they arose during the school day. Spivack (1986) summarized these findings, noting that normal nursery school children exposed to the program were less likely to exhibit signs of behavioral problems than other normal four-and-a-half-year-olds and that programs for older elementary-age children yielded "positive ameliorating effects" and "prevented the negative impact of the stress of school change from elementary to junior high school" (p. 72).

Another well-researched program is the Primary Mental Health Project, which was initiated in Rochester, New York, in 1958 and which has since been adapted to other locations (Cowen, Gesten, & Wilson, 1979; Cowen, Izzo et al., 1963; Cowen, Zax, Izzo, & Trost, 1966). The project began as an attempt at early detection of children at risk for chronic maladjustment to school and gradually grew to include both consultative services for teachers and parents and direct help to children. The program has been expanded to include the training of aides to provide special experiences and coaching to children outside of the classroom, the presentation of after-school programs staffed by volunteers, and the training of mental health professionals so that the program can be transplanted to other settings.

Throughout the project's evolution, the work of Cowen and his colleagues in the Primary Mental Health Project has rested on four principles:

> (a) focusing on elementary school children, who with early intervention can change significantly for the better before early behavioral warning signs become extended serious problems; (b) using active systematic screening procedures to identify children experiencing behavioral, social, and emotional problems that interfere with learning; (c) bringing prompt, effective, preventively oriented help to large numbers of identified children, using care-

fully selected, interpersonally skilled, paraprofessional child aides; and (d) modifying the role of school mental health professionals from individual assessment and treatment of relatively few seriously troubled youngsters toward training and supervision of child aides and increased consultation with teachers so that more children receive effective help. (Weissberg & Allen, 1986, p. 163)

The results of their research have consistently demonstrated that children participating in the intervention program became better adjusted, in contrast with members of the control group (Cowen, Gesten, & Wilson, 1979).

School-based interventions based on behavioral approaches have also shown a great deal of promise for primary prevention. A series of programs carried out in Chicago by Jason and his associates (1980) have "utilized various behavioral technologies to prevent the development of specific maladaptive responses, to establish and build competencies, and to help youngsters navigate through milestone developmental transitions" (p. 114).

One of these programs, aimed at preventing adolescents from smoking, formed support groups among ninth-grade students to help students develop assertive responses that would help them resist pressures to smoke. Evaluation of the program showed that nonsmokers had remained abstinent and that cigarette smoking had declined among those students who had already begun to smoke before the program started.

Another program used operant techniques to improve academic achievement and adjustment to school among elementary-age children. All of the children in one class were taught peer-tutoring skills and had opportunities to serve as both tutors and students. The youngsters "manifested increases in appropriate classroom behavior during nonproject times, earned higher math and spelling grades, and 50 percent of the students indicated they used the peer-tutoring game during nonproject times with friends and relatives" (Jason, 1980, p. 115). Later follow-up showed that the teacher considered the children to have improved in their overall adjustment.

Another series of group interventions used a variety of behavioral techniques to help children cope with transitions. One program used operant techniques to improve the classroom behaviors of first graders. Another helped adolescents entering high school to improve their public speaking skills. Still another helped students who had to transfer to a public school after the closing of their parochial school. All of these programs succeeded in helping the children develop adaptive competencies that would allow them to cope with normal life transitions.

Common to all of the school-based programs is a recognition that a variety of mental and physical health problems and adjustment difficulties can be prevented by timely intervention. If children can be helped in their early years to develop life skills and competencies that can see them through adolescence and adulthood, they can withstand a variety of pressures. Community counselors, whether employed by schools or by community agencies, can play a major role in developing, implementing, and evaluating such important interventions.

Community Mental Health Centers

Community mental health centers are agencies responsible for serving the mental health needs of the general population residing within given geographical boundaries. The Community Mental Health Act of 1963 authorized seed money for such centers provided they offered a broad range of services, including inpatient and outpatient services, partial hospitalization, emergency services, and consultation and education. The federal guidelines that provided direction for the original community mental health centers emphasized community-based prevention programs. As community mental health has evolved over the years, however, centers have differed in their interpretation of the community mental health concept and in their success at implementing truly preventive programs. Those centers that have maintained strong consultation and education components have been at the forefront of preventive education, offering a wide array of workshops and seminars to meet the needs of local community members. One example of a community mental health center with a strong consultation and education component is the Tri-City Community Mental Health Center, which serves several communities in northwest Indiana.

The Tri-City Community Mental Health Center offers a variety of residential and outpatient programs for adolescents, adults, and families at risk. In addition to treatment services, however, the center offers over 12,000 hours of educational programs each year under the auspices of its consultation and education department. In one recent season, the following programs were available free or at low cost to community members:

- *Premenstrual Syndrome:* A lecture for women focusing on the causes, treatment, and self-management of premenstrual syndrome
- *Unemployment:* A free workshop in which the unemployed and their families learn ways to manage transitional stress and rebuild the future

- *Self-Defense for Women and Girls:* A six-session course designed to teach women ways to protect themselves at home, school, or work
- *Eight Ways to Destroy Your Child:* An examination of approaches to child rearing, using a look at what hurts children as an "eye-opener" and a beginning for change
- *Criando Sus Hijos—Buscando Mejores Formas de Relacionarse con Ellos* [Raising Your Children—Looking for Better Ways of Relating with Them]: A program for Spanish-speaking parents
- *Relieving Your Pain:* A pain management and reduction program teaching techniques such as imagery, relaxation, and biofeedback to chronic pain sufferers
- *AIDS Information Session:* An information session offered free of charge to community members and focusing on the emotional impact of the disease on family and friends of affected individuals
- *Horticulture to Feel Better:* An informational session on gardening and its emotional benefits for children and adults
- *Stepping Out—Goodbye to Guilt and Depression:* A seminar offered to help individuals take the first steps out of depression
- *Teen Life—Don't Let It Die:* An information session discussing myths regarding teen suicide, warning signs, preventive measures, and sources of help for suicidal teens
- *Business Special:* A series of breakfast meetings dealing with work issues such as team building, conflict management, and supervision of troubled employees
- *Busy Women's Special:* Lunchtime workshops focusing on interpersonal skills; juggling home, career, and family responsibilities; and stress management and creative problem solving

In addition to these programmed workshops, the center's consultation and education department offers "Workshops To Go," programs and talks ready for presentation at meetings of community groups that choose special topics of interest to their members. Further, agencies, organizations, schools, and the juvenile court consult with the mental health center regularly to assess the needs of community members and to develop special programs. The center also provides consultation and training to the "Tender Loving Caregivers," volunteers in an interfaith coalition who offer respite care to the families of people with Alzheimer's disease and related disorders. Adolescent substance abuse programs operated by the center in two separate communities offer GED classes in the morning and rap groups, activities, counseling, and field trips in the afternoon and evening. Tri-City, like other mental health centers that have maintained a concern for prevention, thus offers community members many opportunities to gain the specific knowledge and skills that answer their needs.

Summary

Recognizing community needs and developing prevention programs capable of reaching large numbers of people who have not yet developed dysfunctions are central components of community counseling. Preventive education programs train community members in life skills and competencies that they can use to buffer the effects of stress and maintain good physical and mental health.

Such programs are most effective if they are designed to meet the needs of the specific community or client population being served. It is possible, however, to identify some general approaches that appear to hold a great deal of promise for primary prevention. Some of the most important preventive educational strategies include stress management training, health promotion programs, life skills training, life planning, parent education, and school-based mental health programs.

Some of the most extensive work in prevention has been done at community mental health centers, many of which maintain strong consultation and education components.

Supplemental Activities

1. Community counselors must frequently develop and implement workshops for community members. They can do this most effectively if they use regular, step-by-step planning procedures. Think of a particular topic and audience you would like to address and develop a workshop plan by following these steps:
    a. State the specific objectives of the workshop. How do you want participants to be different after the workshop than they were before? What new skills, attitudes, or knowledge are you trying to instill?

    b. Select the kinds of activities that are most likely to meet your objective. Consider lectures, discussions, case conferences, media, gaming, role playing, simulations, or any of a variety of other approaches. Which are most likely to achieve your objective?

    c. Consider the resources that would be available, including the nature of your own skills.

    d. Consider the audience you are addressing. What do you need to do to ensure their active involvement and interest?

    e. Develop a detailed design for the workshop, based on your analysis of the above factors.

    f. Design an evaluation method. How will you determine whether or not the workshop's objectives have been met?

2. After reading Chapter 1, you developed in broad outline a community counseling program to meet the needs of a particular population. Now, consider in detail the kinds of community education programs that might be appropriate for this target group. What preventive educational activities might help to build needed competencies?

Related Reading

BOND, L. A., & ROSEN, J. C. (Eds.). (1980). *Competence and coping during adulthood.* Hanover, NH: University Press of New England.

GATCHELL, R. J., & BAUM, A. (1983). *An introduction to health psychology.* Reading, MA: Addison-Wesley.

KETTERER, R. E. (1981). *Consultation and education in mental health: Problems and prospects.* Beverly Hills, CA: Sage Publications.

LARSON, D. (Ed.). (1984). *Teaching psychological skills: Models for giving psychology away.* Pacific Grove, CA: Brooks/Cole.

LEVANT, R. F. (Ed.). (1986). *Psychoeducational approaches to family therapy and counseling.* New York: Springer.

LAZARUS, R. (1966). *Psychological stress and the coping process.* New York: McGraw-Hill.

MEICHENBAUM, D., & JAREMKO, M. E. (Eds.). (1983). *Stress reduction and prevention.* New York: Plenum.

NICHOLAS, D. R., & KELLER, K. E. (1988). Behavioral medicine and the mental health counselor [Special issue]. *Journal of Mental Health Counseling, 10.*

SELYE, H. (1956). *The stress of life.* New York: McGraw-Hill.

References

ARDELL, D. B., & TAGER, M. J. (1982). *Planning for wellness: A guidebook for achieving optimal health* (2nd ed.). Dubuque, IA: Kendall/Hunt.

BARBER, T. X. (1982). Foreword to R. G. Straus, *Strategic self-hypnosis.* Englewood Cliffs, NJ: Prentice-Hall.

BENSON, H. (1975). *The relaxation response.* New York: Morrow.

BLOOM, B. L. (1984). *Community mental health* (2nd ed.). Pacific Grove, CA: Brooks/Cole.

COWEN, E. L., GESTEN, E. L., & WILSON, A. B. (1979). The primary mental health project: Evaluation of current program effectiveness. *American Journal of Community Psychology, 7,* 292–303.

COWEN, E. L., IZZO, L. D., MILES, H., TELSCHOW, E. F., TROST, M. A., & ZAX, M. (1963). A mental health program in the school setting: Description and evaluation. *Journal of Psychology, 56,* 307–356.

COWEN, E. L., ZAX, M., IZZO, L. D., & TROST M. A. (1966). The prevention of emotional disorders in the school setting: A further investigation. *Journal of Consulting and Clinical Psychology, 30,* 381–387.

DANISH, S. J. (1977). Human development and human services: A marriage proposal. In I. Iscoe, B. Bloom, & C. D. Spielberger (Eds.), *Community psychology in transition* (pp. 143–157). New York: Wiley.

DANISH, S. J., & D'AUGELLI, A. R. (1980). Promoting competence and enhancing development through life development intervention. In L. A. Bond & J. C. Rosen (Eds.), *Competence and coping during adulthood* (pp. 105–129). Hanover, NH: University Press of New England.

DANISH, S. J., GALAMBOS, N. L., & LAQUATRA, I. (1983). Life development intervention: Skill training for personal competence. In R. D. Felner, L. A. Jason, J. N. Moritsugu, & S. S. Farber (Eds.), *Preventive psychology: Theory, research, and practice* (pp. 49–66). New York: Pergamon Press.

DINKMEYER, D., & MCKAY, G. (1973). *Raising a responsible child: Practical steps to successful family relationships.* New York: Simon & Schuster.

DINKMEYER, D., & MCKAY, G. (1976). *STEP: Systematic training for effective parenting.* Circle Pines, MN: American Guidance Service.

DINKMEYER, D., & MCKAY, G. (1983). *STEP/Teen.* Circle Pines, MN: American Guidance Service.

DOWNS, H., & ROLL, R. J. (1981). *The best years book.* New York: Delacorte.

FARQUHAR, J. W., MACCOBY, N., WOOD, P. D., ALEXANDER, J. K., BREITROSE, H., BROWN, B. W., HASKELL, W. L., MCALISTER, A. L., MEYER, A. J., NASH, J. D., & STERN, M. (1977). Community education for cardiovascular health. *Lancet, 1,* 1192–1195.

FISHER, D. J., & WALZ, G. R. (1982). Self-exploration in career development. In G. Walz (Ed.), *Career development in organizations* (pp. 47–66). Ann Arbor, MI: ERIC/CAPS (Educational Resource Information Center/Counseling and Personnel Services).

FRIEDMAN, M., & ROSENMAN, R. H. (1974). *Type A behavior and your heart.* New York: Knopf.

GATCHELL, R. J., & BAUM, A. (1983). *An introduction to health psychology.* Reading, MA: Addison-Wesley.

GAZDA, G. M. (1984). Multiple impact training: A life skills approach. In D. Larson (Ed.), *Teaching psychological skills: Models for giving psychology away* (pp. 87–103). Pacific Grove, CA: Brooks/Cole.

GAZDA, G. M., & BROOKS, D. K. (1980). A comprehensive approach to developmental interventions. *Journal for Specialists in Group Work, 5,* 120–126.

GAZDA, G. M., CHILDERS, W. C., & BROOKS, D. K. (in press). *Foundations of counseling and human development.* New York: McGraw-Hill.

GIRDANO, D. A., & EVERLY, G. S. (1979). *Controlling stress and tension: A holistic approach.* Englewood Cliffs, NJ: Prentice-Hall.

GOLDFRIED, M. R., & GOLDFRIED, A. P. (1980). Cognitive change methods. In F. H. Kanfer & A. P. Goldstein (Eds.), *Helping people change* (2nd ed.) (pp. 97–130). New York: Pergamon Press.

GOLDSTEIN, A. P. (1981). *Psychological skill training.* New York: Pergamon Press.

GOLDSTEIN, A. P., GERSHAW, N. J., & SPRAFKIN, R. P. (1984). Structured learning therapy: Background, procedures, and evaluation. In D. Larson (Ed.), *Teaching psychological skills: Models for giving psychology away* (pp. 69–86). Pacific Grove, CA: Brooks/Cole.

GORDON, T. (1971). *A new model for humanizing families and schools.* Pasadena, CA: Effectiveness Training Associates.

GUERNEY, B. G. (1977). *Relationship Enhancement: Skill-training programs for therapy, problem prevention, and enrichment.* San Francisco: Jossey-Bass.

GUERNEY, B. G. (1984). Relationship enhancement therapy and training. In D. Larson (Ed.), *Teaching psychological skills: Models for giving psychology away* (pp. 171–206). Pacific Grove, CA: Brooks/Cole.

GUERNEY, B. G., COUFAL, J., & VOGELSON, E. (1981). Relationship Enhancement versus a traditional approach to therapeutic/preventative/enrichment parent-adolescent programs. *Journal of Consulting and Clinical Psychology, 49,* 927–929.

IVANCEVICH, J. M., & MATTESON, M. T. (1980). *Stress and work: A managerial perspective.* Glenview, IL: Scott, Foresman.

JASON, L. A. (1980). Prevention in the schools: Behavioral approaches. In R. H. Price, R. F. Ketterer, B. C. Bader, & J. Monahan (Eds.), *Prevention in mental health: Research, policy, and practice* (pp. 109–134). Beverly Hills: Sage Publications.

KETTERER, R. F., BADER, B. C., & LEVY, M. R. (1980). Strategies for promoting mental health. In R. H. Price, R. F. Ketterer, B. C. Bader, & J. Monahan (Eds.), *Prevention in mental health: Research, policy, and practice* (pp. 263–283). Beverly Hills: Sage Publications.

KIRN, A. G., & KIRN, M. O. (1978). *Life work planning* (4th ed.). New York: McGraw-Hill.

KOBASA, S. C. (1979). Stressful life events, personality, and health: An inquiry into hardiness. *Journal of Personality and Social Psychology, 37,* 1–11.

LAMB, W. (1986). Parent education. In R. F. Levant (Ed.), *Psychoeducational approaches to family therapy and counseling* (pp. 160–193). New York: Springer.

LEWIS, J. A., & LEWIS, M. D. (1986). *Counseling programs for employees in the workplace.* Pacific Grove, CA: Brooks/Cole.

MARTIN, D., & MARTIN, M. (1982). Nutritional counseling: A humanistic approach to psychological and physical health. *Personnel and Guidance Journal, 61,* 21–24.

MASTERPASQUA, F. (1981). Toward a synergism of developmental and community psychology. *American Psychologist, 36,* 782–786.

MATARAZZO, J. D. (1982). Behavioral health's challenge to academic, scientific, and professional psychology. *American Psychologist, 37,* 1–14.

MATTHES, W. A., & DUSTIN, D. (1980). The counselor as a trainer: Principles of workshop design. *School Counselor, 27,* 310–314.

MICHAEL, J. M. (1982). The second revolution in health: Health promotion and its environmental base. *American Psychologist, 37,* 936–941.

MORACCO, J. C., & MCFADDEN, H. (1982). The counselor's role in reducing teacher stress. *Personnel and Guidance Journal, 60,* 549–552.

NATIONAL MENTAL HEALTH ASSOCIATION COMMISSION ON THE PREVENTION OF MENTAL-EMOTIONAL DISABILITIES. (1986). *The prevention of mental-emotional disabilities: Report of the National Mental Health Association Commission on the Prevention of Mental-Emotional Disabilities.* Alexandria, VA: National Mental Health Association.

PRESIDENT'S COMMISSION ON MENTAL HEALTH. (1978). *Report of the task panel on prevention.* Washington, DC: U.S. Government Printing Office.

REED, M. (1959). Mother study groups. In R. Dreikurs, R. Corsini, R. Lowe, & M. Sonstegard (Eds.), *Adlerian family counseling: A manual for counseling centers.* Eugene: University of Oregon Press.

SARNOFF, D. (1982). Biofeedback: New uses in counseling. *Personnel and Guidance Journal, 60,* 357–360.

SHURE, M. B., & SPIVACK, G. (1982). Interpersonal problem solving in young children: A cognitive approach to prevention. *American Journal of Community Psychology, 10,* 341–356.

SPARKS, D., & INGRAM, M. J. (1979). Stress prevention and management: A workshop approach. *Personnel and Guidance Journal, 56,* 197–200.

SPIVACK, G. (1986). Psychological competencies in mental health prevention research and intervention. In *The prevention of mental-emotional disabilities: Resource papers to the report of the National Mental Health Association Commission on the Prevention of Mental-Emotional Disabilities* (pp. 71–76). Alexandria, VA: National Mental Health Association.

SPIVACK, G., & SHURE, M. B. (1974). *Social adjustment of young children.* San Francisco: Jossey-Bass.

SPIVACK, G., & SHURE, M. B. (1982). The cognition of social adjustment: Interpersonal cognitive problem-solving thinking. In B. B. Lahey & A. E. Kazdin (Eds.), *Advances in child clinical psychology* (Vol. 5, pp. 323–372). New York: Plenum.

STRAUS, R. G. (1982). *Strategic self-hypnosis.* Englewood Cliffs, NJ: Prentice-Hall.

THORESEN, C. E., & EAGLESTON, J. R. (1985). Counseling for health. *Counseling Psychologist, 13* (1), 15–87.

VENINGA, R. L., & SPRADLEY, J. P. (1981). *The work/stress connection: How to cope with job burnout.* Boston: Little, Brown.

WEISSBERG, R. P., & ALLEN, J. P. (1986). Promoting children's social skills and adaptive interpersonal behavior. In B. A. Edelstein & L. Michelson (Eds.), *Handbook of prevention* (pp. 153–175). New York: Plenum.

WEISSBOURD, B. (1986). Parent education and support. In *The prevention of mental-emotional disabilities: Resource papers to the report of the National Mental Health Association Commission on the Prevention of Mental-Emotional Disabilities.* Alexandria, VA: National Mental Health Association.

WILBUR, C. S. (1983). *The Johnson & Johnson Live for Life Program: Technical overview.* New Brunswick, NJ: Johnson & Johnson.

3

Outreach to Vulnerable Client Populations

At the same time that community counselors strive to prevent problems by strengthening the life competencies of the general population they serve, they recognize that some individuals and groups may be especially vulnerable and therefore in need of additional services. People under severe stress—whether because of chronic stressors, such as poverty, or immediate crises, such as the breakup of a family—risk developing physical or mental health problems. Such stress strains the individual's ability to cope, and may consequently bring new clients to counseling.

One way to conceptualize the delicate balance between people's resources and their life circumstances in the development of mental health problems is through an equation first devised by George Albee and cited by the National Mental Health Association (NMHA) Commission on the Prevention of Mental-Emotional Disabilities (1986, p. 13) as follows:

$$\text{Incidence} = \frac{\text{Organic Factors} + \text{Stress} + \text{Exploitation}}{\text{Coping Skills} + \text{Self-esteem} + \text{Social Support}}$$

Though designed for examining the variables affecting the incidence of mental health problems in general populations, the equation is equally valuable applied to specific populations or individuals: "In his formula, Albee balances the deficits of organic factors, stress and exploitation with the resources of coping skills, self-esteem and social support. A change in one or more of the components in the equation has an effect on mental-emotional stability or disability" (NMHA Commission on the Prevention of Mental-Emotional Disabilities, 1986, p. 13). Thus, people may become susceptible to mental or physical health problems when their life circumstances overwhelm their coping resources.

Community counselors attempt to prevent or mitigate such problems by recognizing potentially problematic situations and working to strengthen the ability of community members to cope, reaching out to people when they are at their most vulnerable. How these direct client services fit in the community counseling model is shown in Table 3.1.

As indicated in Table 3.1, outreach programs aimed at vulnerable populations are considered direct services to specific client groups. Such programs target individuals and groups that might at particular times be more vulnerable to stress than the general population and therefore in need of more intensive programming. Outreach can be preventive, as when community counselors, having identified certain situations as particularly stressful, intervene to help healthy individuals develop the resources to cope with them. When prevention is not possible and chronic problems or crises do develop, community counselors use outreach to provide support and assistance for those experiencing them.

Table 3.1 Outreach Strategies and the Community Counseling Model

	Community services	Client services
Direct	/ / / / / / / / / / / / / / / / / / / / / / / / / / / / / / / / / / / / / / / / / / / / / / / / / / / /	Outreach to vulnerable clients: High-risk situations Crises
Indirect	/ / / / / / / / / / / / / / / / / / / / / / / / / / / / / / / / / / / / / / /	/ / / / / / / / / / / / / / / / / / / / / / / / / / / / / / / / / / / / / / /

For example, counselors can significantly improve their clients' well-being by helping them adapt to new or difficult situations, which reduces some of the stress that accompanies change. Any situation that makes demands on an individual can be stressful, and potentially damaging, even one normally perceived as positive. Whether or not a situation will act as a stressor depends on how the person interprets the demand and on his or her ability to cope with it. According to Lazarus (1980), an individual may interpret a situation as irrelevant, benign-positive, or stressful. Lazarus further distinguished among stressful situations that represent harm or loss, threats to the individual's well-being, or challenges.

> The distinction between harm/loss, threat, and challenge may be very important not only in affecting the coping process itself and the effectiveness with which coping skills are utilized in social transactions, but also in their divergent consequences for morale and somatic health. . . . A working hypothesis about the causal antecedents of threat and challenge is that the former is more likely when a person assumes that the specific environment is hostile and dangerous and that he or she lacks the resources for mastering it, while challenge arises when the environmental demands are seen as difficult but not impossible to manage, and that drawing upon existing or acquirable skills offers a genuine prospect for mastery. (pp. 47–48)

Counselors can apply these distinctions by working to help clients take "personal control of their lives, accepting stress as a challenge rather than a harm-loss-threat factor, and finding personal meaning within stressful situations" (Stensrud & Stensrud, 1983, p. 216). Such an attitude helps clients to gain a sense of mastery, even when facing difficult problems or transitions.

In choosing methods they can use to enhance positive coping and decrease stress-related dysfunctions, counselors need to take into account factors that mediate the effects of potential crises. Once counselors become aware of the personal and situational characteristics that favor successful coping, they can develop methods for creating similar conditions. Several factors seem to characterize people who succeed in adapting to trying conditions:

1. *Successful copers have strong social support systems.* The availability of supportive associates seems to provide a buffer against the effects of stressful situations. Such relationships provide both personal validation and practical assistance; people faced with troublesome

situations can turn to family members, friends, or associates for information, advice, and concrete resources as well as emotional sustenance.

2. *Successful copers tend to have a sense of control over the environment.* Whether we term this factor "self-efficacy" or "internal locus of control," we know that people who cope effectively tend to do so because they believe their actions can have an effect on the world. Individuals differ in their general belief sytems concerning their ability to exert power and control when needed. In addition, the sense of control in a specific situation can be affected by the appraisal of the stressor and the presence or absence of adequate resources.

3. *Successful copers have the information and tools needed for effective problem solving.* Individuals' coping success depends, at least in part, on their skill in solving immediate problems and developing appropriate new behaviors. This factor involves both general life competence and situation-specific knowledge.

4. *Successful copers are confident that they can adapt to the new situation.* Realistic feelings of confidence come from the fact that adequate personal and financial resources are available and that the individual has coped successfully with similar transitions in the past. One aspect of confidence-building, then, is recognizing commonalities between the current situation and prior experiences. While the victim of job loss may never have been fired in the past, he or she has been successful in obtaining a position; the planning skills used at that time may still be valid. (Lewis & Lewis, 1986, pp. 177–178)

These factors are all interrelated. People's support systems help them solve problems, increasing both their sense of control and their confidence; confident people are more likely to have strong social support systems and to apply their problem-solving skills effectively.

Recognizing these buffering factors enables community counselors to become "buffer builders" (Aubrey & Lewis, 1983) creating opportunities for people under special stress within their communities to develop the resources they need to survive and grow while helping and supporting one another.

When counselors direct their efforts at encouraging the formation of groups having common interests and concerns, they can simultaneously build new social support systems, provide the context for skill development, and assist people to gain feelings of control over their lives. They can help their clients to create and maintain the buffers they need to withstand stress, both immediately and in the long run. (Aubrey & Lewis, 1983, p. 12)

Buffer building can be used to assist people dealing with expected transitions, unexpected crises, or ongoing stressors.

The key to intervention in outreach to vulnerable client populations is recognizing situations that are likely to lead to crises. We know that certain life events place heavy demands on individuals trying to cope with them. In a now classic study, Holmes and Rahe (1967) identified and ranked a number of life events that are particularly stressful:[1]

Death of spouse
Divorce
Marital separation
Jail term
Death of close family member
Personal injury or illness
Marriage
Fired at work
Marital reconciliation
Retirement
Change in health of family member
Pregnancy
Sex difficulties
Gain of new family member
Change in financial state
Death of close friend
Change to different line of work
Change in number of arguments with spouse
Mortgage over $10,000
Foreclosure of mortgage or loan
Change in responsibilities at work
Son or daughter leaving home
Trouble with in-laws
Outstanding personal achievement
Wife beginning or stopping work
Beginning or ending school
Revision of personal habits
Trouble with boss

[1] From "The Social Readjustment Rating Scale" by T. Holmes and R. Rahe, 1967, *Journal of Psychosomatic Research, 11.* Copyright 1967 by Pergamon Press. Reprinted with permission.

Change in hours or work conditions
Change in residence
Change in schools
Change in recreation
Change in social activities
Mortgage or loan less than $10,000
Change in sleeping habits
Change in number of family get-togethers
Change in eating habits
Vacation
Minor violations of the law

Many of the highest-ranked life changes signify other changes, as well. For instance, the death of or separation from a spouse, a jail term, personal injury, retirement, or the gain of a new family member may also bring about financial changes that can themselves trigger crises.

Model Outreach Programs

Successful programs build on what is known both about high-risk situations and about the resources that enable people to cope with them. Ideally, outreach programs for vulnerable clients should adhere to the following principles:

1. Use whatever sources of support are available, including peers, counselors, and people who can serve as models of successful coping.
2. Give individuals opportunities to help themselves and one another.
3. Inform clients about the nature of the new roles or situations they face.
4. Assist clients in developing the coping skills they are likely to need in their specific situations.
5. Use methods that enhance clients' sense of control over their situations and their lives.

Such actions help clients gain confidence and a greater sense of control as they learn to cope more effectively with their problems.

Many successful programs, serving diverse populations, have been developed to help clients facing high-risk situations.

Several programs can serve as models for outreach. The diverse populations served by these programs include adults and children dealing with marital disruption, families coping with the economic farm crisis, Vietnam veterans, people with chronic mental health problems, and people in crisis. If we consider again the Albee equation showing the balance between people's deficits and resources in relation to their mental health, we can see that what all of these people have in common is the need to ensure that their "denominator values" (coping skills, self-esteem, and social support) are strong enough to withstand powerful negative forces in the numerator. What these programs have in common, and part of the reason for their success, is that they combine timeliness with a clear focus on these denominator values. But the models described below are only examples; community counselors must adapt such programs to the special needs of their own clients.

Helping People Cope with Marital Disruption

As Bloom (1984) has noted, "separation and divorce are consistently judged by samples of professionals or community residents as among the most stressful events of adult life" (p. 267). It is no wonder that marital disruptions put people at risk for mental and physical health problems: when a marriage breaks up, the family members must cope with radical life changes at the same time that their social support systems are severely disrupted.

After reviewing a number of epidemiological and clinical studies, Bloom (1984) summarized the problems associated with marital separation and divorce:

> The findings of these studies converge on identifying a small but important number of problems faced by persons undergoing marital disruption. Such a list would include a generally weakened social support system; the need to work through the variety of psychological reactions to the disruption; problems with child rearing, resocialization, finances, education and employment planning, housing, and homemaking; and protection of legal rights. (p. 272)

Newly separated people report problems with anger, depression, loneliness, finances, disequilibrium, and regression, and difficulty in resolving their attachments to the spouse (Kelly, 1982). Such difficulties heighten physical and mental health problems, with separated and divorced persons as higher risk than persons in intact marriages for psychopathology, physical illnesses, accident proneness, alcoholism, suicide, and homicide (Bloom, Asher, & White, 1978).

Programs for adults   Given the general agreement that marital disruption is a high-risk situation, counselors can intervene preventively by developing programs for people going through this transition. Ideally, such programs should focus on "(a) fostering ongoing support mechanisms and (b) building practical, situationally relevant problem-solving skills" (Cowen, 1985, p. 36). One such program was developed by Bloom, Hodges, and Caldwell (1982).

Bloom and his colleagues put together a six-month preventive program aimed at recently separated people in Boulder, Colorado. Using mass media and mailings to appropriate referral sources, the program developers recruited 153 persons, 101 of whom were assigned to the intervention program and 52 of whom became the untreated control group. Those participating in the separation and divorce program were offered two types of services: individual assistance from paraprofessional helpers and participation in study groups focusing on issues deemed to be of special concern to the newly separated.

Each program participant was assigned to a paraprofessional counselor whose role was to provide emotional support, intervene in possible crises, and link the individual with other program facets. These paraprofessionals, who were called program representatives, "played an active outreach role, contacting the participants on a regular basis, developing opportunities for social interaction on both a group and individual basis, making referrals to other parts of the program and to appropriate community agencies, and following up throughout the period of participation in the intervention program" (Bloom et al., 1982, p. 255).

Participants could also choose to participate in study groups focusing on practical issues commonly faced by those recently separated or divorced. Study group options included the following:

- *Career planning and employment:* A psychologist-led group designed to help participants find or change jobs, make long-range career plans, and develop marketable skills
- *Legal and financial issues:* A group led by an attorney, exploring such issues as establishing credit, loan eligi-

bility, child custody and visitation, child support, and the divorce litigation process

- *Child rearing and single-parenting:* A group in which participants discuss children's reactions to the separation, visitation issues, behavior problems, and ways to help children adjust
- *Housing and homemaking:* A group led by a home economist, addressing such issues as finding a new place to live, making home repairs, managing money, purchasing and preparing food, and managing time
- *Socialization and personal self-esteem:* A group experience designed to help participants deal with their loneliness, damaged self-concepts, and feelings of social and personal inadequacy

Evaluation of the program as a whole indicated that the intervention group reported significantly fewer problems than the control group after six months. Members of the intervention group also showed a significant decrease in general psychological problems across time, along with a reduction in psychological distress, maladjustment, anxiety, and neurasthenia (Bloom et al., 1982). Furthermore, "follow-up, after 2½ years, showed that the early gains were either maintained or increased over time. Those findings suggest that the program achieved its primary prevention objective, i.e., to forestall the psychological fallout that often follows marital dissolution" (Cowen, 1985, p. 36).

Programs for children The psychological fallout of divorce is not limited to the adult partners. Children, too, are put at risk: a number of researchers have identified cognitive, affective, behavioral, and psychological problems in children whose parents have divorced (Hetherington, 1979; Kurdek, 1981; Stolberg & Garrison, 1985; Wallerstein & Kelly, 1980). Recognition of the special needs that children may have during the transition from an intact to a separated family has led to several preventive outreach programs.

One such program is the Divorce Adjustment Project, a "structured two-part primary prevention program intended to enhance prosocial skills and to prevent acting out, poor self-concept, and academic failure in children of divorce" (Stolberg & Garrison, 1985, p. 113). Designed for psychologically healthy children who had never before used mental health services, the program offered both school-based Children's Support

Groups (CSG) and community-based Single Parents' Support Groups (SPSG).

The Children's Support Groups taught cognitive-behavioral skills and provided emotional support to 7- to 13-year-olds to help them adjust to their parents' divorces. In the highly structured, 12-session program, the children both discussed issues directly related to the divorce and received training in skills such as problem solving, anger control, communication, and relaxation.

The assumption underlying the complementary Single Parents' Support Groups was that the children's ability to adjust could be enhanced indirectly by improving the parenting skills and postdivorce adjustment of their parents. This support and skill-building program—also 12 weeks long—helped divorced mothers who had custody of their children work on developing both as single persons and as parents. Personal development topics included "The Social Me," "The Working Me," "The Sexual Me," and "Controlling My Feelings." Parenting topics included "Communicating with My Child," "Disciplining My Child," and "Communicating with My Former Spouse About Childrearing Matters" (Stolberg & Garrison, 1985).

This well-researched project evaluated outcomes for four different groups of children: (1) children who participated in the Children's Support Group alone, (2) children who participated in the Children's Support Group and whose parents took part in the Single Parents' Support Group, (3) children whose only treatment was their parents' participation in the Single Parents' Support Group, and (4) a control group of children receiving no treatment. The researchers found that the self-concepts and social skills of the children who had participated in the Children's Support Group alone (Group 1) improved substantially. In addition, the Group 3 parents, who had participated in the Parents' Support Group but whose children had received no direct treatment, appeared better adjusted at follow-up, in contrast to the parents of the other groups. The combination of the two interventions did not bring about the strong improvements that might have been expected.

> The goals of this program were to prevent psychological problems in children of divorce. Children's self-concept and adaptive social skills improved only for members of the CSG-alone intervention. Although parents' participation in the SPSG-alone intervention facilitated adult adjustment, it did not affect their children's adjustment. Single-parenting skills were not differentially influenced by this intervention. It appears that intervention programs

must emphasize important child development processes to significantly influence child adjustment. (Stolberg & Garrison, 1985, p. 121)

A modified version of the Children's Support Group was implemented in Pedro-Carroll and Cowen's (1985) Children of Divorce Intervention Program. Pedro-Carroll and Cowen, while also emphasizing support and skill building, added more activities related to affect, including discussions and role playing that explored the children's emotional responses to experiences related to divorce. In the first three sessions, the children concentrated on getting to know one another, sharing common experiences, and discussing divorce-related anxieties and other feelings. In Sessions 4 through 6, which focused on cognitive skill building, the children were taught methods for resolving interpersonal problems.

> A key distinction was made between problems beyond children's control and thus not solvable (e.g., parent reconciliation) and those within their control (e.g., appropriate ways of communicating feelings). Understanding and being able to deal effectively with the latter was designed to increase children's sense of mastery and comfort with others. (Pedro-Carroll & Cowen, 1985, p. 605)

Once the children understood the importance of disengaging from their parents' conflicts, they began to work on expressing and controlling their anger. In the last session, the children had a chance to evaluate their group experience and deal with their feelings about its ending.

Evaluation of this project indicated that participants made significantly greater gains in adjustment than did members of the control group. Pedro-Carroll and Cowen attributed these gains in part to the supportive group context that allowed the children to break through their sense of isolation and deal with their feelings about their parents' divorce. They considered the skill-building aspects of the program equally important, however.

> However important a supportive environment is in helping children to identify, express, and deal with salient feelings about their parents' divorce, it may not by itself be enough. . . . Acquiring specific competencies for dealing with the concrete challenges that parental divorce poses is a co-equal need. Interpersonal problem-solving strategies, including the communication and anger control skills that the program offered, stressed a differentiation between problems that could and could not be solved and, for the latter, stressed ways of disengaging. . . . The intervention's positive effects appear to reflect a combination of its support

and skill building components. (Pedro-Carroll & Cowen, 1985, p. 609)

Programs for stepfamilies   Effective coping skills are also needed to deal with the new stresses brought about when one or both partners remarry. Stepfamilies—that is, families formed through remarriage—represent a promising, if sparsely researched, area of intervention.

> Because remarriage families start with children and yet have had no time to build a history, the family must deal with the tasks required of more mature families while possessing the skills of a family just starting out. Because they lack a common set of experiences, remarriage families hold limited or unrealistic expectations that paralyze them into inaction or galvanize them into a reaction against people or events they little understand. (Hayes & Hayes, 1986, p. 7)

The blended families that result from remarriage need to clarify and stabilize members' roles and relationships, replace myths with realistic expectations, develop appropriate limits for children, and acknowledge the impact of children's allegiances to noncustodial parents. Hayes and Hayes (1986) have suggested that counselors can help such families accomplish these tasks by:

- Encouraging family members to relinquish myths they may hold about the remarriage family.
- Helping members to understand the entire family system, its differences from their past families, and the involvement of non–family members in the system.
- Teaching members more effective communications skills.
- Helping members, especially children, to mourn the loss of previous relationships and encouraging the development of new relationships.
- Providing a forum in which members can work out their relationships with one another and with quasi-kin, especially the absent parent.
- Offering structured programs of parent training and lists of readings that family members can use as self-instructional devices.
- Informing members of the latest research findings and clinical evidence that may be helpful to them in the reorganization process.
- Identifying the tasks of parenting and the relationships that are necessary to enact those roles.

- Running groups for remarriage parents in the community or for stepchildren in the schools. (p. 7)

The comprehensiveness of such an approach makes it an appropriate model for preventive outreach to many client populations at risk.

Helping Families Cope with the Farm Crisis

A comprehensive program is especially important when a stressor affects not just individuals but whole communities and regions. Many parts of the United States encountered just such a stressor in the 1980s when a marked downturn in the agricultural economy put farm families at risk. Since then, the worsening economic situation has made poverty-level incomes, debt, foreclosures, bankrupticies, lending institution failures, agribusiness closures, and the loss of generations-old family farms the norm in many rural areas; further, "between 30 and 50 percent of all farms in the United States are expected to fail in the next decade" (Thiers, 1987, p. 1).

This economic crisis has brought in its wake a mental health crisis. The stress associated with the economic downturn has been implicated in a surge of emotional problems, especially depression, anxiety, marital conflicts, abuse, alcohol and drug dependence, and suicide (National Association of Counties Mental Health Project, 1987). These reactions go beyond a simple stress response to strike at the core of many people's existence.

> Farm families view their loss, or their anticipated loss, very personally. They are breaking a generational trust, losing a valued possession which has been an integral part of the family. This sense of loss is complex, for it is a loss of one's history, one's present, and one's future. During the grieving process, the meaning and value of life is called into question primarily because of the discrepancy between one's hopes/expectations and the course of actual events. There is a loss of confidence in the predictability and stability of the environment. (Blundall, undated, pp. 4–5)

The devastating impact of personal loss is exacerbated by the common tendency of others to blame the victims, to assume erroneously that mismanagement and inefficiency are at the root of individual problems.

> The blaming is not only devastating to families at risk and those sliding toward loss but also to the community as a whole. The belief that segments of the community will remain untouched by the crisis often negatively affects the development of strategies that will enhance our ability to survive. The myth that we can

make it through a crisis alone, that we are insulated from the fallout of this crisis, erodes our ability to create a longterm, sustainable lifestyle for our food supply, our people, our state, and our region. (Blundall, undated, p. 3)

Problems of this breadth and depth require interventions that use the resources of the community, that involve natural support networks, and that increase individuals' sense of self-efficacy. A number of excellent programs—all designed to help individuals, families, and communities help themselves—have emerged.

One comprehensive effort has been implemented by the consultation and education department of the Northwest Iowa Mental Health Center in Spencer, Iowa. The center's Rural Response Program received its initial impetus in 1984, when a number of farm women came for help with depression, stress, and family discord that they attributed to the farm crisis. The commonality of their problems led the center to sponsor a mutual support group that would allow these women to help one another. Soon, the support group expanded to include their husbands. In time, the center offered meetings attended by hundreds of people, as well as men's groups and family support groups throughout the center's multicounty catchment area. These groups are well attended, with some people traveling more than 50 miles to participate. Farm families are attracted not because the groups offer a structured agenda but because they offer a chance to share common concerns and seek fresh solutions to chronic problems.

The Northwest Iowa Mental Health Center also provides a peer listener program that has trained 370 volunteers to provide help and support to their neighbors on an individual basis. After receiving 15 hours of training in basic helping skills, volunteers may act as formal listeners, actively letting community members know they are available; informal listeners, simply using their training to be more effective neighbors and friends; or broker-system listeners, providing additional support to individuals or families receiving professional services. The peer listener program offers care and encouragement to people whose isolation or discomfort with more formal helping services would otherwise prevent their receiving the help they need.

Finally, the center sponsors a Rural Renaissance VISTA project, created to encourage the development of income-generating cooperatives and to facilitate and coordinate the mediation of credit disputes. The mediation service, developed as part of the Rural Response Program and now operated by the Iowa/Farmer Creditor Mediation Service, helps to minimize the destructiveness of credit conflicts and, whenever possible, resolve such disputes without costly litigation.

The Northwest Iowa Mental Health Center developed its programs in response to the expressed needs of the communities it serves. Each of the services it provides is aimed at building the resources already present in the community, through the community's members. Programs that appear to be drawing active participation in other locations also depend on farm families' abilities to support and assist one another. The Cooperative Extension Service in Grand Forks, North Dakota, for instance, is one of many agencies offering a Neighbor to Neighbor program based on Roger Williams's guidebook for organizing farm family education/support/action groups.

Neighbor to Neighbor (Williams, 1987) was written to facilitate the formation of support groups, either small groups meeting in the homes of farm families or larger groups sponsored by extension services, churches, organizations, or human-services agencies. Carefully planned sessions and supplemental written materials enable groups to proceed on their own, with or without professional facilitation, choosing what sessions they will use, according to their priorities. The guidebook outlines the following sessions:

1. *Getting Started: Setting Group Goals* In this introductory session, group members use a written exercise to set goals specific to the group. Participants are also encouraged to consider the question of blame for the current financial crisis in agriculture, to recognize the forces over which their families have no control, and to think about specific actions the group can take to "sensitize the public and policy makers to the complex forces affecting farm families" (p. 8).

2. *Farm and Family: A Careful Balancing Act* The materials for this session help participants examine their family's values and strengths. Participants are also encouraged to explore ways in which the group as a whole can better support each family.

3. *Stress Management Strategies: Learning to Cope* In this session, participants examine the stressors that are unique to farming, including such uncontrollable factors as the weather, the capital-intensive nature of farming, seasonal pressures, and accidents. Group members also learn more general ways of managing stress.

4. *Communication Skills: Promoting Self-Worth and Preventing Conflict* The written materials and exercises

for this session introduce basic communication and problem-solving skills. The materials also include examples of issues of concern to farm families, along with directions for role playing and discussion.

5. *Change and Its Impact: Coping with Loss and Grief* For this session, the guidebook provides material explaining both the grieving process and ways of helping others who might be experiencing loss and grief. Participants are also encouraged to learn about professional resources in the community and to refer troubled friends for help.

6. *Reaching Out to Others: The Importance of Support Systems* In this session, group members are introduced to the concept of social support systems and use a self-diagnostic test to examine their own relationships. The group is encouraged to explore ways in which it can support its members; farm-related examples are provided.

7. *Your Personal Financial Situation: Taking Stock* The materials for this session include a self-scored financial health questionnaire that participants can use to analyze their own situations. Supporting materials provide more general information concerning debt-to-asset ratios, loan refusal delinquency rates, and other relevant issues.

8. *If You're Experiencing Financial Problems: Looking at Financial Options* In this session, each person is asked to respond briefly to the phrase, "If I think about the possibility of losing our farm, I feel . . ." In addition, the guidebook provides information about various financial options so that participants can explore their own alternatives. The guidebook also suggests that participants discuss their options with a lawyer.

9. *If You Want to Seek an Off-Farm Job: Looking at Life/Career Options* This session is focused on helping participants to recognize their own talents and skills and to expand the options they are willing to consider. Written exercises are designed to help participants better understand themselves and the work world.

10. *Looking to the Future: Where Do We Go from Here?* Materials for the final session help participants reflect back on the group experience, evaluate the Neighbor to Neighbor Program, and discuss the future. The guidebook also suggests ways in which the group can extend the social commitment it has begun; the suggestions include socializing, sharing resources, working for social policy change, developing community problem-solving efforts, and even working on global issues.

The Neighbor to Neighbor Program, like Northwest Iowa's Rural Response Program, is designed primarily as a preventive tool, encouraging farm families to mobilize their resources and develop support networks before personal crises develop. Farm states are also finding it necessary to provide direct services to families that have already been severely affected. In Kansas, for instance, the Farmers Assistance, Counseling and Training Service (FACTS) provides a toll-free hot line and free information and counseling for the rural community. As the FACTS brochure states,

> Farmers Assistance, Counseling and Training Service . . . was designed to assist Kansas farmers, ranchers, agribusinessmen and their families in avoiding or alleviating the problems and stress resulting from the current agricultural economic crisis. In simpler terms, the FACTS program was developed to serve as the state's point of first assistance for individuals and families in crisis by:
>
> - Helping Kansas farmers, ranchers and agribusinessmen save the family farm or business whenever humanly possible.
> - Helping families cope with the stress and other problems that result from living under today's economic conditions.
> - And, when absolutely no way can be found to save the farm, ranch or business, helping families make a successful transition to other lifestyles.

All of the programs described above attempt to help individuals and families who are under severe stress. They have in common efforts to build buffers against the effects of stress by reducing people's isolation, encouraging them to help themselves, and helping them develop more adaptive coping skills. In the long run, interventions are likely to be most helpful if they build on the community's commitment to change and foster interdependence among families instead of dependence on professional help.

> There are two long and rich traditions that have been interwoven throughout the history of rural America. One is the tradition for *independence.* This is exemplified in the pioneer spirit where individuals and families moved westward, carving out new futures for themselves while facing incredible odds. The pioneer spirit is still alive and well in rural America. . . . What's often overlooked is that our forefathers and mothers really didn't do it all alone. There is another rich tradition woven throughout America's rural history. This is the tradition of *social commitment,* of joint action and mutual support. It is best exemplified by barn raisings and community festivals, by threshing bees and quilting bees, and by other community happenings in the one-room school or local

church. This tradition is still alive—but not well—in rural America. (Williams, 1987, p. 46)

Helping Vietnam Veterans

Dohrenwend and Dohrenwend (1981) defined stressful life events as "proximate to, rather than remote from, the onset of a disorder" (p. 131). According to their stressful life event theory, in the absence of positive mediating factors, a stressful life event can place an individual at immediate risk for maladaptation. The problems that result may be chronic, but their onset occurs shortly after the event.

In recent years, however, increasing attention has been paid to the phenomenon of the delayed stress response. After experiencing unusual traumas, an individual may appear to have adapted well, only to have stress reactions appear later. The stressful life events affecting them are thus remote in time from the recognizable onset of the maladaptive response.

The stressors that tend to trigger delayed reactions are generally both traumatic enough to cause distress in most people and "outside the range of such common experiences as simple bereavement, chronic illness, business losses, or marital conflict" (American Psychiatric Association, 1980, p. 236). Although these stressors may be either natural or humanly induced, *posttraumatic stress disorder* is "apparently more severe and longer lasting when the stressor is of human design" (American Psychiatric Association, 1980, p. 236).

What is now termed posttraumatic stress disorder (PTSD) can be either chronic or delayed, but people suffering from PTSD share a number of experiences and characteristics. They reexperience the trauma, either through dreams or through intrusive recollections; show a numbed responsiveness and express a feeling of detachment from others; and exhibit such symptoms as hyperalertness, sleep disturbance, survival guilt, or memory impairment.

> The traumatic event can be reexperienced in a variety of ways. Commonly the individual has recurrent painful, intrusive recollections of the event or recurrent dreams or nightmares during which the event is reexperienced. . . . Diminished responsiveness to the external world, referred to as "psychic numbing" or "emotional anesthesia," usually begins soon after the traumatic event. A person may complain of feeling detached or estranged from other people, that he or she has lost the ability to become interested in previously enjoyed significant activities, or that the ability to feel emotions of any type, especially those associated with intimacy, tenderness, and sexuality, is markedly de-

creased. . . . Symptoms of depression and anxiety are common. . . . Increased irritability may be associated with sporadic and unpredictable explosions of aggressive behavior, upon even minimal or no provocation. . . . Emotional lability, depression, and guilt may result in self-defeating behavior or suicidal actions. Substance Use Disorders may develop. (American Psychiatric Association, 1980, pp. 236–237)

Though a variety of traumas can cause posttraumatic stress disorder, recognition of the disorder has drawn particular attention to the special needs of veterans of the Vietnam War. Many veterans, whether or not they are diagnosable as suffering from PTSD, have adjustment difficulties that can be attributed to their combat experiences and to the interruption of their lives that Vietnam represents. These individuals may risk developing mental, physical, or substance abuse problems if they are not helped through an aggressive outreach program.

Proactive outreach efforts are all too rare in the field of human services. They do exist, however, and one good example is that of the Chicago Heights Vet Center, which serves Vietnam-era veterans from parts of Illinois and Indiana. The Vet Center staff and volunteers actively work to bring services to veterans who might be hesitant to ask for the help they need. Staff members move out beyond the center's walls, following leads provided by fellow veterans, seeking agency referrals, speaking to community groups, visiting VA hospitals, and intervening in crises. The center reaches many veterans with substance abuse problems because it has been designated to assess individuals who have been arrested for driving while intoxicated and referred there by the courts. Vietnam-era veterans can be assessed without fee through the center's unique DWI program. Because of this service, the center is able to reach a number of troubled clients who would be unlikely to come in themselves.

At the center, veterans may participate in a variety of programs designed to help them meet their psychological, social, health, career, and family needs. These services include:

- Initial assessment, evaluation of the client's mental status, and referral for medical or psychiatric care if needed
- Individual counseling for problems such as depression, anxiety, domestic violence, substance abuse, and sexual dysfunction
- Family counseling
- Information on upgrading one's military discharge status

- Group counseling and rap sessions
- Career counseling, with job placement assistance by a job developer from an employment service

Group sessions are at the core of the center's services because of their usefulness in building mutual support while addressing problems. The rap group approach is used for specific groups (clients dealing with substance abuse, veterans experiencing PTSD, individuals specifically concerned with enhancing their self-esteem) and also for the general client population. A Vet Center counselor described the rap group experience in the center's regular newsletter, *Sit-Rep* (Situation Report):

> The rap group allows the Vietnam Veteran to interact with others who have shared similar experiences. One of the primary complaints vets have is the feeling that others who haven't had the experience cannot understand them. The rap group provides an environment where communication can be honest and spontaneous without the feeling of stigmatization.
>
> A sense of community is cultivated with many vets referring to their experience at the Vet Center as a coming home. Trust is developed quickly and a strong support system forms, facilitating the sharing of feelings which until now have been kept secret. Free expression of emotions along with ventilation of repressed feelings is encouraged. Once the vets feel comfortable in the group and the interactions begin, discussion of a variety of topics ensues.
>
> Sharing of war experiences usually occurs throughout the course of the group along with in-depth discussions of current adjustment problems. Issues such as interpersonal relationships, fears of mental illness, and self-esteem are commonly brought up. Other commonalities among vets include problems such as alcoholism and drug abuse, unemployment, and post traumatic stress. . . . A comment made by many vets is that one of their major issues is learning to feel again. (Gonzales, 1983, p. 6)

Beyond encouraging the vets to share their feelings, the groups help them develop practical methods of coping with and solving problems.

A major concern of many Vietnam veterans is their families. The center's staff thus sees its job as serving not just veterans but also members of their families. Therefore, in addition to providing family counseling, the center's staff and volunteers facilitate rap groups for veterans' spouses and a youth project for their children. The youth project, which involves both discussion groups and peer counselor training, culminates in participants' membership in the Sons and Daughters of the Vietnam Veterans.

Many of the activities sponsored by the Vet Center reflect a focus on the positive. Although the center's problem-oriented counseling services are important, they are considered no more valuable than the opportunities the center provides for veterans to stand together—with their families—and see their lives in a new light. Thus, the center publishes an unofficial, picture-filled newsletter for its clients, sponsors family activities, and coordinates participation in parades honoring Vietnam veterans. On one occasion, veterans and their children went together to Washington, DC, for the opening of the Vietnam Veterans Art Exhibit. They came together for a memorial service at the Vietnam Veterans' Memorial, hearing a benediction by Reverend Allen Wade that said in part:

> Yesterday, we Vietnam Veterans met at the Vet Center in the light of day, and departed on our journey to Washington, D.C., accompanied by our sons, daughters, nephews and nieces . . . the next generation of Americans. We passed through the darkness of Thursday night and early Friday morning. The darkness was a reminder of the darkness we lived through in Vietnam. Today we stand, hand in hand, as one, in silence and in the light, at the center of this Memorial . . . a Memorial dedicated to the men and women who were killed, or who remain listed as missing in action. Please bless them in death as we are blessed in life. . . . Let us always remember, for we dare not forget.

Helping People with Chronic Mental Health Problems

Active outreach efforts are especially important when working with people subject to chronic mental health problems who are currently living in the community. For many long-term psychiatric clients previously treated as inpatients, deinstitutionalization has meant displacement, being either returned to their families of origin for care or put into furnished rooms or out on the street to eke out an existence. Lacking many of the resources usually considered necessary for successful coping, these troubled individuals often resist returning to formal human services agencies for help or even for medication. They can be reached, but only if helpers are willing to seek them out, to give them guidance and support, and to help them make the concrete, practical decisions that can get them through each day. Thresholds, a Chicago-based agency devoted to rehabilitation for people with chronic mental health problems, is an example of a program that provides such help.

Thresholds has grown much larger and more complex since its origin as a social club for emotionally disturbed individuals in 1959. Its mission, however, has remained consistent. Through its multifaceted program, Thresholds endeavors to help each of its members avoid rehospitalization, find and maintain employment, live independently, develop socially, and get whatever education she or he may need. Several programs, adapted for the needs of individuals and special populations, work in tandem to achieve these ends.

Vocational programs   Rehabilitation programs like that at Thresholds are structured on the premise that work is important to recovery but that the transition from unemployment to a full-time job must be made gradually. Individuals who have had chronic mental health problems may need extensive support as they try to gain the confidence and skills that will enable them to obtain and hold jobs. The Thresholds Transitional Vocational Program for Mentally Ill Young Adults is an example of a step-by-step program leading gradually from vocational readiness training to independent job seeking. The program includes the following components:

- *Prevocational Class:* A 20-week class that introduces participants to attitudes and behavior appropriate to the work world
- *Community Experience Program:* A program that allows participants to apply what they learned in the prevocational class while visiting work settings, learning how to use public transportation, and observing other young adult members of Thresholds at work
- *Visiting Chefs Program:* A program in which the young adults work on kitchen crews, preparing and serving meals on-site at Thresholds under the supervision of professional chefs brought in from local restaurants
- *Social Skills Training:* Training sessions designed to teach interpersonal skills that are important in work settings
- *Vocational Assessment:* Evaluation of each participant's work-related skills and aptitudes
- *Volunteer Placement:* Work placement in a not-for-profit community agency, allowing participants to gain work experience in a low-stress, noncompetitive environment
- *Trial Work Day:* Placement in a competitive employment setting with a cooperating employer, providing an opportunity to assess each participant's skills and plan for training that will allow the person to move on to a paid position
- *Young Adult Only Group Placement:* A group placement through which members work together under the supervision of a Thresholds job coach

- *Substance Abuse at the Workplace Group:* A group focusing on issues related to drug and alcohol use and presenting healthy alternatives to substance abuse
- *Job Club:* A structured, intensive approach to helping participants learn how to locate and apply for jobs in which participants spend five half-days per week on job-hunting activities

Through this step-by-step process, young adults can first gain the skills and experience that will enable them to succeed, and then move into real jobs.

Educational programs   Many of Thresholds' members—like other individuals with mental health problems—have had their educations interrupted, whether because their illnesses interfered with learning or because acute episodes have interfered with their attending school. Completing their schooling can help individuals increase their self-esteem and gain self-sufficiency.

Thresholds' first educational intervention was a special program for adults with learning problems who needed very basic help. Thresholds' educational work has expanded considerably since then. Their accredited school now has curricula for adolescents and adults, offering students classes in basic skills, high school level classes, or preparation for college. Members who have completed some college work in the past or who are ready for postsecondary education can receive individual tutoring and assistance in planning a gradual, supported transition to full-time studies.

Social rehabilitation   One of the most important challenges in working with the chronically mentally ill is helping them develop more effective social relationships. Since its earliest days, Thresholds has addressed this challenge, recognizing from the beginning that developing social skills must be a priority for its members. As the Thresholds' director wrote,

> Almost all of the members of rehabilitation facilities have experienced major failure in social relationships, often starting at a very early age. . . . By the time the members come to us, they are feeling isolated, their symptoms have separated them from their peers, and most often their peers have marched past them in the quest for a richer life. What seems to characterize our members is isolation, inability to establish relationships, periodic regressions that alienate their friends, and an overwhelming sense of loneliness and failure. (Dincin, 1975, p. 138)

Thresholds uses both formal and informal mechanisms for breaking through this sense of isolation and building social skills. Problem-solving groups, led by professionals on the staff, give participants an opportunity to explore their feelings, their relationships, and their attitudes, both in general and in relation to selected topics. Practice sessions focus on specific social skills, enabling participants to gain confidence in such areas as grooming, conversation, and dating. Activity groups involve members in leisure activities such as sports, games, hobbies, and community outings, as well as wilderness camping, hiking, canoeing, rock climbing, and bicycling. Even the clublike atmosphere of the agency itself, which provides a drop-in center with a comfortable lounge, serves to enhance members' social skills.

Community volunteers provide valuable assistance by leading activity groups and by spending time with members on a one-to-one basis. This helps individual clients develop relationships with other people; at the same time, it helps the agency as a whole maintain close ties with the community.

Residential programs   One of the primary goals of Thresholds' programs is to help members live as independently as possible. Without active assistance, people with chronic mental health problems often find it difficult to locate appropriate housing; some may even be kept in the hospital when they are ready for release just because decent housing cannot be found. Thresholds owns or rents several properties, enabling it to place members in suitable transitional or long-term residences. Living arrangements include well-supervised group homes, co-ops, shared apartments, and separate apartments. This range of options makes it possible for individuals to move steadily toward independence, limited only by their own readiness. Parallelling Thresholds' residential placement program is an educational program that teaches participants how to find and take care of their own housing.

Programs for special populations   Thresholds continually develops new programs to address the needs of special populations as it recognizes them. The Mother's Project provides intervention and support for mentally ill mothers and their young children; the Young Adult Program addresses issues related to peer groups, education, family involvement, and substance abuse; still another program offers specialized services for the hearing impaired.

No Thresholds program has received more attention than Thresholds' Bridge, an assertive outreach effort that has become a model for serving psychiatric patients who have been repeatedly hospitalized. Because the Bridge is designed to meet the needs of the most disabled of Thresholds' members, its methods are necessarily intensive. Bridge staff members go out into the community, visiting their clients where they can find them and helping them to deal with the day-to-day pressures of life. They help participants obtain financial assistance, manage their money, buy clothes and food, and find housing, thus "reconnecting them with normal social goals and functions" ("Bridge to a Normal Life," 1986).

Few programs have succeeded in connecting with this population at all. The activist approach of Thresholds has demonstrated that rehospitalization can be reduced, even for a highly recidivistic group, and that people with chronic mental health problems can gain the skills they need to live independently and work productively (Dincin & Witheridge, 1982; Witheridge, Dincin, & Appleby, 1982).

Crisis Intervention and Suicide Prevention

A *crisis* is a temporary stage in a person's life when his or her normal ways of dealing with the world are suddenly interrupted. The crisis may stem from a sudden, life-affecting change, or result from a combination of problems. Theorists have distinguished various kinds of crisis situations, primarily in terms of the degree to which the crises are predictable or serious. T. F. McGee (1968, 1980) has suggested that crises can be placed along a continuum ranging from normal developmental crises, such as those associated with entering school, adolescence, marriage, or retirement, to more serious crises, such as those resulting from job loss, a disabling injury, or the death of a close family member. Shneidman (1973) has suggested that crises can be categorized as *intratemporal* (specific to particular life stages), *intertemporal* (occurring as an individual moves from one developmental stage to the next), and *extratemporal* (occurring independently of developmental stages). Aguilera and Messick (1981) have categorized crises as either *maturational* or *situational.*

Regardless of the cause, people in crisis find that they are no longer on an even keel. They need help from other people— help in exploring the immediate problem, finding resources that will enable them to solve the problem, and developing a practical plan of action. Often they also need personal support and encouragement to cope with their feelings of helplessness or frustration.

A crisis does not imply pathology. A crisis can erupt any time a person faces a problem that calls on resources or problem-solving abilities that he or she has not needed before. Although we know that major life changes can place a person at risk, we also know that the source of a crisis is not always apparent. The key is "people's emotional reactions to a situation, not the situation itself" (Okun, 1982, p. 211).

A crisis is temporary, but the way it is handled can have long-lasting effects. A crisis can be seen as a process; after the first impact of the crisis, the individual finds that his or her usual problem-solving methods are unworkable, attempts new approaches, and emerges either stronger or under greater stress than before (Caplan, 1964; T. F. McGee, 1980). Individuals who surmount their difficulties quickly and appropriately may grow from the experience, learning new problem-solving approaches and developing ways to avoid crises in the future. On the other hand, those who are unable to cope effectively may develop chronic problems.

> The Chinese characters that represent the word "crisis" mean both danger and opportunity. Crisis is a danger because it threatens to overwhelm the individual or his [or her] family, and it may result in suicide or a psychotic break. It is also an opportunity because during times of crisis individuals are more receptive to therapeutic influence. Prompt and skillful intervention may not only prevent the development of a serious long-term disability but may also allow new coping patterns to emerge that can help the individual function at a higher level of equilibrium than before the crisis. (Aguilera & Messick, 1981, p. 1)

In a crisis, then, the timeliness of the intervention is very important. To intervene is to enter into a situation and thereby change it in some way. Accordingly, in crisis intervention a helper enters the life of an individual experiencing a crisis in order to affect the outcome of the crisis. Interventions are, of course, temporary, with the goal being to help clients develop the resources they need to regain their independence. Crisis intervention may take place in a center designed specifically for that purpose, or it may occur in an agency with a wider service mandate. In either instance, the same basic principles apply:

1. The focus of crisis intervention is on specific and time-limited treatment goals. Attention is directed toward reduction of tension and adaptive problem solving. The time limits can enhance and maintain client motivation to achieve the specified goals.
2. Crisis intervention involves clarification and accurate assessment of the source of stress and the meaning of the stress to the helpee, and it entails active, directive cognitive restructuring.
3. Crisis intervention helps clients develop adaptive problem-solving mechanisms so that they can return to

the level at which they were functioning before the crisis.

4. Crisis intervention is reality oriented, clarifying cognitive perceptions, confronting denial and distortions, providing emotional support rather than false reassurance.

5. Whenever possible, crisis intervention uses existing helpee relationship networks to provide support and help determine and implement effective coping strategies.

6. Crisis intervention may serve as a prelude for further treatment. (Okun, 1982, p. 216)

Crisis intervention is practical and realistic. The counselor focuses on the client's current situation, encouraging him or her to identify the salient points of the problem as he or she experiences them. Because the client may have difficulty focusing on the problem and identifying alternative solutions, the counselor needs to use a directive approach, following organized problem-solving procedures and helping the client identify more permanent sources of support in his or her social network. The process should include the following steps:

1. *Assess the nature of the crisis.* As step one, the counselor's goal is to learn as much as he or she can about what precipitated the crisis, what coping mechanisms have been attempted, and what patterns the individual usually follows. Of course, the helper must also assess the seriousness of the situation. Is the individual or family in any immediate danger?

2. *Help the client clarify the immediate problem.* At this point, the individual in crisis might be experiencing difficulty in making a realistic assessment of the major issues. The counselor can help by framing the problem in concrete and realistic terms.

3. *Make the problem manageable.* The individual in crisis feels overwhelmed by the demands being faced. He or she can begin to gain control most effectively if the problem is broken down into small, manageable parts. As action is taken to resolve aspects of the problem, the individual can begin to regain a feeling of equilibrium.

4. *Identify additional sources of support.* As the client begins to work on the problems being faced, he or she can identify sources of social support from among family, friends, and associates. In reaching out to others the client gains emotional support and accepts concrete assistance.

5. *Identify personal strengths.* The individual might have lost sight of his or her positive attributes. Helping the

client to identify resources within himself or herself can enhance the struggle tow ard self-responsibility.

6. *Explore feelings.* The client's emotions are deeply engaged in the crisis situation. These feelings can be dealt with most effectively if the individual is helped to identify and express them.

7. *Develop a strategy for coping with the situation and resolving immediate problems.* The counselor works to engage the client in practical problem solving. The strategies employed are similar to those used with clients who are not in a crisis situation. The primary difference is that the client in crisis needs more direction. . . .

8. *Plan for the prevention of future crises.* As the client returns to a more usual level of functioning, he or she can take stock of the situation and identify possible methods for preventing future problems. If new problem-solving skills are accompanied by attempts to maintain personal resources at a higher level, the crisis can prove to be a growth-producing event. (Lewis & Lewis, 1986, pp. 100–101)

The development of crisis intervention models in the late 1950s and early 1960s was paralleled by increased attention to one specific issue: suicide prevention. Contemporary approaches to suicide prevention are largely based on the work of Farberow and Shneidman (Farberow, 1974; Farberow & Shneidman, 1961) and their Los Angeles Suicide Prevention Center. This center developed the concept of the 24-hour telephone crisis line and was the first to train volunteers to actively intervene in crises. Workers there developed and studied effective methods of counseling over the telephone and then shared this information widely so that crisis intervention programs could be initiated throughout the nation. At the same time, suicide began to be seen as an urgent problem, one needing study as well as active preventive measures.

The Los Angeles Suicide Prevention Center has served as a model not only because it broke ground in developing scientific methods of intervention but also because it has consistently generated significant research on the nature of suicidal thinking and behavior. This research began with Farberow and Shneidman's discovery and analysis of hundreds of suicide notes.

However one chooses to tell the story, certain elements must be included, such as the fortuitous discovery by two behavioral scientists of several hundred actual suicide notes filed in the office of the Los Angeles County Medical Examiner-Coroner. This discovery, together with the realization of its scientific worth, led Norman Farberow and Edwin Shneidman to make the first of many explorations into the psychological processes of a person to take his own life. They analyzed the thinking processes and identified the "logic of suicide"; they looked into affective states and uncovered the ambivalence; they dissected the communications and discovered the clues which foretell an act of self-destruction. Thus, they became convinced that suicide could be prevented. (R. K. McGee, 1974, p. 5)

This research has continued, with Shneidman (1987) developing the *psychological autopsy,* a detailed postmortem mental history that provides insight into the thoughts of people who have decided that suicide is their only remaining option. Such research provides a base of knowledge about the terrain of suicide that enables suicidologists to develop more effective preventive interventions.

Suicide, I have learned, is not a bizarre and incomprehensible act of self-destruction. Rather, suicidal people use a particular logic, a style of thinking that brings them to the conclusion that death is the only solution to their problems. This style can be readily seen, and there are steps we can take to stop suicide, if we know where to look. (Shneidman, 1987, p. 56)

Shneidman has suggested a number of guidelines for preventing suicide. Because we know that the suicidal person is feeling unendurable pain, we have to reduce that distress as quickly as possible, sometimes by actively intervening with others in the person's life. Because we know that suicidal people are acting out of different needs, we must tailor our interventions to the individual's specific pain. Because we know that suicidal people have been unable to find alternative solutions, we need to show them that other options are available. Because we know that suicidal people indicate their intentions in advance, we can learn to intervene in time.

Summary

In addition to working to prevent dysfunctions through communitywide educational activities, community counselors, recognizing that some individuals are especially vulnerable to mental health problems, offer more intensive services. One way to conceptualize vulnerability is through an equation that balances the deficits of organic factors, stress, and exploitation against the resources of coping skills, self-esteem, and social support. A change in any of these factors affects the degree to which an individual is vulnerable at any given point. Clients may thus need extra assistance when their life circumstances have the potential to overwhelm their coping resources.

People under severe stress are subject to a number of physical, psychological, and social problems. We can intervene in these stressful, high-risk situations even without being able to connect a specific stressor to a specific disorder.

Whether individuals are able to cope with chronic or acute stress may depend on the existence of buffers such as their social support systems, their sense of self-efficacy, and their problem-solving skills. Community counselors can identify groups or individuals at risk in their particular settings and develop programs that both provide support and strengthen problem-solving skills.

A number of community-based programs have begun to demonstrate the tremendous potential of outreach to vulnerable clients. Among the examples presented in this chapter are (1) programs designed to help families going through separation and divorce, (2) programs assisting farm families affected by the economic crisis in agriculture, (3) an agency devoted to meeting the needs of Vietnam veterans, (4) an assertive outreach program for people with chronic mental health problems, and (5) crisis intervention and suicide prevention programs. The programs described in this chapter are simply examples that demonstrate outreach in action, illustrating general approaches that can be adapted to the situations each counselor faces in his or her own community or work setting.

Supplemental Activities

1. Think about a specific population. What particular transitions or situations might make members of this population more likely to develop problems? Can these high-risk situations be prevented? If not, how can individuals' ability to cope with them be strengthened?
2. Consider again your own hypothetical community counseling program. For the client population you have identified, what would you do to make sure that crisis situations were prevented, or at least handled promptly? Develop in more detail the facet of your program involving outreach to vulnerable populations.

Related Reading

AGUILERA, D. C., & MESSICK, J. M. (1981). *Crisis intervention: Theory and methodology.* St. Louis: C. V. Mosby.

BANDURA, A. (1982). Self-efficacy mechanism in human agency. *American Psychologist, 37,* 122–147.

BLOOM, B. L. (1984). *Community mental health: A general introduction.* Pacific Grove, CA: Brooks/Cole.

COELHO, G. V., & AHMED, P. I. (Eds.). (1980). *Uprooting and development: Dilemmas of coping with modernization.* New York: Plenum.

KELLER, P. A., & MURRAY, J. D. (Eds.). (1982). *Handbook of rural community mental health.* New York: Human Sciences Press.

KOBASA, S. C. (1979). Stressful life events, personality and health: An inquiry into hardiness. *Journal of Personality and Social Psychology, 37,* 1–11.

NATIONAL MENTAL HEALTH ASSOCIATION COMMISSION ON THE PREVENTION OF MENTAL-EMOTIONAL DISABILITIES. *The prevention of mental-emotional disabilities: Report of the National Mental Health Association Commission on the Prevention of Mental-Emotional Disabilities.* Alexandria, VA: National Mental Health Association.

SHNEIDMAN, E. (1980). *Voices of death.* New York: Harper & Row.

SHNEIDMAN, E. (1985). *Definition of suicide.* New York: Wiley.

WALLERSTEIN, J. S., & KELLY, J. B. (1980). *Surviving the breakup: How children and parents cope with divorce.* New York: Basic Books.

WILLIAMS, R. T. (1987). *Neighbor to neighbor: A do-it-yourself guide for organizing farm family support groups.* Madison: Cooperative Extension Service, University of Wisconsin, & Wisconsin Department of Health and Social Services.

References

AGUILERA, D. C., & MESSICK, J. M. (1981). *Crisis intervention: Theory and methodology.* St. Louis: C. V. Mosby.

AMERICAN PSYCHIATRIC ASSOCIATION. (1980). *Diagnostic and statistical manual of mental disorders* (3rd ed.). Washington, DC: Author.

AUBREY, R. F., & LEWIS, J. A. (1983). Social issues and the counseling profession in the 1980s and 1990s. *Counseling and Human Development, 15*(10), 1–15.

BANDURA, A. (1982). Self-efficacy mechanism in human agency. *American Psychologist, 37,* 122–147.

BLOOM, B. L. (1984). *Community mental health: A general introduction.* Pacific Grove, CA: Brooks/Cole.

BLOOM, B. L., ASHER, S. J., & WHITE, S. W. (1978). Marital disruption as a stressor: A review and analysis. *Psychological Bulletin, 85,* 867–894.

BLOOM, B. L., HODGES, W. F., & CALDWELL, R. A. (1982). A preventive program for the newly separated. *American Journal of Community Psychology, 10,* 251–264.

BLUNDALL, J. (undated). *Community and family: Responding to immediate needs.* Unpublished manuscript.

Bridge to a Normal Life. (1986, January 6, p. 18). *Newsweek.*

CAPLAN, G. (1964). *Principles of*

preventive psychiatry. New York: Basic Books.

CAPLAN, G. (1974). *Support systems and community mental health.* New York: Basic Books.

COWEN, E. L. (1985). Person-centered approaches to primary prevention in mental health: Situation-focused and competence-enhancement. *American Journal of Community Psychology, 13,* 31–48.

DINCIN, J. (1975). Psychiatric rehabilitation. *Schizophrenia Bulletin, 13,* 131–147.

DINCIN, J., & WITHERIDGE, T. F. (1982). Psychiatric rehabilitation as a deterrent to recidivism. *Hospital and Community Psychiatry, 33,* 645–650.

DOHRENWEND, B. S., & DOHRENWEND, B. P. (1981). Life stress and psychopathology. In D. A. Regier & G. Allen (Eds.), *Risk factor research in the major mental disorders* (DHHS Publication No. ADM 81–1068). Washington, DC: U.S. Government Printing Office.

FARBEROW, N. L. (1974). *Suicide.* Morristown, NJ: General Learning Press.

FARBEROW, N. L., & SHNEIDMAN, E. S. (1961). *The cry for help.* New York: McGraw-Hill.

GONZALES, M. (1983, January). Rap groups with Vietnam veterans. *SIT-REP* (Veteran's Center newsletter), I(1), p. 3.

HAYES, R. L., & HAYES, B. A. (1986). Remarriage families: Counseling parents, stepparents, and their children. *Counseling and Human Development, 18*(7), 1–8.

HELLER, K., & SWINDLE, R. W. (1983). Social networks, perceived social support, and coping with stress. In R. D. Felner, L. A. Jason, J. N. Moritsugu, & S. S. Farber (Eds.), *Preventive psychology: Theory, research, and practice* (pp. 87–103). New York: Pergamon Press.

HETHERINGTON, E. M. (1979). Divorce: A child's perspective. *American Psychologist, 34,* 851–858.

HOLMES, T., & RAHE, R. (1967). The social readjustment rating scale. *Journal of Psychosomatic Research, 11,* 213–218.

KELLY, J. (1982). Divorce: The adult perspective. In B. Wolman & G. Stricker (Eds.), *Handbook of developmental psychology* (pp. 734–750). New York: Prentice-Hall.

KOBASA, S. C. (1979). Stressful life events, personality and health: An inquiry into hardiness. *Journal of Personality and Social Psychology, 37,* 1–11.

KURDEK, L. A. (1981). An integrative perspective on children's divorce adjustment. *American Psychologist, 35,* 856–866.

LAZARUS, R. (1980). The stress and coping paradigm. In L. A. Bond & J. C. Rosen (Eds.), *Competence and coping in adulthood* (pp. 28–74). Hanover, NH: University Press of New England.

LEWIS, J. A., & LEWIS, M. D. (1986). *Counseling programs for employees in the workplace.* Pacific Grove, CA: Brooks/Cole.

McGEE, R. K. (1974). *Crisis intervention in the community.* Baltimore: University Park Press.

McGEE, T. F. (1968). Some basic considerations in crisis intervention. *Community Mental Health Journal, 4,* 319–325.

McGEE, T. F. (1980). Crisis intervention. In M. S. Gibbs, J. R. Lachenmeyer, & J. Sigal (Eds.), *Community psychology: The-*

oretical and empirical approaches (pp. 239–266). New York: Gardner Press.

NATIONAL ASSOCIATION OF COUNTIES MENTAL HEALTH PROJECT. (1987). *Factsheet for county officials.* Washington, DC: National Association of Counties.

NATIONAL MENTAL HEALTH ASSOCIATION COMMISSION ON THE PREVENTION OF MENTAL-EMOTIONAL DISABILITIES. (1986). *The prevention of mental-emotional disabilities: Report of the National Mental Health Association Commission on the Prevention of Mental-Emotional Disabilities.* Alexandria, VA: National Mental Health Association.

OKUN, B. F. (1982). *Effective helping: Interviewing and counseling techniques* (2nd ed.). Pacific Grove, CA: Brooks/Cole.

PEDRO-CARROLL, J. L., & COWEN, E. L. (1985). The Children of Divorce Intervention Program: An investigation of the efficacy of a school-based prevention program. *Journal of Consulting and Clinical Psychology, 53,* 603–611.

PRICE, R. H., BADER, B. C., & KETTERER, R. F. (1980). Prevention in community mental health; The state of the art. In R. H. Price, R. F. Ketterer, B. C. Bader, & J. Monahan (Eds.), *Prevention in mental health: Research, policy, and practice* (pp. 9–20). Beverly Hills: Sage Publications.

SHNEIDMAN, E. S. (1973). Some thoughts and perspectives. In G. Specter & W. Claiborn (Eds.), *Crisis intervention.* New York: Behavioral Publications.

SHNEIDMAN, E. S. (1987, March). At the point of no return. *Psychology Today,* pp. 54–58.

SHURE, M. B., & SPIVACK, G. (1982). Interpersonal problem solving in young children: A cognitive approach to prevention. *American Journal of Community Psychology, 10,* 341–356.

STENSRUD, R., & STENSRUD, K. (1983). Coping skills training: A systematic approach to stress management counseling. *The Personnel and Guidance Journal, 62,* 214–218.

STOLBERG, A. L., & GARRISON, K. M. (1985). Evaluating a primary prevention program for children of divorce. *American Journal of Community Psychology, 13,* 111–124.

THIERS, N. (1987). Farm crisis causing emotional difficulties. *Guidepost, 29*(15), pp. 1, 5, 8, 19.

WALLERSTEIN, J. S., & KELLY, J. B. (1980). *Surviving the breakup: How children and parents cope with divorce.* New York: Basic Books.

WILCOX, B. L. (1981). Social support, life stress, and psychological adjustment: A test of the buffering hypothesis. *American Journal of Community Psychology, 9,* 371–386.

WILLIAMS, R. T. (1987). *Neighbor to neighbor: A do-it-yourself guide for organizing farm family support groups.* Madison: Cooperative Extension Service, University of Wisconsin, & Wisconsin Department of Health and Social Services.

WITHERIDGE, T. F., DINCIN, J., & APPLEBY, L. (1982). Working with the most frequent recidivists: A total team approach to assertive resource management. *Psychosocial Rehabilitation Journal, 5,* 9–11.

The Community Counseling Model: Implications for the Counseling Process

Inherent in the community counseling model is a set of values that unify a variety of services, even in highly diverse settings. Community counselors emphasize the strengths and competencies of community members, instead of focusing on their deficits. They recognize that the social environment affects each individual's development. They seek to prevent problems, instead of merely reacting to them. They know that people can be helped most effectively if given the skills and resources they need to help themselves.

In accordance with these values, community counselors create multifaceted programs that go far beyond individual counseling to include preventive education, outreach to people coping with high-risk situations, attention to public policy issues, and advocacy for stigmatized populations. Despite the emphasis here on nontraditional services, however, counseling remains an important part of community counseling programs.

Counselors, by definition, counsel, helping clients directly, one-to-one, and "although the individual counseling interview can no longer be considered an end in itself, it will always be a basic building block in [community counseling] programs" (Lewis, 1981, p. 7).

The community counseling context strongly affects the nature of the counseling process, however. Counselors following the community counseling model simultaneously emphasize that clients are responsible for their own lives while recognizing that environmental factors do influence human behavior. Accordingly, community counselors work to strengthen their clients' sense of mastery by encouraging them to take responsibility for solving each problem without necessarily shouldering the blame for causing it.

As Brickman, Rabinowitz, Karuza, Coates, Cohn, and Kidder (1982) have made clear, how one attributes responsibility fundamentally determines one's approach to the helping process: "Whether or not people are held responsible for causing their problems and whether or not they are held responsible for solving these problems are the factors determining four fundamentally different orientations to the world, each internally coherent, each in some measure incompatible with the other three" (p. 369). Brickman and his colleagues defined these four orientations in terms applicable to helping:

1. *The moral model:* People are responsible both for creating and for solving their problems.
2. *The medical model:* People are responsible neither for creating their problems nor for solving them.
3. *The enlightenment model:* People are responsible for creating their problems but not for solving them.
4. *The compensatory model:* People are not responsible for creating their problems but are responsible for solving them.

Using substance abuse as an example, we can see how differently adherents of these four models would conceptualize the same problem (Lewis, Dana, & Blevins, 1988). Adherents of the moral model attribute full responsibility for each problem to the individual; if drinking or drug use is the problem, therefore, willpower is the solution. In contrast, adherents of the medical model hold that neither the problem nor the solution is under the control of the client; substance dependent clients are, therefore, not to blame for their disease but cannot recover without treatment. According to the enlightenment model, though people bear the responsibility for their past actions, and thus for any resulting problems, they can find help in surrendering to an outside force that is stronger than themselves; the Alcoholics Anonymous program thus encourages its members to "make amends" for past actions and turn their lives over to a "higher power." Finally, adherents of the compensatory model expect individuals to assume responsibility for solving their own problems despite the fact that these problems are not of their own making; Marlatt and Gordon (1985) have suggested that the etiology of an addiction may involve totally different factors than the process of recovery and that "a sense of detachment between the problem behavior and the person's identity and self-concept" (p. 17) can help substance abusing clients change their behavior.

The models described by Brickman and his colleagues are applicable to any human problem. Regardless of the problem, "models in which people are held responsible for solutions . . . are more likely to increase people's competence than models in which they are not held responsible for solutions" (Brickman et al., 1982, p. 375). At the same time, models in which problems are attributed to external causes are less likely to provoke guilt or self-blame, the effects of which can be debilitating. The compensatory model thus offers a double advantage: "The strength of the compensatory model for coping is that it allows people to direct their energies outward, working on trying to solve problems or transform their environment without berating themselves for their role in creating these problems, or permitting others to create them, in the first place" (Brickman et al., 1982, p. 372). The compensatory model balances the issues of environmental influence and individual responsibility, allowing counselors a dual focus that is clearly consistent with the community counseling model.

Individual Responsibility

"A truly human responsibility emerges from a person's being able to conceive of himself or herself as an agent or actor in making life happen" (Young-Eisendrath, 1985, p. 11). To foster such responsibility, a primary goal of the counseling process must be to help individuals recognize their own power; this, in turn, leads them to recognize and accept responsibility for exercising that power.

Self-Efficacy

Bandura's (1982) concept of self-efficacy clarifies this objective. *Efficacy* refers to a person's ability to mobilize whatever cognitive and behavioral skills he or she needs to deal with the environment. *Perceived self-efficacy* refers to the person's beliefs about his or her ability to deal with challenges. How people judge their self-efficacy greatly affects their behavior: those who judge themselves as lacking efficacy will tend to avoid challenges or to give up quickly when encountering obstacles, while those with a strong sense of self-efficacy will persevere.

> In any given activity skills and self-beliefs that ensure optimal use of capabilities are required for successful functioning. If self-efficacy is lacking, people tend to behave ineffectually even though they know what to do. . . . The higher the level of perceived self-efficacy, the greater the performance accomplishments. Strength of efficacy also predicts behavior change. The stronger the perceived efficacy, the more likely are people to persist in their efforts until they succeed. (Bandura, 1982, pp. 127–128)

Clients are most likely to resolve their problems if they perceive their self-efficacy positively. Thus, self-efficacy is important both as an end in itself and as a means for continued success. Counselors can help to strengthen their clients' sense of self-efficacy by encouraging clients to see their problem behavior as controllable and themselves as capable of mastering their problems.

Self-Managed Behavior Change

Many people seek counseling because they want to change their behavior but have been unable to do so on their own. If they can learn the principles of behavior change, however, they can gain greater control over their own lives. In fact, the ideal use of behavior change technology is for counselors to teach clients skills that they can use to manage their own behavior, both immediately and in the future.

> Training in self-management requires strong early support from the helper, with the client gradually relying more and more on his [or her] newly developed skills. These include skills in (1) self-monitoring; (2) establishment of specific rules of conduct by contracts with oneself or others; (3) seeking support from the environment for fulfillment; (4) self-evaluation; and (5) generating strong reinforcing consequences for engaging in behaviors which achieve the goals of self-control. The concept of self-control implies that an individual can be taught to rearrange powerful contingencies that influence behavior in such a way that he [or she] experiences long-range benefits. (Kanfer, 1980, p. 344)

The technology of behavioral management is based on established learning principles. In simple terms, people learn to repeat or to avoid particular behaviors according to the consequences of those behaviors. If a behavior is positively reinforced, the person tends to attempt it again in the future; the more regular the reinforcement, the more likely the response becomes. If a behavior is either punished or never reinforced, it becomes less frequent and may, in time, be extinguished. People can also learn to associate a behavior with a specific stimulus from the environment: the stimulus serves as a cue that a given action is likely to be positively reinforced, making that action more likely to be repeated.

Individuals can learn to change their behavior by purposefully manipulating cues and reinforcements in their environment. They can increase their performance of positive behaviors by choosing special rewards for themselves and making those rewards contingent on successful performance of the desired behaviors. They can decrease their performance of negative behaviors by changing the environmental cues, eliminating or nullifying consequences they have identified as reinforcing, substituting positive behaviors that are incompatible with the undesired behaviors, or even using punishment.

The first step in changing behavior is to establish measurable objectives. The client learns to identify and describe the specific behaviors he or she wants to learn, translating what may at first be vague goals into concrete, measurable terms. The client can then select a positive reinforcement to follow successful performance of the behavior at the desired rate. If the desired behavior is difficult or complex, the client can establish subgoals, accomplishing the change gradually.

Before people can set realistic goals, they must obtain base rates for their activities, observing and recording how frequently they currently perform the behavior they want to change. Once they have collected baseline data and established behavioral objectives, individuals can plan their own intervention, with, again, the personally chosen reinforcement contingent on their performance of the target behavior at the specified rate.

As an individual implements this plan, he or she should continue to keep records so that changes from the baseline will be readily apparent. At first, the target behavior should be reinforced each time it occurs. Later, reinforcement should be intermittent. Eventually, natural reinforcers should replace the artificial reinforcement, at which point keeping records is no longer necessary or desirable. By this time, the behavioral management skills should be part of the individual's repertoire, enabling him or her to feel that life can, indeed, be controlled. Throughout this process, the counselor plays an educational and supportive role, providing the initial encouragement, training, and ongoing support (Kanfer, 1980).

Developmental Stages

For many clients, true empowerment may require not just learning behavioral skills but also making *developmental changes.*

> Changes that one can legitimately call developmental are those major transitional alterations that are persistent, complex, and lead to qualitative differentiation. . . . Developmental changes represent transformational shifts in a person's previous manner of thinking, perceiving, feeling, and relating to others. . . . From a developmental point of view, higher stage functioning is discernibly "better," in the long run, in terms of effectively coping with the demands of a sophisticated post-industrial society. (D'Andrea, 1984, p. 3)

If higher developmental levels are preferable in the sense of being more adaptive, counseling should promote development; accordingly, while counselors work to strengthen each client's sense of personal power and efficacy, they also try to move the individual toward higher stages of development, guided by various structural developmental theories.

The *structural developmental model* is based on the idea that, because of an inherent tendency toward structure, individuals develop through invariant stages, each of which brings a new set of expectations, a new frame of reference, and a new perspective.

> Each stage is a more differentiated, comprehensive, and integrated structure than the one before it. Each succeeding stage represents the capacity to make sense of a greater variety of experiences in a more adequate way. . . . The fundamental reason for movement from one stage to the next, therefore, is that a later stage is more adequate in some universal sense than an earlier stage. (Hayes, 1986, pp. 43–44)

According to structuralists, movement to each stage depends on completion of the preceding stage, so no stage can be skipped. But not everyone proceeds through every stage: "When further development is not supported by environmental factors, a person may stop developing" (Young-Eisendrath, 1985, p. 4). One purpose of counseling is to provide an environment that can trigger and facilitate the client's development (Hayes, 1986).

Although all structuralists use a hierarchical model of stages of development, they apply the model to different aspects of development. Loevinger, for instance, has described the stages of ego development, while Kohlberg has investigated moral development and Perry, intellectual.

Ego development Loevinger (1976) has done extensive research to identify the stages of *ego development,* "the process by which personal being evolves from less to more complexity, from less to more differentiation, and from less to more adequacy of self-reflection" (Young-Eisendrath, 1985, p. 6). The *ego,* as defined by Loevinger, brings coherence to a person's life and provides a way for the individual to make sense of experience. As the individual moves to higher levels of ego development, he or she becomes increasingly able to deal with complex concepts. Loevinger's stages of ego development include the following:

1. *Presocial:* The individual is autistic and unable to differentiate self from other.
2. *Impulsive:* The individual is dependent, preoccupied with bodily feelings and aggressiveness, and conceptually confused.
3. *Self-protective:* The individual controls his or her impulses out of fear of being caught and is manipulative and self-protective.
4. *Conformist:* The individual conforms to external rules, is concerned with belonging and "niceness," understands simple concepts, and seeks approval.
5. *Conscientious-conformist:* The individual is able to differentiate norms, values, and goals and shows increasing awareness of self in relation to groups.
6. *Conscientious:* The individual behaves according to self-determined standards, feels guilt for the consequences of his or her actions, acts responsibly, is concerned with communication, shows increasing differentiation of feelings and motives, and understands complex concepts.
7. *Individualistic:* The individual adds respect for individuality to the character development achieved in the previous stage, is concerned with independence and dependency, is able to distinguish process and outcome, shows concern for broad social problems, is able to make commitments, and has transcended perfectionism.
8. *Autonomous:* The individual is able to cope with conflicting inner needs and tolerate ambiguity, shows respect for others' autonomy, shows greater concern for self-fulfillment than for achievement, is able to be ob-

jective, understands complex concepts, and is able to approach issues broadly.

9. *Integrated:* In addition to the abilities gained in previous stages, the individual is now able to resolve inner conflicts and renounce the unattainable, cherishes individuality, and is concerned with integrity and identity.

Although these stages always occur in the same order, people do not invariably move through them all. In fact, only about 1% of the population is thought to reach the stage of integration.

Moral development The highest stage in Kohlberg's (1984) stages of moral development is also reached by only a small number of adults. For Kohlberg, *moral development* refers to "the reasoning process by which individuals determine what is right or fair in resolving moral conflicts, which are really conflicts of perspective or interest" (Hayes, 1986, p. 74). The reasoning an individual uses in dealing with moral dilemmas determines his or her stage of development. Kohlberg (1984) has identified three levels of moral development, with each level divided into two stages:

Level 1: Preconventional
> Stage 1 *Heteronomous Morality:* The individual tries to avoid punishment and accepts the power of authorities in making moral choices; the rights of others are considered only in relation to actual physical damage.
> Stage 2 *Individualism, Instrumental Purpose, and Exchange:* The individual judges behavior to be right or wrong based on self-interest while recognizing that others also have interests; right is considered to mean equal exchange.

Level 2: Conventional
> Stage 3 *Mutual Interpersonal Expectations, Relationships, and Conformity:* The individual is concerned with living up to the expectations of others and caring for others and believes in the "Golden Rule."
> Stage 4 *Social System and Conscience:* The individual is concerned with upholding laws, performing his or her social duties, and preventing the breakdown of the system.

Level 3: Postconventional, or Principled
> Stage 5 *Social Contract or Utility and Individual Rights:* The individual understands that most values and opinions are relative but tries to

uphold them in the interest of the social contract, tries to reason, and tries to identify the greatest good for the greatest number.

Stage 6: *Universal Ethical Principles:* The individual chooses his or her own ethical principles and maintains a personal commitment to them; principles such as justice and the dignity of human beings override the law in cases of conflict.

Counselors can promote moral development by presenting individuals with cognitive conflicts and exposing them to higher levels of thinking.

Intellectual and ethical development   Though based on research with college students, the work of Perry (1970) has clear implications for the general adult population. Perry's model traces intellectual development from dualism to relativism and, finally, to commitment. These three general categories are divided into nine positions, along with a number of transitions, as is shown in Figure 4.1 on page 122.

Like other theories of structural development, Perry's identifies stages that bring increasing tolerance for ambiguity, increasing recognition of complexity, and, finally, an acceptance of the need for commitment within a context of relativism. In this direction lie empowerment and mastery.

Systems Theory and Environmental Influences

Community counseling, with its attention to environmental factors, is also influenced by systems theory. *General systems theory* (von Bertalanffy, 1968) is an alternative to the reductionistic thinking underlying Newtonian science. Newtonian thought was reductionistic in that it attempted to study complex phenomena by breaking them down into their smallest possible parts; it was also linear in that it attempted to understand these small parts as a series of less complex cause and effect relationships. Von Bertalanffy's general systems theory is based on a different way of thinking, in which all living things are viewed as open systems and the focus is on consistent patterns of interaction, interrelationships, and general organizing principles, not on linear, causal relationships.

If a *system* is defined as a set of units or elements standing in some consistent relationship or interactional stance with each other, then the first concept is the notion that any system is

Dualism Modified

Position 1	Authorities know, and if we work hard, read every word, and learn right answers, all will be well.		*Basic Duality*
Transition	But what about those others I hear about? And different opinions? And uncertainties? Some of our own authorities disagree with each other or don't seem to know, and some give us problems instead of answers.		
Position 2	True authorities must be right; the others are frauds. We remain right. Others must be different and wrong. Good authorities give us problems so we can learn to find the right answer by our own independent thought.		*Prelegitimate Multiplicity*
Transition	But even good authorities admit they don't know all the answers *yet!*		
Position 3	Then some uncertainties and different opinions are real and legitimate *temporarily*, even for authorities. They're working on them to get to the truth.		*Subordinate Multiplicity*
Transition	But there are *so many* things they don't know the answers to! And they won't for a long time.		
Position 4a	Where authorities don't know the right answers, everyone has a right to his or her own opinion; no one is wrong!		*Coordinate Multiplicity (Solipsism)*

Relativism Discovered

Transition	But some of my friends ask me to support my opinions with facts and reasons. *and/or:* Then what right have authorities to grade us? About what?		
Position 4b	In certain courses authorities are not asking for the right answer; They want us to *think* about things in a certain way, *supporting* opinion with data. That's what they grade us on.		*Subordinate Relativism*
Transition	But this "way" seems to *work* in most courses, and even outside them.		
Position 5	Then *all* thinking must be like this, even for them. Everything is relative but not equally valid. You have to understand how each context works. Theories are not truth but metaphors to interpret data with. You have to think about your thinking.		*Generalized Relativism (Contextual)*
Transition	But if everything is relative, am I relative too? How can I know I'm making the right choice?		

Commitments Developed

Position 6	I see I'm going to have to make my own decisions in an uncertain world with no one to tell me I'm right.		*Commitment Foreseen*
Transition	I'm lost if I don't. When I decide on my career (or marriage or values), everything will straighten out.		
Position 7	Well, I've made my first commitment!		*Initial Commitment*
Transition	Why didn't that settle everything?		
Position 8	I've made several commitments. I've got to balance them— how many, how deep? How certain, how tentative?		*Coordinating Commitments*
Transition	Things are getting contradictory. I can't make logical sense out of life's dilemmas.		
Position 9	This is how life will be. I must be wholehearted while tentative, fight for my values yet respect others, believe my deepest values right yet be ready to learn. I see that I shall be retracing this whole journey over and over— but, I hope, more wisely.		*Evolving Commitments*

Note: Adapted from "Cognitive and Ethical Growth: The Making of Meaning" by W. G. Perry in A. Chickering (Ed.), *The Modern American College* (p. 79), 1981, San Francisco: Jossey-Bass. Copyright 1981 by Jossey-Bass. Adapted by permission.

Figure 4.1   **Perry's stages of intellectual and ethical development**

composed of elements that are *organized* by the consistent nature of the relationship between these elements. Consistency is the key; consistent elements are related to each other in a consistently describable or predictable fashion. (Steinglass, 1978, p. 305)

Living organisms can be defined as *open systems* because they interact with their environments. Their boundaries are sufficiently permeable for them to take in and discharge information in transactions with their environments. Within these living systems are *subsystems,* which interact predictably within the context of the larger system. Umbarger (1983) listed some of the characteristics of living systems:

1. *Part and whole:* The system as a whole is greater than the sum of its parts.
2. *Information, error, and feedback:* Feedback loops within living systems indicate error when the system encounters dissimilarities to the system's overall design.
3. *Feedback and homeostasis:* The feedback loops enable the system to maintain a steady state.
4. *Feedback and growth:* Feedback can also trigger changes that may be necessary to the system's continued life.
5. *Life and tension:* Periods of growth alternate with periods of stability.
6. *Circularity:* Cause and effect relationships, which are linear, are secondary to ongoing processes, which are circular.
7. *Change:* Change in one part of the system affects changes in other parts and in the system as a whole.

Thinking in terms of systems shapes the way a counselor perceives all of the issues and problems affecting clients. To date, however, the most widespread application of systems theory has been in working with families and other microsystems with which clients interact directly.

> Clearly, the human family can be characterized as an open system that conforms to the principles listed by Umbarger. Each family has its own homeostasis, or preferred steady state, that may or may not be "healthy" but that is monitored through feedback and control mechanisms and protected by the system as a whole. Each family has a set of rules that governs its interactions and makes them predictable. Each includes subsystems (e.g., spousal, parental, or sibling) that carry out specialized functions and attempt to preserve the integrity of the overall system. Each is an organized whole, making it impossible to consider intervening in one part without taking the others into account. (Lewis et al., 1988, p. 160)

Family Counseling

Family systems have an obvious impact on the outcomes of individual counseling. Even more important, many counselors see the family system itself as the most appropriate target for intervention. Counselors who concentrate on working with families feel that the individual cannot really be separated from the family, or the sick from the well, or the cause of a dysfunction from its effect.

> Problems are recast to take into consideration the fact that relationship difficulties and an individual's behavior cannot be understood without attention to the context in which that behavior occurs. Rather than seeing the source of problems or the appearance of symptoms as emanating from a single "sick" individual, the family therapy [or counseling] approach views that person simply as a symptom bearer—the identified patient— expressing a family's disequilibrium. (Goldenberg & Goldenberg, 1985, p. 7)

This attention to context is a key element in family counseling approaches, as it is in the community counseling model.

There are as many approaches to family counseling as there are to individual counseling. Satir (1967, 1972) has focused on improving the family's communication patterns to enhance the self-esteem and growth of each family member. Bowen (1982) has emphasized increasing the differentiation of each member of the family system. Minuchin's structural approach (1974, 1979) helps family counselors understand the structure of specific family systems and ways to make such systems more functional within their own environments. The strategic therapy of Haley (1976) and Madanes (1981) exemplifies the communications approach to family therapy, which derives from Gregory Bateson's work in Palo Alto in the 1950s. In the communications approach, resolving problems is seen as dependent on "discovering the social situation that makes the problem necessary" (Haley, 1976, p. 9). Finally, in behavioral family counseling (Liberman, 1981), problem behaviors are considered socially reinforced, learned behaviors.

Although these perspectives vary in their emphases, each recognizes the importance of the family as a social context that affects and is affected by the behavior of individuals. Systems thinking can be just as useful in examining the impact of other systems, or other levels of the larger environmental system, on the well-being of individuals.

> In human ecology, the person-environment context constitutes the totality of relationships among individuals and their environment. Each person-to-person and person-to-environment interaction forms a linkage in an intricate network of interconnections. Viewed over time, this network of interactions establishes a dynamic equilibrium as each individual strives to adapt to changing social and environmental conditions. . . . Theoretically, system levels can be identified from the smallest subatomic

particles to the interaction of galaxies. In human services, the focus extends from the level of physiological functioning to that of social and cultural influences. Given this range, selection of the system levels relevant to a specific problem is a crucial first step in the process of diagnosis and treatment. (Stachowiak and Briggs, 1984, pp. 8–9)

Practical Applications

Community counselors' dual focus on individual responsibility and environmental factors shapes the practical, day-to-day activities they carry out in providing direct counseling services to clients. Both the process of initial assessment and the selection and implementation of counseling interventions are affected.

Assessment[1]

The client is responsible for running his or her own life. The counselor can identify problem areas and suggest possible solutions, but to be most effective, the assessment process must elicit the client's active participation. When clients actively participate in assessing their situations, they can simultaneously learn about themselves and begin to increase the sense of control they feel over their actions. These benefits can be realized only through an assessment process that is practical, multifaceted, and easily understood by clients.

The basic question to be answered through assessment is not "What is wrong with this person?" but "What is keeping this person from effectively managing his or her life right now?" The goal of assessment is not necessarily to place clients in appropriate treatment but to devise a plan through which they can transcend problematic situations and improve the quality of their lives. The best method of answering this question and meeting this goal is through an assessment process that has the following characteristics:

1. The assessment focuses on the individual's strengths and resources as well as his or her deficits.
2. The assessment is based on active involvement and understanding on the part of the client.
3. The assessment process flows naturally into the planning process, so that each difficulty that is identified is addressed in a plan of action.

[1]This section is based on material in *Counseling Programs for Employees in the Workplace* by J. A. Lewis and M. D. Lewis, 1986, Pacific Grove, CA: Brooks/Cole. Copyright 1986 by Wadsworth. Used with permission.

4. The assessment takes into account both the stressors in the individual's environment and the supports available to him or her.

Whatever other issues might bring them to a counselor's office, most clients have in common the need to increase their sense of control over events. In Bandura's (1982) terms, they need to strengthen their perceived self-efficacy, their expectation that they can take action that will lead to positive results. If assessment is taken out of their hands and performed by an "expert," clients' presenting problems might be solved, but their sense of control and personal responsibility will be damaged. Assessment in the community counseling context, then, is a mutual effort through which counselor and client strive to identify components of the client's life that can be changed as the client works to gain mastery over his or her life, to increase his or her sense of self-efficacy, and to withstand stress.

As we saw in Chapter 3, the following equation (National Mental Health Association Commission on the Prevention of Mental-Emotional Disabilities, 1986, p. 13), which expresses the relationships among the variables affecting the development of mental health problems, can be applied equally well to whole communities, high-risk populations, and individuals.

$$\text{Incidence} = \frac{\text{Organic Factors} + \text{Stress} + \text{Exploitation}}{\text{Coping Skills} + \text{Self-esteem} + \text{Social Support}}$$

Moreover, it can serve as a general guide in both the assessment and the prevention of mental health problems. As a tool for assessing individual clients, it provides a way of organizing data and a method of teaching people how stress and coping factors interrelate. Earlier versions of this equation did not include exploitation. The addition of this term clarifies Albee's belief that social, economic, and political exploitation place members of powerless populations at risk.

When using the equation in the assessment process, the counselor's first step is to teach the client how to use it as a guide for thinking about his or her own circumstances. Clients generally have no trouble understanding that anyone might, because of genetic or other physiological factors, be vulnerable to specific problems or disorders. This susceptibility might never be triggered unless the individual, because of a critical event or long-term exposure to an environmental stressor, is subjected to severe stress. But even under such stress, people are protected from dysfunction by their abilities to mobilize social supports, to use effective coping skills, and to maintain their self-esteem.

Familiarity with the equation helps clients understand that they can take steps both to reduce stress, thereby decreasing the values of the numerator, and to strengthen their resources, thereby increasing the values of the denominator. Moreover, analyzing their own particulars according to the variables in the equation shows clients what strengths they can build on and what areas they need to change. They can then plan what actions they will take to work on the issues that have come to light.

Counselors can use a structured form to focus on the variables to be assessed and remind themselves to assess all aspects of the client's well-being instead of concentrating on only one issue or problem. The Lewis-Fussell Case Conceptualization Form, for example, is a handy means of documenting the multifaceted assessment process. Further, using this form, counselors can clearly conceptualize their recommendations to the client. The form is a practical, though unorthodox, record-keeping tool that uses an open-ended questionnaire format to allow counselors to record their perceptions systematically. The form is shown in Figure 4.2 beginning on page 128.

The case conceptualization form provides space for the assessor to list recommendations pertaining to each factor. The completed form thus serves as both a personal record of the assessment interview and a set of guidelines to follow in continuing the counseling process. Consequently, the form enables counselors to proceed naturally from assessment to problem solving.

Individual and Environmental Change

When community counselors work with individual clients, they work with the whole person as well as with the person's environment, attending both to detrimental factors and to possible sources of help and support. If an individual's natural support systems cannot meet his or her needs, additional sources of support must be sought. If aspects of the individual's environment are destructive, then those aspects must, if possible, be changed.

Troubled individuals must, of course, examine, and perhaps change, those aspects of their own behavior that are adding to their problems. Obviously, people have more control over their own actions than they have over the actions of others. And if the individual can resolve his or her problems through personal change, there is no need to change the environment.

Client: _____ Address:_____	Dates Seen: _____ _____ _____
Telephone: Work _____ Home _____	

Employer Providing Coverage: _____ _____ _____ Employee _____ Family Member of Employee	Employment: Present Job Title _____ How Long in Present Position? _____ How Long with Company? _____ Referred by: _____

Marital Status:	Dependents:	Age:	_____ Male _____ Female

Reason for Referral (Presenting Problem):

Physical Vulnerabilities

Physician:

Medical Problems/Medications:

Pattern of Alcohol Use (Self and/or Family):

Pattern of Drug Use (Self and/or Family):

Previous Treatment (for Substance Abuse):

Level of Health/Fitness:

General Impressions (Physical Strengths/Vulnerabilities):

Assessor's Recommendations for Decreasing Physical Vulnerabilities:

Figure 4.2   The Lewis-Fussell Case Conceptualization Form

Stress
Significant Life Changes (Last 12 Months):
Marital/Family Stressors:
Work-Related Stressors:
Client's Perception of Stress Factors:
General Level of Stress:
Recommendations for Decreasing Stress:
Life Skills
Professional/Educational Level:
Problem Solving/Decision Making Skills:
Interpersonal Skills:
Life Planning Skills:
Aptitudes/Interests/Hobbies:
Ability to Handle Life Situations:

Figure 4.2   *(continued)*

General Impressions of Life Skills:
Recommendations for Increasing Life Skills:
Self-Concept
Level of Life Satisfaction:
Client's Perception of Strengths:
Client's Perception of Weaknesses/Problems:
Level of Self-Esteem:
Level of Work Satisfaction/Perceived Competence:
General Impressions:
Recommendations for Increasing Self-Esteem:
Social Supports
Stability of Present Home Situation:
Relationship to Family:
Family-Related Problems:

Figure 4.2 (*continued*)

Degree of Family Support for Problem Resolution:

Significant Other Relationships/Support:

Work Relationships/Support:

General Level of Available Support:

Recommendations for Increasing/Using Social Support:

General Level of Adjustment

Psycho-Social Problem Areas:

Developmental History of Problems:

Previous Treatment/Response to Treatment:

General Assessment

Nature of Problem	Recommendation/Referral
_____ Everyday Living Issue (No Long-Term Treatment Needed)	
_____ Psychological	
_____ Substance Abuse _____	
_____ Family	
_____ Medical _____	
_____ Legal/Financial	
_____ Other _____	
Date of Referral:	Date of Follow-up:

Figure 4.2 (*continued*)

Usually, however, the individual, the family, and the community are so closely related that the client's social system must be taken into account. Purely personal change may be impossible, impractical, or damaging to the individual's integrity. Then the counselor must help the client (1) identify sources of help in the environment, (2) create additional sources of support if necessary, and (3) reduce or eliminate stressful elements in the environment by either avoiding them or directly confronting and changing them.

Identifying possible sources of support must be done jointly by the counselor and the client; no one can tell another what his or her support system should be. Relationships are supportive or helpful only if people experience them that way. Thus, no objective standard can help us distinguish between a "good" environment and a "bad" one. It is the interaction between individuals and their surroundings that determines this, and only the people involved can know when their own needs are being met.

The attention given the environment in counseling within the community counseling context distinguishes it from traditional counseling. Most counselors have, in the past, assumed that the attitudes, feelings, or behavior of the client should be the objects of change. We are becoming more aware every day, however, that the obstacles that keep people from meeting their goals may be in the environment, rather than in themselves. Intervention in the environment is therefore often imperative if an individual's problems are to be truly resolved. At the same time, even when environmental factors have clearly contributed to the development of a problem, as when economic changes have caused an individual's unemployment,

> it may be important to separate responsibility for the *etiology* of the problem from responsibility for the *resolution* of the problem. Otherwise there is a danger that the individual will suffer passivity and helplessness from being portrayed as a victim of economic and social circumstances beyond his or her control. (Monahan & Vaux, 1980)

This approach accords with the compensatory model defined by Brickman et al. (1982) in recognizing that people are not to blame for their predicaments but can still act to resolve them.

As is clear from Albee's equation, personal factors and environmental factors are interrelated. To choose sides, therefore—that is, to insist either that most problems arise within the individual or that a destructive environment is usually to blame—is unrealistic. In fact, sometimes individuals have the power to solve their own problems and sometimes they don't.

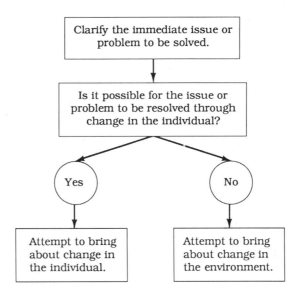

Figure 4.3   The first juncture in the counseling process

It is therefore helpful to look at the counseling process in terms of a number of junctures. These junctures are points at which the counselor and the client together decide who has the power to resolve the issue at hand.

The first juncture in the counseling process is shown in Figure 4.3. Working together, the counselor and the client are trying to determine what changes the client can make to resolve a specific problem, identified through the initial assessment. In considering alternatives, the counselor and the client must consider whether or not the client actually has the power to implement the best possible solution.

If the issue can be resolved through personal change, the client and the counselor work to bring about that change. But if at this point the individual seems unable to change—if some destructive force in the environment is blocking change—then the two try to change the environment.

Suppose that a counselor and client have decided that the client is able to change in a way that will solve the immediate problem. Figure 4.4 on page 134 indicates the next juncture in the process.

The next step is to choose what method will best facilitate the client's change. For some clients, continuing with one-to-one counseling may suffice; others may need more help. Counselors may try to foster closer ties between such clients and others in their natural support systems or work with them in a

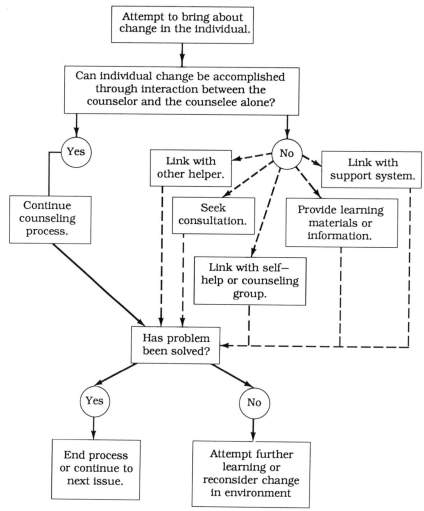

Figure 4.4   Juncture in individual change

group setting. Direct counseling and consultation with a specialized helper might be combined. Further, counselors can supply
the client additional opportunities to learn, such as programmed
materials in decision making or participation in a seminar dealing with self-modification techniques.

Whatever methods are used, the counselor and the client
must ultimately evaluate the success of their efforts. If the client
has been able to solve the problem, he or she can either end the
counseling relationship or go on to deal with another issue or
problem. If the initial problem is still unresolved, the counselor
and client must decide whether the client needs additional help
or whether, in fact, the environment must be changed.

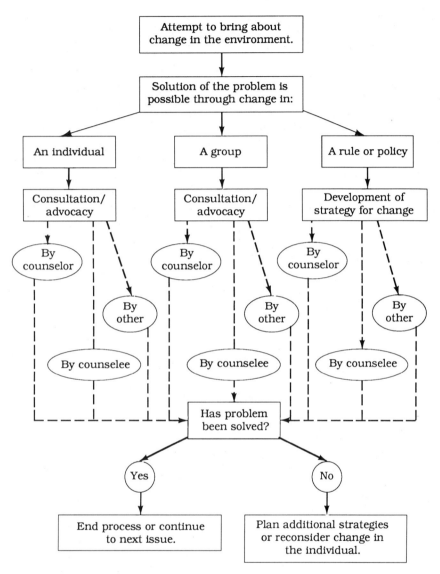

Figure 4.5   Juncture in environmental change

If the counselor and the client decide that the solution to a problem lies in changing an external factor, new questions must be asked. Figure 4.5 illustrates the nature of this juncture.

If the client does not have the power to solve the immediate problem, who does? If a change in the attitudes or behavior of another person or group would solve the problem, an appropriate step might be to consult that person or group, or to speak up on behalf of the client. The person who does this might be the counselor, the client, or someone else, such as a citizen advocate or an official. If solving the problem requires a change in the rules or policies of some agency or institution, then a strategy for bringing about the change must be devised. The appropriate person to take leadership in this process might, again, be the counselor, the client, or another person or group. The counselor is most likely to take an active role in promoting such a change if the rule or policy in question is detrimental to a number of clients.

If the environment is changed and the problem is solved, then counseling can end, or the counselor and client can go on to deal with other issues or problems. If the problem is not solved, they must devise new ways to deal with the environment or consider once more the possibility that the individual must change.

At each of the junctures, the counselor and client decide what elements they will emphasize at that time. When counselors help individuals to change, they are, at the same time, aware of the effects of the environment. When they concentrate on environmental change, they are aware of the individual's complex responses.

The interactive counseling process should not, of course, be oversimplified. At each juncture, the counselor and client must determine not only what kind of change—individual or environmental—will most effectively solve the problem at hand but also how ready for change the individual or significant others in the environment are. Thus, they must first ask what change is preferable, then what change is possible.

The point is that community counselors need not choose between helping individuals and confronting the environment. They need not choose between being counselors and being agents of change; rather, the two roles constantly interact. Dealing with the environment can and should be an important part of counseling individuals. In the process, as clients recognize that more than their own behavior must change, they are learning to actively confront the systems that affect them; thus, their attitudes and behavior are also being changed.

The following examples illustrate the need to examine both personal and environmental factors in choosing strategies for change.

Example #1: A Runaway Youth

An adolescent boy runs away from home and finds himself alone in an unfamiliar neighborhood. He turns to the local runaway center, where a counselor asks questions like the following:

1. Is the youth's own family a source of emotional support for him? Could it be?

2. What changes in the family situation might make his home environment supportive enough for him to consider returning?

3. What changes in the youth's behavior might make the family more supportive of him? Can he make those changes?

4. If the conflicts at home cannot be resolved, what alternative living situations are available? Does the youth know of a family with whom or a group home where he could be comfortable?

5. What kinds of relationships does the youth have with relatives outside of his immediate family? Are any of them potential sources of support?

6. Have the police been involved?

7. Can the youth support himself? What work skills does he have? What job opportunities are or might be open to him?

8. Does the youth or his family need financial aid? What sources of aid might be appropriate?

9. Does the youth have a group of friends with whom he identifies strongly? How can this support system be of help to him now?

10. What is the youth's school situation? Is that where the real conflict lies? Are there any people or programs at the school that can provide additional support? Can any negative factors be changed?

11. Has anyone else tried to help the youth? Have the two established any kind of relationship?

12. Is child abuse or substance abuse a factor in this situation? If so, what steps have been taken to deal with either issue?

These questions seem obvious, but it is surprising how many of them may be left unasked in the immediacy of a crisis. The questions reflect a clear recognition that children don't run away in isolation; they run to or from something. It is more than coincidence that many runaway centers that initially concentrated on counseling or placing individual adolescents have now developed group counseling programs for parents as well as young people. What they are doing, in effect, is working to build more effective support systems for their young clients.

Example #2: A Physically Disabled Adult

A recent accident has left a young, single woman physically disabled. As she prepares to leave the hospital, a counselor on the staff tries to help her answer the following questions:

1. What living situation would best suit the woman? Is she able to live alone? Are members of her family available to provide attendant care? Must an attendant be hired?
2. What financial assistance is available, not only to help her meet her basic needs but also to cover attendants' salaries or technical necessities? Does she need an advocate to obtain assistance?
3. What are her career goals? What work is she able to do? Does she need additional skills? What educational resources are available to her?
4. How are her relationships with family members and friends? Have they been able to offer psychological support throughout the crisis? How have they adjusted to her disability? Are they allowing her to be as independent as possible?
5. How can she maintain social relationships and continue to enjoy recreation?
6. Does she need help and information to deal with what may be a crisis in her sexuality?
7. Does she have ready access to whatever legal and medical assistance she needs?
8. How can she maintain the greatest possible degree of physical mobility and independence?
9. To what degree does the community provide the resources and accessibility that are her right?

In traditional approaches, one helper might help this woman with her vocational goals, another with her physical needs, and still another with her psychological adjustment. Her needs for socializing and recreation might never be addressed.

In contrast, the community counselor sees this woman as a whole person whose interactions with the total environment constitute her potential support system. The basic, underlying questions thus become: Is her former support system holding up under the pressures of change, or does she need supplemental help to meet all of her needs effectively? Where can she find additional support, and how can she be helped to make the most of the opportunities that now exist for her? To what degree does she need an advocate to maximize these opportunities?

Example #3: A Mature Woman Continuing Her Education

A woman who has worked full time at raising a family and maintaining a household decides to return to school to complete an education interrupted by the birth of her first child. Her success, of course, depends on her own motivation, talent, and good fortune, but the environment does make an important difference. The community counselor asks the following questions:

1. Is her family supportive and enthusiastic about her new endeavor? If not, how can they be helped to understand her situation more fully?
2. Do her friends and associates understand her goals? Are any of them in similar situations, or do their values differ? Are they likely to encourage or discourage her?
3. Is she aware of other women taking similar steps who might prove to be supportive new contacts?
4. How is her move affecting the family's immediate finances? Are sources of aid available?
5. Is the educational institution meeting her special needs by providing such services as day care, flexible scheduling, and career counseling?
6. Are extracurricular activities on campus aimed solely at young, resident students, or are some relevant to her and other mature students? Can new, appropriate activities be developed?
7. What steps have been taken to integrate mature students into campus life? What kinds of interaction exist between age groups?
8. Who is handling the household tasks that she used to do? Do other family members understand their responsibilities? Are other sources of help available?
9. When she has completed her education, what job opportunities will she find? Do local businesses discriminate against women or middle-aged people in hiring? Is a part-time or flexible job possible? Could it be?

In this instance, what appears to be an individual step really involves the family, the educational institution, and the community. A change in this one individual's behavior creates stress on all of her interactions with the environment. Her support system, which might have been strong, must adapt. If her former support system proves inadequate, new sources of help must be created or found, or some changes must be made.

Each of these examples makes clear that individual, intrapsychic change cannot be the sole focus of the counseling process. Instead, multiple levels of the whole system, from the family to the culture as a whole, must be considered: "The limits of individual growth, evolution, or health are constrained by the health of their immediate contexts—their families. Families in turn must help to maintain the health of the contexts which embody them; and so on until we can conceive of a healthy planet" (Keeney, 1984, p. 37).

Summary

Inherent in community counseling is a set of values that includes an emphasis on the strengths and competencies of clients, a recognition of the impact of the social environment, an emphasis on prevention, and a belief that people can be helped most effectively if given the resources they need to help themselves. These values lead community counselors to develop multifaceted programs that include preventive education, outreach efforts, attention to public policy issues, and client advocacy. By definition, of course, counselors also provide direct, one-to-one counseling. The nature of the process of counseling, however, is affected by the community counseling context, which emphasizes both individual responsibility and environmental influences.

Brickman and his colleagues have defined four models of helping and coping according to how responsibility is attributed. According to the moral model, people are responsible both for creating and for solving their own problems; according to the medical model, people are responsible neither for creating nor for solving their problems; according to the enlightenment model, people are responsible for creating their problems but not for solving them; and according to the compensatory model, people are not responsible for creating their problems but are, nevertheless, responsible for solving them. The compensatory model, which allows a dual focus on individual responsibility and environmental influences, is most compatible with community counseling.

At its most effective, counseling enhances the client's sense of personal power and responsibility. Counselors can help clients gain mastery over their lives by training them in the principles of behavioral change. They can also promote clients' progress toward higher levels of development following various structural developmental models. Such models trace the development of various psychological functions through specific, invariant stages. Loevinger has identified the stages of ego development; Kohlberg, those of moral development; and Perry, those of intellectual and ethical development. In general, later stages of development are better in that they are more adaptive than earlier, less complex stages.

Counseling in the community counseling context is also characterized by an attention to systems theory. Systems thinking focuses on consistent patterns of interaction, on interrelationships, and on general organizing principles. Although clients may be affected by many systems or levels of systems, the one that counselors have addressed most successfully is the family. Counselors who work with families see the family system itself as the target of their interventions; they identify the source of difficulties as a dysfunctional system instead of a "sick" individual. Although there are a number of approaches to family counseling, each recognizes the importance of the family as a social system that affects and is affected by the behavior of its members.

The dual focus on individual responsibility and systems has practical implications for the counselor's day-to-day work with individual clients, affecting both assessment and intervention.

In following the community counseling model, counselors use multifaceted assessments that build on the individual's strengths and resources, that take into account the stressors and supports present or available in the environment, and that flow naturally into a practical intervention plan addressing each difficulty that has been identified. An effective assessment tool is Albee's equation; in keeping with the equation, strategies can be aimed either at reducing environmental stress or at strengthening the individual's social supports, coping skills, and self-esteem. The Lewis-Fussell Case Conceptualization Form uses the variables in the equation to organize the information obtained during assessment about the individual's situation.

In selecting an intervention strategy, counselors must consider both personal and environmental factors. In many instances, change in the individual client's behaviors or attitudes will fall short of what is needed to resolve troublesome issues. The counselor and client must then consider changing the client's social system. One can think of the counseling process in terms of a number of junctures, points at which the counselor and the client together decide who has the power to resolve the issue at hand. An effort is made to resolve each issue through personal change, but if this is not possible, environmental change must be considered. Counselors do not need to choose between helping individuals and confronting their environments. The two roles alternate constantly as clients interact with their respective systems.

Supplemental Activities

1. Find a friend, colleague, or fellow student who is willing to work with you. Ask the individual to act as a client, either

role playing an imaginary problem or sharing a real concern. Spend a few minutes exploring the issue with your "client" by listening carefully and asking for clarification of any point you do not fully understand. When you think you have a good grasp of the problem, state it in your own words and have your partner verify whether or not your understanding is accurate. If it is, you can now begin to consider ways of resolving the problem. Working together, the two of you should list a number of possibilities that you might explore if this were a real counseling situation. Include both methods of bringing about change in the individual's behavior and strategies for bringing about change in the environment. In a real counseling situation, do you think you would have explored environmental change as completely as you would have individual change?

2. Consider once more your own hypothetical community counseling program. What would you consider to be the most important issues to consider in counseling members of this group? How might the community counseling model affect your approach to counseling these individuals?

Related Reading

BANDURA, A. (1982). Self-efficacy mechanism in human agency. *American Psychologist, 37,* 122–147.

BRICKMAN, P., RABINOWITZ, V. C., KARUZA, J., COATES, D., COHN, E., & KIDDER, L. (1982). Four models of helping and coping. *American Psychologist, 37,* 368–384.

GOLDENBERG, I., & GOLDENBERG, H. (1985). *Family therapy: An overview.* Pacific Grove, CA: Brooks/Cole.

HAYES, R. L., & AUBREY, R. F. (Eds.). (1988). *New directions for counseling and human development.* Denver: Love.

KANFER, F. H., & GOLDSTEIN, A. P. (Eds.). (1980). *Helping people change.* New York: Pergamon Press.

LEWIS, M. D., HAYES, R. L., & LEWIS, J. A. (Eds.). (1986). *An introduction to the counseling profession.* Itasca, IL: F. E. Peacock.

O'CONNOR, W. A., & LUBIN, B. (Eds.). (1984). *Ecological approaches to clinical and community psychology.* New York: Wiley.

VON BERTALANFFY, L. (1968). *General systems theory.* New York: Braziller.

YOUNG-EISENDRATH, P. (1985). Making use of human development theories in counseling. *Counseling and Human Development, 17*(5), 1–12.

References

BANDURA, A. (1982). Self-efficacy mechanism in human agency. *American Psychologist, 37,* 122–147.

BOWEN, M. (1982). *Family therapy in clinical practice.* New York: Aronson.

BRICKMAN, P., RABINOWITZ, V. C., KARUZA, J., COATES, D., COHN, E., & KIDDER, L. (1982). Four models of helping and coping. *American Psychologist, 37,* 368–384.

D'ANDREA, M. D. (1984). The counselor as pacer: A model for revitalization of the counseling profession. *Counseling and Human Development, 16*(6), 1–15.

GOLDENBERG, I., & GOLDENBERG, H. (1985). *Family therapy: An overview.* Pacific Grove, CA: Brooks/Cole.

HALEY, J. (1976). *Problem-solving therapy.* New York: Harper & Row.

HAYES, R. L. (1986). Human growth and development. In M. D. Lewis, R. L. Hayes, & J. A. Lewis (Eds.), *An introduction to the counseling profession* (pp. 36–95). Itasca, IL: F. E. Peacock.

KANFER, F. H. (1980). Self-management methods. In F. H. Kanfer & A. P. Goldstein (Eds.), *Helping people change* (pp. 334–389). New York: Pergamon Press.

KEENEY, B. P. (1984). An ecological epistemology for therapy. In W. A. O'Connor & B. Lubin (Eds.), *Ecological approaches to clinical and community psychology* (pp. 24–40). New York: Wiley.

KOHLBERG, L. (1984). *Essays on moral development: Vol. 2. The psychology of moral development.* New York: Harper & Row.

LEWIS, J. A. (1981). Transition: From school to community mental health counseling. *Counseling and Human Development, 14*(2), 1–8.

LEWIS, J. A., DANA, R. Q., & BLEVINS, G. A. (1988). *Substance abuse counseling: An individualized approach.* Pacific Grove, CA: Brooks/Cole.

LIBERMAN, R. (1981). Behavioral approaches to family and couple therapy. In G. D. Erickson & T. P. Hogan (Eds.), *Family therapy: An introduction to theory and technique* (2nd ed.) (pp. 152–164). Pacific Grove, CA: Brooks/Cole.

LOEVINGER, J. (1976). *Ego development: Conceptions and theories.* San Francisco: Jossey-Bass.

MADANES, C. (1981). *Strategic family therapy.* San Francisco: Jossey-Bass.

MARLATT, G. A., & GORDON, J. R. (1985). *Relapse prevention: Maintenance strategies in the treatment of addictive behaviors.* New York: Guilford Press.

MINUCHIN, S. (1974). *Families and family therapy.* Cambridge: Harvard University Press.

MINUCHIN, S. (1979). Constructing a therapeutic reality. In E. Kaufman and P. Kaufmann (Eds.), *Family therapy of drug and alcohol abuse* (pp. 5–18). New York: Gardner Press.

MONAHAN, J., & VAUX, A. (1980). The macroenvironment and community mental health.

Community Mental Health Journal, 16, 14–26.

NATIONAL MENTAL HEALTH ASSOCIATION COMMISSION ON THE PREVENTION OF MENTAL-EMOTIONAL DISABILITIES. (1986). The prevention of mental-emotional disabilities: Report of the National Mental Health Association Commission on the Prevention of Mental-Emotional Disabilities. Alexandria, VA: National Mental Health Association.

PERRY, W. G., JR. (1970). *Forms of intellectual and ethical development in the college years.* New York: Holt, Rinehart & Winston.

SATIR, V. M. (1967). *Conjoint family therapy* (2nd ed.). Palo Alto, CA: Science and Behavior Books.

SATIR, V. M. (1972). *Peoplemaking.* Palo Alto, CA: Science and Behavior Books.

STACHOWIAK, J., & BRIGGS, S. L. (1984). Ecosystemic therapy: A treatment perspective. In W. A. O'Connor & B. Lubin (Eds.), *Ecological approaches to clinical and community psychology* (pp. 7–23). New York: Wiley.

STEINGLASS, P. (1978). The conceptualization of marriage from a systems theory perspective. In T. J. Paolino & B. S. McCrady (Eds.), *Marriage and marital therapy: Psychoanalytic, behavioral, and systems theory perspectives* (pp. 298–365). New York: Brunner/Mazel.

UMBARGER, C. C. (1983). *Structural family therapy.* New York: Grune & Stratton.

VON BERTALANFFY, L. (1968). *General systems theory.* New York: Braziller.

YOUNG-EISENDRATH, P. (1985). Making use of human development theories in counseling. *Counseling and Human Development, 17*(5), 1–12.

The Community
Counselor and
Social Policy

Community counselors know that human beings constantly interact with their surroundings. Knowing this, they also recognize that they must consider the impact of social, political, and economic factors on their clients. Confronting social issues is thus a natural continuation of the counseling process. Helping individuals and dealing with social-political systems are two aspects of the same task.

Bronfenbrenner (1979) has asserted that, though "human development is a product of interaction between the growing human organism and its environment," there is "a marked asymmetry, a hypertrophy of theory and research focusing on the properties of the person and only the most rudimentary conception and characterization of the environment in which the person is found" (p. 16). Conyne (1985) has made it clear that this "asymmetry" applies also to counselors, pointing out that counselors have tended to ignore Kurt Lewin's formulation that $B = f(P \times E)$—that is, behavior is a function of the interaction between the person and the environment—acting instead on the basis of a far more limited formula: B = f(P); that is, behavior is a function of the person.

Though the helping professions as a whole have awakened in recent years to the need to participate in political action, still rarely recognized is the importance of using such action not just to protect funding and services but also to address issues more directly affecting clients' well-being. Counselors are more likely to recognize and address such issues if they first make a "transition in their own thinking from assuming intrapsychic causality of their clients' problems to recognizing that political explanations are sometimes more appropriate" (Aubrey & Lewis, 1983, p. 13). On the contrary, however, counselors sometimes assume intrapsychic causality of even political phenomena. Iscoe (1981), for instance, has pointed out that many broadly based social movements have been misinterpreted as clinical manifestations:

> In the late '60s and early '70s . . . there was concern about ethnic minorities, the distribution of power, the rights of subordinate counselors, and persons who generally did not fit into the clinical mold. It is instructive, however, to note that many explanations of the motivations of persons using drugs, of urban riots, of demonstrations on university campuses were cast into clinical molds; thus, concepts like mass insanity, acting-out behavior, and unresolved hostility towards autority were invoked to explain social movements and, of course, failed to do so. (pp. 125–126)

Counselors need to address the environmental factors that make their clients susceptible to problems, not the least of which concerns the distribution of power.

Specific environmental factors that affect many community members must, of course, be addressed. But counselors also need to recognize that the degree to which individuals feel that they can control their own environments is important in and of itself. If people within a community feel powerless to control their own lives, that, in itself, is a major mental health problem. Mental health and competence in living depend on a level of self-esteem that, in turn, may depend on the belief that one's behavior can affect the world. Such confidence comes less from self-exploration or deliberate modification of one's attitudes than from experience.

The well-being of a community may well rest on the sense of power, effectiveness, and self-determination felt by its individual members and permeating the community as a whole. Social action, then, must be a major concern of the community counselor because:

1. Specific aspects of the community environment may be detrimental to the growth and development of individuals.
2. Other aspects of the community environment can support individual growth and development.
3. Community counselors cannot help individuals unless environmental factors change along with individuals.
4. Self-determination is not only a political goal, but a mental health goal.
5. Working alone, neither community counselors nor individual citizens can make the community responsive to the needs of its members.

The bottom-line rationale for community counselors' involvement in social and political issues is that their clients are victims of political, social, and economic pressures. If they are not to blame their clients for being victims, they must seek ways to change the environment.

> Blaming the victim means application of a psychological intervention aimed at fitting an individual into existing social conditions, which are presumed to have victimized him or her in the first place. Implied is the notion that the individual has some sort of deficit or emotional difficulty that is the basis of his or her problem in living. . . . It matters little whether one applies the medical model or any other if the interventions are victim blaming while the problems are social systemic in nature. (Rappaport, Davidson, Wilson, & Mitchell, 1975, p. 525)

Problems that derive from social systems must be addressed through interventions in the system. Such interventions can take place at any of several systemic levels. A model described by Bronfenbrenner (1976, 1979) represents one way of defining these levels. According to Bronfenbrenner (1976),

> The ecology of human development is the scientific study of the progressive, mutual accommodation, throughout the life span, between a growing human organism and the changing immediate environments in which it lives, as this process is affected by conditions obtaining within and between these immediate settings and the larger social contexts, both formal and informal, in which the settings are embedded. (p. 2)

Each person's growth and development is thus affected both by the immediate systems in which he or she participates and by broader systems that are more indirect in their effects. These systems, which form a "nested arrangement," comprise the following:

> A *microsystem* is the complex of relations between the develop-
> ing person and environment in an immediate setting containing
> that person (e.g., home, school, work place). . . . A *mesosystem*
> comprises the interrelations among the major settings contain-
> ing the developing person at a particular point in his or her life. . . .
> The *exosystem* is an extension of the mesosystem embracing the
> concrete social structures, both formal and informal, that impinge
> upon or encompass the immediate settings containing the develop-
> ing person. . . . These structures include the major institutions
> of the society, both deliberately structured and spontaneously
> evolving, as they operate at the local level. . . . *Macrosystems*
> refer to the overarching institutions of the culture or subculture,
> such as the economic, social, educational, legal, and political
> systems, of which local mesosystems are the concrete manifesta-
> tions. . . . (Bronfenbrenner, 1976, p. 3)

Community counselors intervene at all of these levels. The
place of these systemic interventions in the community counseling model is shown in Table 5.1.

As indicated in Table 5.1, interventions aimed at shaping
social policy use indirect methods to affect the social, political,
and economic environment of the community at large. In interventions at all levels of systems, the object of change is the
environment as it affects people who have not necessarily been
identified as dysfunctional. Macrosystem interventions, however, are broad enough to address the "profound, widespread
social injustices" (Cowen, 1985, p. 32) that are considered by
many to be at the root of a significant number of psychological
problems, while interventions at other system levels affect community members' more immediate surroundings.

Microsystem Interventions: School-Based Programs

Bronfenbrenner cited the school as an example of a microsystem
setting, and clearly, interventions in schools can have a major
impact on young people's development. But such interventions

Table 5.1   Social Policy Strategies and the Community Counseling
Model

	Community services	*Client services*
Direct	/ /	/ /
Indirect	Interventions at the microsystem, meso- system, exosystem, and macrosystem levels	/ /

are difficult to implement, largely because the status quo is highly resistant to change. As Aubrey (1972) pointed out years ago, "nonnegotiable factors" within the educational system thwart the aspirations of many counselors.

> These nonnegotiable factors are institutional constraints that have been ingrained and long-established by custom and tradition, e.g., the ultimate authority of the principal in instructional and noninstructional matters, the inviolate sovereignty of the teacher in his [or her] classroom, the rigid time schedule in schools, the inflexible methods in the grouping of children, the premium placed on docility and conformity, and so on. In the course of time, they become sanctioned and therefore present themselves to counselors as routine procedures, structural patterns, organizational practices, hierarchical processes, and conventional observances. Collectively, these school heirlooms represent tremendous impediments to counselors wishing to innovate programs and practices for children. (p. 90)

These "heirlooms" are as much a part of American school systems today as they were when Aubrey described them. Consequently, most efforts at primary prevention, even those aimed at young children, tend to be focused on individuals instead of the environment (Wolff, 1987). As useful as direct competency-building programs are, however, more programs aimed at school-age children must focus concurrently on the school environment, if not to change it, then at least to understand its effects.

> While person-centered approaches to competence or social skills may be legitimate interventions for the prevention of individual problems in living . . . we are also concerned with how such programs affect the social context in which they take place. What, we want to know, are the metacommunications of the program to the children in it and those not in it?
>
> When such programs are developed in schools we want to know something about the impact on the teachers, the administrators, the social climate, and the educational policies. We want to know about more than changes in test scores. We want to understand how it is that some children grow up with a sense of their own ability to influence the outcomes of their life and the life of their various communities, while other children do not. (Rappaport, 1987, p. 133)

The Quality of School Life Program

Adults and children can work together to bring about positive changes, as the Quality of School Life Program implemented in Washtenaw County, Michigan, demonstrates. "The Quality of School Life for Elementary Schools Program (QSL-E) of the

Washtenaw County Community Mental Health Center is a social systems intervention whose goal is to promote a beneficial school climate through improved pupil and staff participation and more positive mutual expectancies'' (Schelkun, Cooper, Tableman, & Groves, 1987, p. 8). Based on the Quality of Work Life/Quality Circle programs developed for business and industry, the systemwide QSL-E program uses a variety of organizational development methods to enhance participation and problem solving. The program, which was funded by the Michigan Department of Mental Health, was described by its developers as follows:[1]

> QSL procedures join with other efforts associated with the movement toward excellence and effectiveness in the schools, focusing on the following issues and objectives:
>
> - *Appropriate school climate:* the attainment of a safe, friendly, and orderly learning environment.
> - *Effective student/staff motivation and morale:* a realistic belief in one's ability to affect the outcomes of relevant decisions, with resulting staff/student support and acceptance of school and classroom activities, rules, and norms.
> - *Congruent staff/student/parent expectations:* the explicit sharing of expectations in a context which encourages consensus.
> - *Mutual understanding:* the development of a shared vocabulary, conceptual base, and systematic operating guidelines for problem solving at all levels of the system.
> - *An effective participative organizational culture:* a realistic and predictable system of communication, structures, and procedures for involving others in problem identification, problem solving, and decision-making— where appropriate—in school and classroom.
>
> The total QSL program consists of four levels: (1) Pupil Involvement (PI) clubs, (2) Teacher/Staff Involvement (TI/SI) groups, (3) School Climate Coordination (SCC), and (4) Family/Community Involvement (FI & CI) groups.

Pupil Involvement Clubs

The Pupil Involvement (PI) process encourages students and their teachers to cooperate in identifying, researching, goal-setting, planning, implementing, and evaluating activities which contribute to solving problems and maximizing opportunities in their own classrooms. Teachers utilize a standard curriculum to teach children concepts and skills helpful for group problem-

---

[1]The Quality of School Life program: Improving school and classroom climate by problem solving with people. A program of the Washtenaw County Community Mental Health Center, funded by the Michigan Department of Mental Health.

solving activities. During PI club meetings, students and their teacher meet regularly—first, to learn the skills and concepts, and then to apply these to their ongoing classroom challenges and opportunities. . . .

Training goals include improved problem solving by individuals and groups, cooperativeness in the classroom, improved individual and group responsibility, and mutually understood expectations regarding ability to learn and do. Students learn the "chain of command" functions and responsibilities within the school district, effects of changing the physical environment of the classroom, the need for developing explicitly stated classroom norms, the various stages and techniques related to problem solving and action planning, and various skills needed for responsible self-control. They are encouraged to apply these skills throughout the school day.

Teacher Involvement/Staff Involvement

At the building level, the Teacher Involvement (TI) or Staff Involvement (SI) steering committee is the primary problem-solving mechanism in the participating elementary school. This group always includes the building administrator and, where bargaining units exist, a representative of the relevant bargaining unit(s): in addition, volunteers are recruited from the rest of the school's personnel. Professional staff development training in QSL processes is offered to all participants, operating guidelines are presented and refined, and the TI/SI steering committee then meets regularly for the remainder of the school year. The group indentifies building-based problems and opportunities; engages in fact-finding; suggests goals; reviews recommendations of volunteers, task forces, and work groups; develops and utilizes feedback procedures for the entire staff; makes recommendations to the building administrator; and assists the administrator in other activities which affect his or her decisions. In this way, the TI/SI group serves as a facilitating bridge between administrator and staff. . . .

School Climate Coordination Structures

Once a school district legitimizes the creation of TI/SI steering committees, it is important to monitor and standardize the operating procedures and guidelines of the various buildings so that changes in administrative personnel will not unduly disrupt the participatory process. There is no standard set of coordination and communication structures; however, the program suggests a number of ways a district may choose to ensure the durability and usefulness of participatory methods in a manner which suits the style and structure of the system.

Family Involvement/Community Involvement

Increasingly, school districts are seeking ways to involve parents and community leaders in identifying and solving school-related problems. One major difficulty lies in the various expectations and styles which "outsiders" bring to such endeavors, and school personnel are frequently frustrated to find that family or community participation takes problem solving in so many directions that it ends nowhere or, even worse, into seemingly insurmountable conflicts.

The QSL model suggests that community/family participation can be coordinated in the same way that TI/SI participation is managed: a central figure coordinates, communicates, and monitors these activities, and participatory groups are trained in similar skills and concepts before getting down to work. Operating guidelines and procedures are clarified in advance, boundaries are established, and staff responsibilities to the group and to the school district are clearly established.

The strength of the QSL program lies in its systematic attempt to bring so many role groups into the problem-solving process. Significant effort has been put into designing and implementing a curriculum that directly enhances children's competencies. What makes the program unusual is its complementary effort to make each school an environment in which children can use their problem-solving skills meaningfully. Adults and children in the targeted school systems have a chance to learn new skills; because of the program's participatory structure, they also have a chance to practice them.

Mesosystems: The Relationships between Settings

Mesosystems have to do with the boundaries between microsystems. Bronfenbrenner, in his concept of the mesosystem, acknowledged that the interactions between settings can have as much impact on human development as the characteristics of the settings themselves. Mesosystem interventions may be focused on the interaction between two settings, such as between a child's home and his or her school. Mesosystem interventions may also address ecological transitions, such as a child's entry into preschool or his or her transfer from one school to another.

In 1979, Bronfenbrenner hypothesized that the quality of home-to-school and school-to-school connections might be found to affect children's development over the long run. Years later, when the American Psychological Association's (APA) Task Force on Promotion, Prevention, and Intervention Alternatives sought to identify programs that had proven to be effective, several of the 14 "showcase" programs it selected dealt in some way with these issues (Bales, 1987).

The Perry Preschool Project

The High/Scope Perry Preschool Project was one of the programs identified as exemplary. Implemented in Ypsilanti, Michigan, the project provided a preschool program for children from "poor, undereducated families" and followed participants up through the age of 19. The preschool experience, as described by one of the project's codirectors, was based on the following set of assumptions about the components of high quality programs:

1. A developmentally appropriate curriculum.
2. Supervisory support and inservice training for program staff.
3. Low enrollment limits and an adequate number of adults, with teaching/caregiving teams assigned to small groups of children.
4. Staff trained in early childhood development.
5. Parents involved as partners with program staff.
6. Sensitivity to the noneducational circumstances of the child and family.
7. Developmentally appropriate evaluation procedures. (Schweinhart, 1987, p. 9)

The project, which included home visits by teachers, has been heavily studied. Participating children were compared with a matched group of children who did not attend preschool. Results showed that members of the preschool group did better in school: they scored significantly higher on standardized tests, fewer of them were classified as mentally retarded, and as a group, they spent fewer years in special education. The differences between the two groups remained significant as the participants approached adulthood.

> Interviews at age 19 showed the preschool group dropped out of school less, relied on welfare less, had lower arrest and self-reported delinquency rates, and higher employment rates than the control group. Those who went to preschool also had lower illiteracy rates, were more likely to go on to college, and the women had fewer pregnancies. (Bales, 1987, p. 18)

The Transition Project

Another of the exemplary programs identified by the APA task force dealt with an ecological transition: entry to high school. Felner, Ginter, and Primavera (1982) have pointed out that young people at risk for school failure are especially vulnerable during the transition to high school. A key factor is the nature of the setting itself.

One feature of the school setting which may exacerbate students' difficulties in coping with the transition into high school is that the entire local social system is in a state of flux with all incoming students . . . attempting to adapt to the new setting at the same time. All students in the entering class are simultaneously confronted by a new physical environment and a larger and generally unfamiliar set of peers and school personnel. . . . Teachers and guidance staff are confronted with getting to know and providing information and support for large numbers of new students. Thus in addition to those tasks typically confronted by a student transferring into a new school, the students entering high school are also confronted by a less stable, less predictable environment in which the resources available to aid them in their coping efforts may be seriously taxed. (Felner et al., 1982, p. 279)

The Transition Project, under Felner's direction, was designed to increase the level of support available to vulnerable students from both peers and teachers during this important transition. Interventions included both restructuring the role of homeroom teachers and reorganizing the school environment to reduce the degree of flux students encountered and facilitate the establishment of new peer support systems. Randomly selected students participated in the project, which assigned them to homerooms and primary academic classes with other project students. Their teachers—all volunteers—were selected on the basis of the physical proximity of their classrooms. Thus, for these students, the school became a stable, cohesive, and familiar environment.

Like the Perry Preschool Project, the Transition Project had clear results. Project students, when compared with controls, were more successful in coping with the transition to high school, showing significantly better grade point averages, attendance records, and self-concepts, and expressing more positive views of the school environment.

This study demonstrates that low-cost changes in the roles of school personnel and the social ecology of the high school environment can effectively prevent academic and personal difficulties associated with school change by increasing the levels of social support available to students and decreasing the confusion and complexity of the setting being entered. . . . Overall, these findings support the arguments that attempts to understand and modify social environments . . . can be adapted fruitfully to preventive programs designed to increase people's ability to cope with the adaptive tasks of life transitions. (Felner et al., 1982, p. 288)

Exosystem Interventions: Neighborhood Organizations

The exosystem affects the developing organism indirectly, through its impact on the microsystems it encompasses. Although there are many examples of exosystems (for instance, the world of work, mass media, and informal social networks), Bronfenbrenner emphasized that of the neighborhood.

As Bronfenbrenner (1979) has noted, "the developmental potential of a setting is enhanced to the extent that there exist direct and indirect links to power settings through which participants in the original setting can influence allocation of resources and the making of decisions that are responsive to the needs of the developing person and the efforts of those who act in his [or her] behalf" (p. 256). Accordingly, the potential of the neighborhood to promote human development can be realized through the vehicle of the *neighborhood organization*. Through neighborhood organizations, people can exert influence to change their environments. These organizations serve a dual purpose, dealing with specific local issues and, at the same time, affecting the ways in which community decisions are made.

The process of organizing may be as important as the outcomes that are attained. As Alinsky (1969), the dean of American community organizers, wrote,

> If people are organized with a dream of the future ahead of them, the actual planning that takes place in organizing and the hopes and the fears for the future give them just as much inner satisfaction as does their actual achievement. The kind of participation that comes out of a people's organization in planning, getting together and fighting together completely changes what had previously been to John Smith, assembly-line American, a dull, gray, monotonous road of existence that stretched out interminably, into a brilliantly lit, highly exciting avenue of hope, drama, conflict, with, at the end of the street, the most brilliant ending known to the mind of man—the future of mankind.
>
> This, then, is our real job—the opportunity to work directly with our people. It is the breaking down of the feeling on the part of our people that they are social automatons with no stake in the future, rather than human beings in possession of all the responsibility, strength, and human dignity which constitute the heritage of free citizens of a democracy. (pp. 49–50)

The most effective community organizations win reforms that bring concrete improvements to people's lives, give participants a sense of their own potential, and alter existing power relations (Midwest Academy, 1973). Although outsiders may help with the organizing and share concrete skills, real leadership must emerge from within the group itself. Only then can the group be assured that the issues addressed will be those that are most meaningful to neighborhood residents. Only then can a genuine, ongoing power base be developed that is likely to endure.

Neighborhood organizations should be structured to allow maximum participation and to take advantage of all opportunities for positive change. This means selecting appropriate issues and targets for action and developing the strongest possible organization.

Experience seems to indicate that community organizations work most effectively when they begin by focusing on concrete issues that are amenable to change. People will rally around a practical issue that is important to their lives. Working together on an issue that is relevant and manageable lends cohesiveness to the group. And once the group experiences success—once it actually accomplishes a necessary change—the organization can attract more people to take on new projects. A success can break through people's apathy, countering the feeling of helplessness that is common among many by giving participants a sense of their own power. Many successful organizations have begun in response to one problem and then gone on to build successful coalitions dealing with many related issues.

Coalitions enable orgnaizations to combine active citizen involvement and the strength available in numbers. Individuals tend to become most actively involved in small organizations with which they have a close identification and in which they feel important. The smaller the organization, the more central to its success or failure each of its members can feel. Strength, however, is found in numbers. By banding together, small, close-knit organizations can have the advantages of both an active, involved membership and large numbers of people working together for a common cause.

For a community organization to work successfully, then, it must:

1. Allow leadership to emerge from within the group.
2. Attack specific, concrete issues and then deal with broader goals from a base of success.
3. Use coalitions to combine both active involvement and large numbers of people.

The workings of a group organized along these lines can best be illustrated through an actual example. The Woodlawn Organization, based in Chicago, demonstrates the kinds of gains possible through and in an organization that began as an effort by a few people and grew into a large, broad-based neighborhood coalition. Its history exemplifies community organization concepts in action.

The Woodlawn Organization[2]

Woodlawn is a mile-square neighborhood in the heart of Chicago, Illinois. It has the potential to be an exceptional place to live, since it is close to Lake Michigan, close to Chicago's thriving downtown areas, close to some of the world's finest museums, and adjacent to the University of Chicago.

Yet, in 1960—the year its citizens decided to organize themselves—Woodlawn's potential seemed grim. True, the University of Chicago bordered it to the north. Also true, however, was that a barbed wire fence clearly separated the university and the community.

In Woodlawn, the rates of unemployment, school dropouts, infant mortality, venereal disease, and premature births were among the highest in the city. The people of Woodlawn were paying high rents for substandard housing, high prices for low-quality food and clothing. Health care, social services, and educational facilities were all inadequate. No one in the public or private sector took responsibility for making either goods or services more accessible, and every day more local businesses disappeared. It was to wipe out hopelessness and to bring about community self-determination in its place that The Woodlawn Organization (TWO) was created.

TWO's beginnings   As the 1950s drew to a close, four of Woodlawn's religious leaders realized that, unless something was done to break the cycle, the community's descent into despair would never stop. Doctors Leber and Blakely of the First Presbyterian Church, Father Farrell of the Catholic Church, and Reverend Profrock of the Woodlawn Emanuel Lutheran Church examined the problems they saw around them and turned to their churches for help. By 1960, Leber, Blakely, and Farrell had secured funds from the Catholic Archdiocese of Chicago, the Schwarzhaupt Foundation, and the First Presbyterian Church of Chicago. Forming the Greater Woodlawn Pastors' Alliance from what had been the entirely Protestant Woodlawn Minis-

[2]The following material is adapted from *The Woodlawn Organization: Community action and mental health* by M. D. Lewis and J. A. Lewis, 1978, Chicago: Governors State University and The Woodlawn Organization. Developed under a grant from the National Institute of Mental Health (Grant No. 5T41MH–14 5662–02MHST).

ters' Alliance, they took the first major step toward community organization. They called in Saul Alinsky and his Industrial Areas Foundation (IAF), formed to provide technical assistance to communities attempting to build their own people's organizations.

The IAF's strategy for change involved the development of indigenous people's organizations, which provide the only possible means for obtaining broadly based power. In a community like Woodlawn, the only resource available to the residents is their own number. The IAF's initial organizational approach was (1) to attract people by dealing with the concrete issues about which they were really concerned, (2) to give them an avenue through which they could raise and resolve conflict, and (3) to provide an opportunity for local leadership to arise.

In January of 1961, a meeting of representatives of the Woodlawn Block Club Council, the Woodlawn Businessmen's Association, the Greater Woodlawn Pastors' Alliance, and the United Woodlawn Conference (the UWC subsequently dropped out) resulted in the creation of the Temporary Woodlawn Organization, with the IAF serving as technical advisor. It was important that the organization be deemed "temporary," since the goal of those present was to build a community-based organization that would respond to the needs and desires of a broad range of civic groups in Woodlawn. Toward this end, the Temporary Woodlawn Organization embarked on a series of activities aimed at resolving the most important issues immediately facing the community, while building a base of support capable of supporting a permanent organization.

TWO's successes   The most difficult and immediate concern of the Woodlawn community in 1960 was an expansion plan that the University of Chicago had announced the previous summer. The university intended to clear a strip of land one mile long and one block wide along the southern boundary of the campus, on which it would then build its South Campus. Having the area declared a blighted slum would mean that the university could expand cheaply, while the city would benefit by becoming eligible for federal urban renewal funds.

The residents of Woodlawn were concerned not just about that one-mile-long parcel of land but also about the long-range implications for the community of the South Campus plan. TWO wanted an overall plan for urban renewal, a plan that would involve community members as full participants, that would set out objectives with the people's interests in mind, and that would prevent the university from swallowing up the whole Woodlawn community over time. The fledgling organization rallied support within the community, opposed the plan in Washington on the basis of lack of citizen participation in planning, and embarked on a long and bitter conflict with a seemingly unbeatable adversary. TWO even hired independent city planners to draw up alternatives to the plans developed by the university and by the city.

Finally, an agreement was reached. A citizen's committee, of which a majority of the members came from TWO, would take part in all urban renewal planning in Woodlawn. The South Campus plan would take effect, but only after the broken-down nonresidential buildings on another large plot of land were cleared and low-cost, low-rise housing was erected in their place.

TWO had won recognition as the organization that could speak for Woodlawn. It had won recognition of the right of Woodlawn residents to participate in all planning affecting their lives. At the same time, this struggle brought the organization into a new and long-lived stage in its own development. TWO, with the Kate Maremont Foundation, developed the newly acquired land under the auspices of the TWO–Kate Maremont Development Association, and built, owns, and manages the 502 apartment units of Woodlawn Gardens.

Just as important to many Woodlawn residents as the university's expansion plan was the exploitation of residents by businesses within the boundaries of their community. The primary problems involved false advertising, unfair credit practices, overcharging, and, in the case of food stores, inaccurate weighing. Woodlawn residents had few shopping alternatives, and while they resented being cheated by unscrupulous business people, they felt powerless as individuals to deal with the problem. At the same time, honest business owners within the community were concerned about these grievances, too.

The Temporary Woodlawn Organization created the Square Deal campaign, beginning with a large parade along one of the main shopping streets in the area. The follow-up to this very visible beginning included setting up a checkout counter in the yard of a church. People who had just completed their grocery shopping could bring their purchases there, have them weighed accurately, have their cash register totals checked, and find out immediately whether or not they had been cheated. Stores identified as exploitive were subjected to widespread negative publicity and threats of a boycott. Individuals who had been cheated were encouraged to share this information with their neighbors.

The result of this concerted campaign was that Woodlawn merchants agreed to sign a Code of Business Ethics drawn up by a group of community leaders and representatives of the

Woodlawn Businessmen's Association. A board of arbitration, with representatives from the Businessmen's Association and consumer groups, was set up to deal with future problems. Through these tactics, the people of Woodlawn not only improved local business practices but also became increasingly aware of the new force within their community.

One of the primary motivations for organization in Woodlawn had always been the actual physical deterioration of the buildings in which the residents lived. Many of these buildings were medium-sized structures that had been subdivided again and again and allowed to fall into disrepair by absentee landlords. Neglect of the buildings often extended to refusal to take care of even emergency repair needs like broken windows, faulty plumbing, and nonexistent heating. Yet, because of a lack of alternatives, tenants were paying high rents.

When a majority of tenants within a building found their situation intolerable and formed a tenants' committee, TWO would help them negotiate with the landlord, sometimes turning to such tactics as going to the owner's suburban neighborhood to picket in front of his or her home. When all else failed, rent strikes were organized, with the tenants putting their rent checks into an escrow account until needed repairs were made. Ideally, landlords would complete repairs upon notification of the committee's demands: this happened more frequently after a few hard-fought battles had been won. The tenants' organizations helped to strengthen the young TWO, which was beginning to have a visible impact on concrete problems.

Another emotionally charged issue was the public school system. In Woodlawn, parents saw their children packed into over-crowded schools and forced to attend in double shifts, while a few miles away, white, middle-class children studied in half-empty classrooms. TWO again turned to dramatic demonstrations of community concern.

"Truth squads" visited white schools and took pictures of vacant classrooms to point up the fact that Chicago's schools were, in fact, segregated. Hundreds of community members appeared at a city-wide public hearing. At their own hearing in the Woodlawn community, parents heard reports from masked schoolteachers, afraid of reprisals if their identities were known. Each meeting of the Board of Education was attended by the "Death Watch," groups of parents wearing black capes to symbolize the fate of their children in the Chicago public schools.

All of these activities, along with a major voter registration campaign, made the Temporary Woodlawn Organization a powerful force in the community. Those with political and economic power in Chicago were becoming aware of the organization. More important, the community members themselves were becoming aware of it. It was time to create a permanent organization.

The Woodlawn Organization was set up not as an association of individual members but as an umbrella organization for member groups, including block clubs, religious institutions, business associations, and other civic action groups. Each member organization would send delegates to delegate meetings and the annual convention, with ongoing functions carried on by a steering committee and a number of standing committees. Through this organizational mechanism, TWO had in the beginning—and continues to have—the ability to speak for masses of Woodlawn residents. The organization could now turn its attention to building programs able to provide long-range solutions.

TWO and community development   In the 1970s, TWO created the Woodlawn Community Development Corporation (WCDC) to implement programs in real estate development and management, commercial development, manpower training and education, neighborhood improvement, and health. TWO/WCDC, which remains, as always, a people's organization, now creates and maintains a variety of its own human services programs. Among them are programs for children and youth, including day care and Head Start programs, youth advocacy programs, adoption and foster care programs, and child abuse prevention; employment and training programs; and counseling and residential programs for special groups, such as Woodlawn citizens with developmental disabilities. Real estate development has continued, with the organization involved in building, renovation, and management. Commercial ventures also have brought financial investments to the area.

In the decades that have passed since its creation, The Woodlawn Organization has continued to represent the people of its neighborhoods. The issues that are important to community residents have changed over the years, and the organization's priorities have kept pace. But the basic meaning and purpose of the organization remain constant. What was true in 1970 remains true today. In comparison with other poor, urban neighborhoods, "there is an important difference which distinguishes Woodlawn. . . . The Woodlawn Community has a voice" (The Woodlawn Organization, 1970, p. 28).

Shaping Policies at the Macrosystem Level

Policies at the level of the macrosystem concern the way a society as a whole solves its problems and treats its members. If community counselors need to address human concerns of this scope, it is because the health and well-being of their clients depend on it. If social injustice and a lack of personal power interfere with healthy human development, "it follows that informed social action, policy change and reform, based on concepts such as justice, empowerment, and provision of life-opportunities, rather than changing people, are keys to achieving primary prevention's ultimate goal" (Cowen, 1985, p. 32). Policy changes and reforms that can prevent problems and promote health are those aimed at eliminating *oppression*—defined by Wilson (1987) as "that state or condition within an ordered society where one segment of the society is differentially and involuntarily limited access to all the available opportunities, resources, and benefits of that particular society" (p. 19)—and replacing it with *empowerment,* which counters oppression by "enhancing the possibilities of people to control their own lives" (Wilson, 1987, p. 20).

Many theorists doubt that these ideals can be translated into concrete, practical programs. Such efforts can occur in a political context, however. We must ask, with California Assemblyman John Vasconcellos (1986),

> How do we provide environments (including human relationships) which enable persons to grow themselves into healthy human beings—persons who are:
>
> - self-aware and self-esteeming,
> - self-realizing and self-determining,
> - free and responsible, competent and caring,
> - faithful rather than cynical, open rather than closed,
> - gentle rather than violent, ecologically responsible, motivated rather than apathetic,
> - moral rather than immoral or amoral,
> - political rather than apolitical? (pp. 1–2)

In 1986, Vasconcellos introduced a legislative program entitled "Toward a Healthier State—California '86." This comprehensive agenda for change included numerous separate pieces of proposed legislation, all linked by a common concern for fostering personal power and promoting healthy development. This legislative agenda has implications beyond the time and place in which it was introduced because it demonstrates how idealism may be turned into realism, empowerment themes into accepted policies. Many of the proposals contained in this package have, in fact, been enacted in California. The proposed bills that together form the legislative agenda address the general areas of public health, social health, economic health, family health, environmental health, governmental health, political health, educational health, public safety, and human survival. The brochure describing the program includes suggestions for each of the following areas:

Public health: More than 8,000 people have died of AIDS since 1981, including some 1,700 in California. Incentive for developing an AIDS vaccine depends on funding for clinical trials, guaranteeing vaccine sales, and curtailing product liability.

Social health: Each year hundreds of millions of dollars are spent in California for crucial social service programs. It makes sense to investigate the causes of our numerous social problems. With this goal in mind, we will be promoting healthy self-esteem via a statewide commission, as poor self-esteem is related to personal and thus social dysfunctions.

Economic health: Even as local industries struggle, tax reform legislation is actively being considered that would disadvantage our domestic corporations in their competition with foreign companies. We propose that California's unitary tax be reformed to provide parity between domestic and foreign multinational corporations, protect the state general fund, and create incentive for economic development in California.

Family health: We can facilitate the development of healthy families by following the recommendations of the task force on birthing, by expanding parenting education, and by improving licensing laws for marriage and family counselors.

Environmental health: Using the Silicon Valley's burgeoning public–private partnership prototype, we can create a safer environment by developing a toxics prevention model in the Santa Clara Valley.

Governmental health: At the first annual statewide symposium for state, city, and county and education managers, public management can learn to apply the principles of excellence that have revolutionized management technique and productivity in the private sector.

Political health: With no limits on expenditure or contributions, spending in California legislative campaigns has increased 750 percent in real dollars in less than 30 years . . . To ensure that the legislature is more responsive to the public interest than to special interests, let's limit contributions and spending stringently, and provide limited public financing.

Educational health: Providing ready and equal access to higher education in California, especially in the community colleges, is of particular importance.

Public safety: The Californians Preventing Violence Pilot Project will continue to operate, and we will encourage the rehabilitation of troubled youths in California Youth Authority detention facilities.

Human survival: We will encourage peace-making by designating August 6 as "Peace Day" in California, by designing a nuclear-age education curriculum for our schools, and by developing an exchange program for students in California and the USSR.

Among the diverse issues addressed by specific bills were:

The provision of incentives for development of an AIDS vaccine

The establishment of a statewide commission on self-esteem

Reforms in the state's unitary tax

The establishment of free-standing, humane birthing clinics by addressing malpractice liability insurance problems and implementing standards for the training of lay and nurse midwives

A comprehensive survey of parent education programs, and a direction to counties to inform parents of such services

Reforms in the state licensing of marriage, family, and child counselors

The implementation of measures to protect against toxic wastes

Campaign funding reforms

The establishment of a pilot project for an individualized educational program for troubled youths

The establishment of an academic exchange and sister state program with the Soviet Union

Designation of a "Peace Day" and provision of an honorarium for Peace Prizes to California residents

The training of teachers to encourage critical thinking about the nuclear age, conflict resolution, and creating alternatives solutions to current world problems

A study of the needs of adults who were molested as children

The demand that the Department of Health Services be required to develop a feasibility plan for implementing AIDS hospice treatment services

Allowing the Department of Corrections to place inmates with AIDS in appropriate public or private care facilities, especially hospices

Some of these bills have yet to be passed, but many have become law. Among the bills passed by the California state legislature was AB 3659, which established the California Commission to Promote Self-Esteem, Social and Personal Responsibility. In his discussion of the rationale, for that bill, Vasconcellos (1986) stated,

> We need not resign ourselves to a malfunctioning society. To do so is fatalism at best, self-fulfilling prophesy at worst. If we continue merely to treat symptoms rather than search for causes, we abandon hope of solutions. Continually treating symptoms is neither cost-effective nor responsible. It's like looking for better ways to drag bodies out of the river instead of attempting to fix the bridge.

The 1986 California initiative demonstrates the possibility of implementing broad, systemic policies that can aid in the prevention of many kinds of problems. In each state and locality, comparable issues can be identified and changes that address their citizens' specific needs fostered.

Indirect Community Programs as Empowerment Strategies

Whether they operate at the level of the individual, the institution, the community, or the society at large, indirect community programs are, in fact, empowerment strategies, designed to increase the degree of control people have over their lives.

> By empowerment I mean that our aim should be to enhance the possibilities for people to control their own lives. If this is our aim, then we will necessarily find ourselves questioning both our public policy and our role relationship to dependent people. We will not be able to settle for a public policy that limits us to programs we design, operate, or package for social agencies to use on people, because it will require that the form and the metacommunications as well as the content be consistent with empowerment. We will, should we take empowerment seriously, no longer be able to see people as simply children in need or as only citizens with rights, but rather as full human beings who have both rights and needs. We will confront the paradox that even the

people most incompetent, in need, and apparently unable to function, require, just as you and I do, more rather than less control over their own lives. (Rappaport, 1986, p. 154)

The precise directions that these programs take in various locales must depend on the priorities set by the people most affected, since "locally developed solutions are more empowering than single solutions applied in a general way" (Rappaport, 1987, p. 141). Individuals, groups, and communities can all move toward empowerment with the help of interventions that create the right environmental conditions.

Community counselors, like other citizens, need to be involved in organized action affecting public policy. The potential role of the community counselor must, however, be defined. What unique contributions can the community counselor offer? Community counselors who participate in social action are entering a new arena. Many have been trained primarily in one-to-one or small-group counseling techniques; their concern for social change arises from their experiences rather than their training. They must forge a new identity as professionals concerned both with individuals and with the environment. That identity should be based on the unique attributes that community counselors can bring to tasks related to social policy.

1. Community counselors have a unique awareness of the common problems faced by community members.

In their work with individuals, counselors become aware of recurring themes, of like difficulties and the obstacles faced in common by large numbers of people. This enables counselors to identify specific aspects of the environment that may be detrimental to community members. Trying to help all of the individuals that are affected, however, can become an exercise in frustration, as new victims continually appear. Such occurs when community counselors work in neighborhoods overwhelmed by poverty. This also occurs when career counselors become aware of inequitable hiring practices, when rehabilitation counselors note the obstacles their clients face in trying to obtain equal treatment, when school counselors encounter inhumane educational practices, when agency counselors dealing with special populations try to stop the community from stigmatizing particular groups of people. It happens whenever a counselor trying to help his or her clients finds that their strength and power are overwhelmed by environmental forces that weaken or stifle growth.

When counselors become aware of specific difficulties within the environment, they can bring those problems to the surface. They can encourage action for change:

- by making the community as a whole aware of specific problems and their consequences for human beings,
- by alerting existing organizations that are already working for change and that might have an interest in the issue at hand, and
- by joining with others to support citizens fighting for change on their own behalf.

Community counselors have a special perspective that allows them to recognize the seriousness of community problems and help others in the search for new solutions.

2. Community counselors can encourage the development of new leadership and provide support to new organizations.

Because of the nature of their work, community counselors have intimate contact with the least powerful segments of the population. In the past, many have used this contact to teach these groups to adjust to the demands of the larger community. More and more, however, community counselors are trying to encourage and support the growth of active self-help organizations that instead make demands of the community.

It is not unusual for human services workers to bring together groups of community members who wish to share mutual concerns and develop new coping skills. As leadership emerges in the group, it is a short step to its becoming a self-help organization that can provide a base for a coalition for action. Thus, a natural transition from direct to indirect community services can occur. Groups of people participating in a workshop or class may evolve into groups ready to confront community problems more actively. Counselors can provide active support to such groups while allowing local leadership to emerge.

3. Community counselors can share their human-relations skills with groups trying to help themselves.

If effective community counselors share one common skill, it is in the area of interpersonal relations and communication. They can contribute significantly to a community by sharing these skills with people who are attempting to organize for change. Community counselors can act as consultants to such groups and can provide training in the skills that community members themselves see as important. Such activity might include providing leadership training, analyzing communication patterns within the group, and training members in interpersonal skills that can help them function together as an effective unit. Community counselors may also be able to help people's organizations develop expertise in research and evaluation—that is, in gathering the hard data that they need to support their claims. Ideally, counselors can also share what expertise they may have in understanding social systems and the nature of change itself.

4. Community counselors can help coordinate groups working to bring about change.

Effective community counselors have a finger on the pulse of the community. Familiar with all of the local agencies that provide direct services to individuals, they can also familiarize themselves with the groups and organizations working to bring about more fundamental changes. As links between individuals and agencies within the helping network, they can also link individuals and groups addressing specific needs.

Many agencies—particularly those serving special populations—act as clearinghouses for information and as home bases for a number of self-help groups. Community counselors can participate, along with others, in actions relevant to those who use their services. Often a number of organizations join forces to act on a specific issue. Community counselors and their agencies can, whenever appropriate, be a part of such a force for change.

Summary

Indirect, communitywide interventions play an important part in the work of the community counselor because environmental factors have a powerful impact on the well-being of community members. Because problems develop within social systems, they must be addressed through systemic interventions.

Bronfenbrenner's ecological model of human development defines four systemic levels: the microsystem, the mesosystem, the exosystem, and the macrosystem. An example of a microsystem is the school, which directly affects the development of its young participants. A Michigan-based quality-of-school-life program exemplifies intervention at this level. The mesosystem involves the relationships between settings; the Perry Preschool Project and Felner's Transition Project are examples of tested programs designed to facilitate ecological transitions. The neighborhood is an example of an exosystem, with neighborhood organizations such as The Woodlawn Organization demonstrating the process of local empowerment. Policies at the level of the macrosystem concern the way society as a whole treats its members; macrosystem interventions involve social action, policy change, and reform.

All of these interventions represent empowerment strategies designed to increase the degree of control that people have over their own lives. Community counselors have a role to play in empowerment because they have a unique awareness of the common problems faced by community members. Among the contributions they can make are increasing community awareness of problems, encouraging the development of new leaders and organizations, sharing human-relations skills with people organizing for change, and helping to coordinate groups and organizations.

Supplemental Activities

1. Read through a current local newspaper. As you read, try to be alert to issues that might affect the clients of a local community counseling program. Are there aspects of your community environment that might have a detrimental effect on individuals? Are there things going on that you feel should be changed? Assign priorities to the issues you identify, and try to come up with one thing in your community that should be changed. Consider this change in relation to the following questions:
   a. What other individuals or groups might share a concern about this issue?
   b. What individuals or groups might actively oppose this change?
   c. Can the desired change be broken down into smaller objectives that might be more easily met?
   d. What specific activities might help to bring about this change?
2. Consider again the hypothetical agency that you have been designing. What changes in policy might make the community as a whole more responsive to the needs of the population you plan to serve? Does your program deal with problems that could be prevented through changes in social policy? Try to develop this facet in more detail.

Related Reading

ALBEE, G. W. (1986). Toward a just society: Lessons from observations on the primary prevention of psychopathology. *American Psychologist, 41,* 891–898.

ALINSKY, S. D. (1969). *Reveille for radicals.* New York: Vintage.

AUBREY, R. F., & LEWIS, J. A. (1983). Social issues and the counseling profession in the 1980s and 1990s. *Counseling and Human Development, 15*(10), 1–15.

BRONFENBRENNER, U. (1979). *The ecology of human development.* Cambridge: Harvard University Press.

CONYNE, R. K. (1987). *Primary preventive counseling: Empowering people and systems.* Muncie, IN: Accelerated Development.

COX, F. M., ERLICH, J. L., ROTHMAN, J., & TROPMAN, J. E. (Eds.). (1979). *Strategies of community organization* (3rd ed.). Itasca, IL: F. E. Peacock.

EGAN, G. (1985). *Change agent skills in helping and human service settings.* Pacific Grove, CA: Brooks/Cole.

JEGER, A. M., & SLOTNICK, R. S. (Eds.). (1982). *Community mental health and behavioral-ecology: A handbook of theory, research, and practice.* New York: Plenum.

JOFFE, J. M., & ALBEE, G. W. (Eds.). (1981). *Prevention through political action and social change.* Hanover, NH: University Press of New England.

O'CONNOR, W. A., & LUBIN, B. (Eds.). (1984). *Ecological approaches to clinical community psychology.* New York: Wiley.

SEIDMAN, E., & RAPPAPORT, J. (Eds.). (1986). *Redefining social problems.* New York: Plenum.

References

ALINSKY, S. D. (1969). *Reveille for radicals.* New York: Vintage.

AUBREY, R. F. (1972). Power bases: The consultant's vehicle for change. *Elementary School Guidance and Counseling, 7,* 90–97.

AUBREY, R. F., & LEWIS, J. A. (1983). Social issues and the counseling profession in the 1980s and 1990s. *Counseling and Human Development, 15*(10), 1–15.

BALES, J. (1987, April). Prevention at its best. *APA Monitor,* pp. 18–19.

BRONFENBRENNER, U. (1976). Reality and research in the ecology of human development. *Master lectures on developmental psychology.* Washington, D.C.: American Psychological Association.

BRONFENBRENNER, U. (1979). *The ecology of human development.* Cambridge: Harvard University Press.

CONYNE, R. K. (1985). The counseling ecologist: Helping people and environments. *Counseling and Human Development, 18*(2), 1–12.

COWEN, E. L. (1985). Person-centered approaches to primary prevention in mental health: Situation-focused and competence-enhancement. *American Journal of Community Psychology, 13,* 31–48.

FELNER, R. D., GINTER, M., & PRIMAVERA, J. (1982). Primary prevention during school transitions: Social support and environmental structure. *American Journal of Community Psychology, 10,* 277–289.

ISCOE, I. (1981). Conceptual barriers to training for the primary prevention of psychopathology. In J. M. Joffe & G. W. Albee (Eds.), *Prevention through political action and social change* (pp. 110–134). Hanover, NH: University Press of New England.

MIDWEST ACADEMY. (1973). *Building the community: Modes of personal growth.* Chicago: Author.

RAPPAPORT, J. (1986). In praise of paradox: A social policy of empowerment over prevention. In E. Seidman & J. Rappaport (Eds.), *Redefining social problems* (pp. 141–164). New York: Plenum.

RAPPAPORT, J. (1987). Terms of empowerment/exemplars of prevention: Toward a theory for community psychology. *American Journal of Community Psychology, 15,* 121–148.

RAPPAPORT, J., DAVIDSON, W. S.,

WILSON, M. N., & MITCHELL, A. (1975). Alternatives to blaming the victim or the environment. *American Psychologist, 30,* 525–528.

SCHELKUN, R. F., COOPER, S., TABLEMAN, B., & GROVES, D. (1987). Quality of School Life for Elementary Schools (QSL-E): A system-wide preventive intervention for effective schools. *Community Psychologist, 20* (2), 8–9.

SCHWEINHART, L. J. (1987, Fall). When the buck stops here: What it takes to run good early childhood programs. *High Scope Resource,* pp. 8–13.

THE WOODLAWN ORGANIZATION. (1970). *Woodlawn's model cities plan: A demonstration of citizen responsibility.* Northbrook, IL: Whitehall.

VASCONCELLOS, J. (1986). *A new human agenda* (Capitol Report, 23rd Assembly District). Sacramento, CA.

WILSON, M. (1987). Classnotes on the psychology of oppression and social change. *Community Psychologist, 20*(2), 19–21.

WOLFF, T. (1987). Community psychology and empowerment: An activist's insights. *American Journal of Community Psychology, 15,* 151–166.

6

Client Advocacy

The community counselor should always emphasize not the client's weaknesses but his or her potential strengths. An individual may seem to have many needs involving the services of the community counselor; perpetual dependence is never one of them.

These guidelines appear obvious, but mental health workers have traditionally had difficulty following them. People seeking counseling services often feel a lack of power over their own lives, a sense that they are being forced to relinquish control over environmental contingencies to others. Therefore, "how we structure the services we offer to clients may have a significant impact on their perceived personal power. If services are structured in such a manner that experiences seem noncontingent to clients, we are encouraging learned helplessness and perceived external control—powerlessness" (Stensrud & Stensrud, 1981, p. 301).

Clients who need specialized services may need assistance in making the environment more responsive to their individual or group needs. Such responsiveness depends on the ability of the community to value the contributions of all its members and to develop helping networks that enhance clients' feelings of power and self-worth.

When an individual suffers some disability or impairment, whether mental or physical, he or she is labeled accordingly. Unfortunately, such labels carry with them an assumption of dependence and limited worth. Similarly, when a person's past or present behavior departs from what is considered socially acceptable, whether because of drug or alcohol abuse, delinquency, institutionalization, or merely the process of aging, the same labeling and devaluation occurs. People may also be devalued when they fail to make money or hold a job. For those labeled disabled or impaired as children, the powerlessness of childhood may compound their overall sense of worthlessness.

Almond (1974) described the process by which an individual is labeled deviant, or undesirably different. His or her behavior arouses increasing anxiety in others, until finally: "The individual becomes characterized by his problem behavior. . . . As such, he may be dealt with differently; his deviance becomes the overriding consideration and he may be arbitrarily deprived of certain rights and freedoms. Handling him becomes the special province of experts in his sort of deviance" (p. xxiii).

Whether the "expert" involved is a physician, a psychotherapist, or a jailer, individuals exiled to the province of professional care become separated from their peers and wholly or partially excluded from normal community life. The "overriding" conditions in their lives are emphasized to the point that, sometimes, those conditions *become* their lives.

Those whose labels become central to their interactions with others are, in effect, stigmatized. As Goffman (1963) pointed out in his now-classic work on the process of stigmatization:

> An individual who might have been received easily in ordinary social intercourse possesses a trait that can obtrude itself upon attention and turn those of us whom he meets away from him, breaking the claim that his other attributes have on us. He possesses a stigma, an undesired differentness from what we had anticipated. . . . By definition, of course, we believe the person with a stigma is not quite human. (p. 5)

In the long run, stigmatization can be overcome only through changes in perception, through efforts to adapt society itself to new ways of accommodating everyone's humanness. In the short run, stigmatization can be addressed by strengthening its victims.

When an individual or group has been categorized as likely to benefit from additional help—additional, that is, to that offered to the community as a whole—some kind of labeling has taken place, if only through the procedure of identification itself. The solution is not to avoid identifying such groups, however, but, instead, to work to reduce the victimization that results from labeling and increase the value individuals place on themselves. When community counselors work with socially devalued populations, they assume that it is possible to:

1. Place the stigma, label, or problem behavior in perspective as only one part of the individual's total being.
2. End the self-devaluing that often results from external limitations.
3. Bring individuals who have been excluded into the mainstream of social interaction.
4. Increase the power of the group to fight for needed social changes.
5. Increase the community's responsiveness to the needs and rights of affected individuals and groups.

Such goals cannot be reached solely through a relationship between an individual and a professional helper. Instead, community counselors should concentrate on bringing clients into contact with others through self-help groups, offering and encouraging advocacy, and enhancing the effectiveness of the helping network. The place of such efforts in the community counseling model is shown in Table 6.1 on page 176.

Empowerment through Self-Help

Dependence on professional assistance is part of the whole exclusionary process. When individuals accept the role of client, the gap between them and their community is, if anything, widened. When people have the opportunity to participate in the helping process with others, however, their ties to the community are strengthened. Helping becomes a mutual occupation in which each participant can become aware of his or her value to others. In self-help organizations, people with common bonds are able to make contact with one another, mutually support one another, request or offer active assistance, and deal with common problems in an understanding but realistic group. All decisions are made collectively by the group members, who are

Table 6.1   Client Advocacy and the Community Counseling Model

	Community services	Client services
Direct	/ /	/ /
Indirect	/ /	Self-help groups Class advocacy Fostering a responsive helping network

not categorized as service givers or service receivers. All are both helpers and "helpees."

Steele (1974), discussing the self-help phenomenon in general terms, identified several factors that seem to make such organizations effective:

1. Reference identification is to a peer group.
2. Attitudes are altered through emphasis on action and experience.
3. Communication is facilitated by peers; members do not have to overcome initial cultural, social, and educational barriers.
4. Opportunities for socialization are improved.
5. Group action, free and open discussion, and confrontation by peers help to remove individual defensiveness.
6. Because members are from the same community, they are better able to provide emotional support and understanding.
7. Status is not such a problem with peer group members as when different classes are represented.
8. In self-help groups some semblance of conditions existing in the outside world appears in the group. (p. 106)

These factors are particularly significant for people who have been excluded, for whatever reason, from the social mainstream. In the self-help setting, they can experience normal social contact, as well as communication that is unhampered by irrelevant barriers. Most important, they can have an opportunity to develop and exercise leadership skills. Although some self-help groups allow professional participation or sponsorship, their potential for success always rests on the active participation and commitment of their members.

When new members enter a self-help organization, they are encouraged to believe that the group and its members are special and that they can share in this specialness. Full membership is valued and is based on behaving according to the particular norms of the group. The same kind of behavior is expected from every member of the group; through that behavior, an initiate becomes a full-fledged group member, a caregiver rather than solely a care receiver.

The fact that each member of a self-help group becomes a caregiver is the key to the efficacy of this approach.

> Self-help converts . . . problems or needs into resources. Instead of seeing 32 million people with arthritis as a problem, it is possible to see these people as resources, service givers, for dealing with the everyday concerns of the arthritic. . . . At the same time, people will acquire a new sense of independence and empowerment as a consequence of dealing effectively with their own problems. (Gartner, 1982, p. 64)

The "Helper Therapy" Principle

One of the reasons self-help succeeds corresponds to the "helper therapy" principle: although receiving help is beneficial, giving help is even more so. Skovholt (1974) summarized the benefits of giving help as follows:

> (1) The effective helper often feels an increased level of interpersonal competence as a result of making an impact on another's life, (2) The effective helper often feels a sense of equality in giving and taking between himself or herself and others, (3) The effective helper is often the recipient of valuable personalized learning acquired while working with a helpee, and (4) The effective helper often receives social approval from the people he or she helps. (p. 62)

Gartner and Riessman (1984) have pointed out three additional mechanisms that account for the beneficial results of helping: "(1) the helper is less dependent; (2) in struggling with the problem of another person who has a like problem, the helper has a chance to observe his or her problem at a distance; and (3) the helper obtains a feeling of social usefulness by playing the helping role" (p. 20).

A good example of the helper therapy principle in action is Recovery, Incorporated, an organization for self-described "nervous and former mental patients." The organization's initial impetus in 1937 came from a professional, Dr. Abraham Low. Now, however, the group's leaders are all lay people who came to the group as patients. (Patients are defined as people recently discharged from inpatient settings or others who identify themselves as under psychiatric care or as having symptoms such as anxiety or depression.) At weekly meetings, group discussion is combined with structured panel presentations during which members contrast old and new ways of dealing with problems.

Recovery members emphasize the degree to which they have been helped by practicing the steps outlined by Dr. Low. They are probably also helped, however, by the new awareness that they are not alone in their problems, by the exposure to successful models that are like themselves, and by the realization that they, too, can assist others while helping themselves.

In addition to their regular meetings, experienced members also present programs to educational or community groups. This service increases public knowledge and awareness about mental health and points up another strength of self-help groups: they give people a collective voice that they would not have as individuals.

Ideology

Self-help organizations usually expect their members to adhere to some mutual belief system regarding the problems or issues on which the group is focused. As Gartner and Riessman (1984) have pointed out, the ideological character of self-help groups brings an involvement beyond the self that gives members a sense of commitment and gives the organization its "force and conviction" (p. 22). The ideology of self-help organizations tends to conform to what Borkman (1984) has termed an "experimental-knowledge" framework.

> Experiential knowledge is specialized information on a problem based on a first-hand experience of it. . . . Experiential knowledge is developed within self-help groups through a process of individuals reflecting upon and trusting as valid their experiences in a context of other people with similar experiences. (p. 207)

The specific content of an organization's ideology may be less important than the fact of its existence as a unifying force and as an explanation for members' successes. In general, however, the longest-lived of the self-help organizations tend to have coherent philosophies that are readily understood by new members and capable of inspiring lifelong adherence, whether or not they are scientifically valid. Among self-help organizations, none has been more successful than Alcoholics Anonymous (AA) in affecting the belief systems of its adherents.

The ideology of Alcoholics Anonymous has its basis in Twelve Steps that guide each member's recovery and Twelve Traditions that give direction to the fellowship. The Twelve Steps fit Borkman's experiential knowledge framework in that they were based on the experiences of AA's earliest members. The Twelve Steps are:

1. We admitted we were powerless over alcohol—that our lives had become unmanageable.
2. Came to believe that a Power greater than ourselves could restore us to sanity.
3. Made a decision to turn our will and our lives over to the care of God as we understood Him.
4. Made a searching and fearless inventory of ourselves.
5. Admitted to God, to ourselves, and to another human being the exact nature of our wrongs.
6. Were entirely ready to have God remove all these defects of character.
7. Humbly asked Him to remove our shortcomings.
8. Made a list of all persons we had harmed, and became willing to make amends to them all.
9. Made direct amends to such people wherever possible, except when to do so would injure them or others.
10. Continued to take personal inventory and when we were wrong promptly admitted it.
11. Sought through prayer and meditation to improve our conscious contact with God as we understood Him, praying only for knowledge of His will for us and the power to carry that out.
12. Having had a spiritual awakening as a result of these steps, we tried to carry this message to alcoholics and to practice these principles in all our affairs. (Alcoholics Anonymous, 1953)

The steps listed above are designed to guide individuals toward long-term recovery. Created by Alcoholics Anonymous, these 12 steps have been adapted for the needs of other populations. Current "12-step groups" include, among others, Al-Anon, Alateen, Narcotics Anonymous, Families Anonymous, and Overeaters Anonymous.

The Twelve Traditions, designed to give unity and coherence to AA as an organization, consist of the following:

1. Our common welfare should come first; personal recovery depends on AA unity.
2. For our group purpose there is but one ultimate authority—a loving God as He may express Himself in our group conscience. Our leaders are but trusted servants—they do not govern.
3. The only requirement for AA membership is a desire to stop drinking.

4. Each group should be autonomous, except in matters affecting other groups or AA as a whole.
5. Each group has but one primary purpose—to carry its message to the alcoholic who still suffers.
6. An AA group ought never to endorse, finance or lend the AA name to any related facility or outside enterprise lest problems of money, property, and prestige divert us from our primary purpose.
7. Every AA group ought to be fully self-supporting, declining outside contributions.
8. Alcoholics Anonymous should remain forever non-professional, but our service centers may employ special workers.
9. AA, as such, ought never to be organized; but we may create service boards or committees directly responsible to those they serve.
10. Alcoholics Anonymous has no opinion on outside issues; hence the AA name ought never to be drawn into public controversy.
11. Our public relations policy is based on attraction rather than promotion; we need always maintain personal anonymity at the level of press, radio and films.
12. Anonymity is the spiritual foundation of all our traditions, ever reminding us to place principles above personalities. (Alcoholics Anonymous, 1953)

The Twelve Traditions have helped Alcoholics Anonymous maintain its integrity as a self-help organization. Over the decades, AA has avoided such pitfalls as dependence on outside funding, co-optation by other institutions, and deference to individual personalities. Instead, the fellowship has successfully combined autonomy for its separate groups and commonality of purpose for the organization as a whole.

Mutual Support

As Borkman (1984) has pointed out, members of self-help groups, because of gaps in their natural support networks, frequently need the social support provided by such organizations. Family members, friends, and others in group members' personal networks may be unsupportive in regard to the individual's focal problem: they may stigmatize the individual, lack understanding of the problem, relate poorly to the person, or react only to the negative consequences of the individual's problems. Sometimes this unsupportiveness can be subtle and indirect. What Borkman termed "stigmatizing reactions," for instance, includes behaviors such as ignoring, denying, or minimizing the problem; manipulating situations to protect the troubled individual and thereby avoid stigmatization; stereotyping the individual; or reacting to interactions with unease, embarrassment, or discomfort.

Individuals dealing with special problems may benefit from developing mutually supportive relationships with other people whom they can expect to understand. Self-help groups provide an opportunity for emotional and social support that might be difficult to find in everyday interactions. This need seems especially important for individuals with health-related problems; participation in mutual self-help groups helps them realize that they are not alone in their fears and struggles and, at the same time, instills hope by introducing them to people who have overcome their problems. From among the many national health-related self-help groups, Stanford and Perdue (1983) have listed the following:

> Alcoholics Anonymous
> AMEND (Aid to Mothers Experiencing Neonatal Death)
> American Schizophrenic Association
> Association for Children with Learning Disabilities
> Candlelighters (for parents of young children with cancer)
> The Compassionate Friends (for bereaved parents)
> Daughters United (for young women who have been victims
>   of incest)
> DES-Watch (for women who took DES during pregnancy
>   and their daughters)
> Emotions Anonymous (a 12-step program for people with
>   emotional problems)
> Epilepsy Foundation
> Families Anonymous
> Gamblers Anonymous
> Gay Men's Health Crisis (for gay men concerned about
>   AIDS)
> Gray Panthers
> Heart to Heart (a one-to-one visitation program for people
>   with coronary problems)
> Juvenile Diabetes Foundation
> La Leche League
> Make Today Count (for persons with cancer and their
>   families)
> Muscular Dystrophy Association
> Narcotics Anonymous
> National Alliance for the Mentally Ill
> National Association for Retarded Citizens

National Federation of the Blind
National Foundation for Sudden Infant Death
National Gay Task Force
National Society for Autistic Children
Neurotics Anonymous
Overeaters Anonymous
Parents Anonymous
Parents of Stillborns
Parents Without Partners
Parents of Premature and High Risk Infants
Reach to Recovery (for women who have had mastectomies)
Recovery, Inc.
Resolve, Inc. (for individuals who are infertile)
Sisterhood of Black Single Mothers
Share (for parents who have lost an infant)
Smokenders
Theos Foundation (for the widowed and their families)
United Cerebral Palsy
Widowed Persons

In these and other organizations designed to foster mutual help and support, people can experience a sense of empowerment. The length of this list indicates the pervasiveness of the self-help phenomenon. Ironically, because of the important service they provide, mutual help groups have entered the social mainstream.

> When people help themselves . . . they feel empowered; they are able to control some aspect of their lives. . . . Empowerment expands energy, motivation, and help-giving power that goes beyond helping one's self or receiving help. In addition, this self-help-induced empowerment may have significant political relevance because, as people are enabled to deal with some aspects of their lives in a competent fashion, the skills and positive feelings they acquire may contagiously spread and empower them to deal with other aspects of their lives. (Riessman, 1985, pp. 2–3)

Self-Help and Political Action: Disability Rights

Riessman (1985) noted that self-help groups have traditionally been nonpolitical, focusing on strengthening individuals rather than on ameliorating adverse social conditions. Some organizations, however, have become more politically oriented, recognizing that the power and competencies they have developed can be applied to larger issues.

> An advocacy focus may appear as the self-helpers discover the external causes of their problems. In some cases this takes the

form of criticism regarding the provision of services, in other cases it is concerned with the media and the images presented of the particular self-help problem or condition. Underlying all of this is the basic self-help ethos that emphasizes the indigenous strengths of the people involved in contrast to a dependence on external, elite experts. (Riessman, 1985, pp. 3–4)

The Center for Independent Living (CIL), an organization operated by and for disabled people since 1972, exemplifies this self-help ethos. Based on the notion that "disabled people know what is best for disabled people," CIL began in Berkeley, California, as a support service for blind and physically disabled people and as a movement advocating the rights of the disabled. The CIL brochure describes the accomplishments of this groundbreaking organization:

> CIL is a non-profit organization operated by and for disabled people. It was founded in 1972 in Berkeley by a small group of disabled people who wished to live independent lives away from isolating and costly institutions or dependency upon family. Funding first came from [the University of California at] Berkeley and private foundations, soon to be followed by government grants for pilot and model programs never before offered. CIL quickly grew to become the nation's leading advocate for people with all types of disabilities. A pioneer in the disability movement, CIL offered hope and opportunity for many disabled people whose lives had been locked behind institutional doors or similar dependent situations. Disabled people came from all over the country to form an umbrella organization which led to major changes for disabled people. By the late '70s, barriers were broken in all areas as curb cuts opened accessibility; ramps replaced stairs; doors widened as did opportunities in the classroom, workplace, transportation and housing.
>
> For thousands of disabled people and their families these changes opened a world of choices, making a difference between unnecessary confinement, which meant a tax burden as well as isolation, and full participation in our society as tax paying and productive members. Thanks to the efforts of CIL and our many friends, disabled people take their rightful places alongside students, employees in all kinds of corporations and businesses, commuters on the bus and BART (Bay Area Rapid Transit), and in all kinds of social and receational activities as self-sufficient people demonstrating their abilities. Because CIL's staff members are primarily disabled people, they provide a positive role model for other disabled people seeking to live independently. Because of CIL over 200 similar organizations have sprung up throughout the world. (Center for Independent Living, undated, p. 1)

The Center for Independent Living offers a number of programs designed to help its clients live independently in the community. Although what specific services are offered at any one time depends on funding, CIL's basic programs include the following:

- *Attendant Referral:* Interviewing and referral of prospective attendants to disabled and elderly clients who need special housekeeping and personal care in order to live independently
- *Benefits Counseling:* Counseling, education, and representation to ensure that disabled individuals receive financial and medical benefits to which they are entitled
- *Blind Services:* Instruction in mobility and orientation; reader referrals; talking book certification; counseling, information, and referral services for the visually impaired; special outreach to elderly visually impaired people
- *Deaf Services:* Peer Counseling, referral, and special services to give deaf and hearing-impaired individuals access to all CIL services
- *Housing Department:* Help for disabled and elderly clients in locating and securing accessible and affordable housing; consultation on issues such as building ramps and moving
- *Independent Living Skills Classes:* Instruction by peer counselors on practical issues such as home modifications, cooking, budgeting, homemaking, nutrition, personal care, vocational planning, and socialization
- *Job Development:* Assistance in job seeking; disability awareness workshops with employers and affirmative-action officers
- *Mental Disabilities Independent Living Program:* Peer counseling and Independent Living Skills training for mentally disabled individuals
- *Peer Counseling:* Support for individuals, groups, couples, and families in coping with issues such as interrelationships and social situations
- *Youth Services:* Program to help young disabled people and their families make the transition from dependence to independent living at the earliest possible age; includes on-site programs at schools
- *Wheelchair Repair:* Servicing and modification of wheelchairs, sale of wheelchair accessories, advice on purchasing orthopedic equipment

Direct services are an important component of CIL's work, but they are offered within a context of advocacy. Staff members recognize that independent living depends not just on the disabled individual's skills and attitudes but on the degree to which the environment allows integration into the community. Thus, they take pride in the changes that have taken place in their home city of Berkeley and in the United States as a whole since CIL's formation in 1972. As CIL's executive director wrote at the outset of the center's 15th year,

> Fifteen years ago in Berkeley/USA, severely disabled individuals were living in nursing homes and institutions.
>
> Fifteen years ago a group of disabled people had an idea, a dream, a vision that they and other people in similar situations should and could live in the community.
>
> Fifteen years ago disabled people had to protest in the streets of Berkeley in order for the city to provide curb cuts.
>
> Fifteen years ago parents of disabled children had to fight for the right of disabled children to be educated alongside non-disabled children in public schools.
>
> Ten years ago over 100 disabled persons sat in the federal building for over 100 days until their civil rights bill, Section 504, was signed into law by Jimmy Carter.
>
> Just within 10 years disabled people had to wage a fight to have bus lifts and make BART accessible.
>
> As a result of CIL and the independent living movement . . . the ruling philosophy is that disabled people should live in the community and not in institutions. (Winter, 1986, p. 1)

Self-Help and Volunteerism

Volunteers can provide a valuable link between client populations and the community at large. At one time, the use of non-salaried volunteers to provide services seemed necessary because of the limited number of professionals available to deal with problems. It is becoming more apparent, however, that volunteers also offer much that is unique to them. Frequently, they offer a depth of personal involvement, a freshness of approach, and a link to the community that salaried personnel cannot duplicate.

Volunteerism is growing far beyond "helping others who are less fortunate." Under this traditional definition, the distance between the helper and the person being helped might be as great as that between the person and a professional mental health worker. Both the concept of volunteerism and our notion of who constitutes a potential volunteer are expanding, however. As Wilson (1976) has pointed out, "Instead of being the privilege of the already privileged, volunteering must become the right of everyone: minorities, youth, seniors, the handicapped, blue-collar workers, business people, the disadvantaged'' (p. 118). The trend is ''away from the concept of 'doing for' toward the concepts of 'doing with' and 'helping to help themselves' '' (Cull & Hardy, 1974, p. 112).

This orientation is particularly important when volunteers work with socially devalued populations. Such populations can, indeed, help themselves. Volunteers are needed because of their ability to link the individual or group being helped and the community as a whole. They can:

1. Facilitate two-way communication between the excluded population and the community at large.
2. Assist in shedding light on the particular concerns of the group being served.
3. Mobilize community support for needed programs and changes.

The best efforts allow volunteers and those they are serving to work together, grow together, and learn together. The best programs do not replace self-help but complement it.

As early as 1972, Wolfensberger described a three-day course during which developmentally disabled adults and volunteers took a trip together.

> The nonretarded often arrive with the thought that they are to be the teachers, and the retarded will be their pupils. However, soon after arrival, all participants discover that they are taking part in a course common for all. As tourists, they are going to learn and be enriched through new experiences and meeting new people. All are given the same amount of money for budgeting their weekend needs and activities, such as meals, shopping, sightseeing, and entertainment. When they are exploring the city in small mixed groups of three or four persons (which are changed at intervals), they gradually learn not only about the life and assets of this new city, but they also learn from being together. They find out about public transit, price levels of various restaurants, the amusement possibilities for their Saturday night, and the interesting sightseeing places for the Sunday morning walk.
>
> Through these experiences, occasional lectures, and comparative reports and discussions, the nonretarded gradually learn more and more about the proper ways of being together with the mentally retarded, as well as vice versa; and when they later listen to the report from the retarded, and to their reactions to the attitudes of the nonretarded they have met, the nonretarded (volunteers) commonly experience that they were the pupils and the retarded the teachers. (p. 182)

Volunteers in programs such as the one described above certainly help the people with whom they work. At the same time, however, the volunteers also gain new knowledge and new perceptions that they take back to their communities. While strengthening the stigmatized group, volunteers' efforts thus also help counter the very process of stigmatization.

A similar process takes place when volunteers work in corrections. Some of the most common activities through which volunteers help offenders include developing personal relationships with juvenile offenders, probationed offenders, or prison inmates; locating job possibilities for ex-offenders; providing tutoring, vocational training, or other educational opportunities to prison inmates; helping to create recreational programs or other services within prisons; and working with the families of inmates.

But more important than the specific services they offer is the volunteers' recognition that correctional facilities are a community responsibility and that offenders are a part of the community. Volunteers create links through their presence and through their recognition of the humanness of the offender and his or her family. As this attitude spreads, the corrections process can be removed from its customary isolation, and the community at large can address problems traditionally consigned to so-called experts.

No expert can solve the problems of the stigmatized. Too many of these problems lie in the attitudes of the community itself; seeking solutions is therefore up to the community. Many citizens are beginning to recognize this responsibility and to seek their own roles in fulfilling it.

Contemporary efforts to develop effective volunteer programs thus break from traditional forms. The volunteer can no longer be viewed as someone with excessive leisure time, someone who can fit in to perform whatever task has been left or overlooked. What the volunteer has to give is as valuable as what the professional can offer, and this "new volunteer" has the right to expect new attitudes and opportunities.

Volunteers should be encouraged to examine their own needs and to develop work styles and assignments that meet those needs. They should receive immediate training during an orientation period and then in-service education that responds to questions they themselves raise. They should have the opportunity to use their work as part of their own career development, whether receiving academic credit or being considered for paid human services positions. Most important, volunteers should be allowed to use their own creativity in developing roles and programs that meet needs they have observed in the community.

Volunteerism, along with self-help, "may be the treatment of choice for many individuals whose need to become involved with other community members is greater than their need to become clients. When community members help themselves and one another, resources increase geometrically" (Lewis & Lewis, 1983, p. 101).

Fostering a Responsive Helping Network

Self-help groups and volunteers form part of the total network of caregivers in any community. Clients sometimes need additional help, however, from human services agencies or institutions.

In most communities, a number of agencies and institutions offer services to enhance the well-being of individuals. Examples include:

- Mental health facilities that attempt to treat or prevent psychological problems
- Educational and religious institutions
- Specialized agencies dealing with specific problem areas, such as substance abuse, legal or medical problems, family conflicts, disabilities, poverty, or homelessness
- Agencies providing services to specific populations, such as women, gay men and lesbians, children, adolescents, or the elderly
- Crisis or suicide prevention centers providing immediate intervention in personal crises
- Employment or rehabilitation centers that help individuals gain the skills and opportunities they need to achieve independence and economic security
- Employee assistance programs providing services at the work site

These entities may be government supported, charitable, or self-help; large or small; formal or informal. They have in common the goal of providing helping services to their clients. Others may also share this goal, particularly individuals whose occupational roles give them a special opportunity to work with people. Teachers, police officers, welfare workers, and employers, for example, can act as important helping resources if they are sensitive to the human needs of the individuals they affect.

All of these individuals and agencies, in combination with self-help groups, constitute a *helping network* that makes up part of the social environment. But the helping network is helpful only if it is responsive to the needs of the people it seeks to serve. And it can be termed a network only if all of its parts are interconnected. A responsive helping network can be fostered through a number of mechanisms, including (1) class advocacy, (2) community-based planning, and (3) consultation.

Class Advocacy

Self-help efforts expand people's ability to control their own lives, but, as we have already seen, true empowerment often depends on changes beyond the individual or the group. Making the social, political, and economic environment conducive to the development of people with special needs requires active advocacy efforts. The term *advocacy* refers to the act of speaking up for people whose rights might be in jeopardy; *class advocacy* involves protecting the rights of an entire category of people.

When community counselors see the rights of less powerful individuals or groups infringed upon, they take action. Ideally, counselors act to empower and strengthen oppressed individuals or groups to the point where they can protect themselves. In the interim, however, community counselors may need to act as advocates, defending those who need defense and working to limit the power of those who abuse it.

Advocates are needed not just to fight against dehumanization but to fight for humanization. People have more than the right not to be mistreated. They also have the right to develop their own creativity and their own values, to have access to whatever benefits our culture may have to offer, and to increase the numbers and kinds of choices they may make in their lives. When community counselors see individuals being confined and restricted, they seek to alter the situation, whether by trying to change a policy or attempting to make those in authority accountable. They struggle not just to eliminate constraints but to create opportunities.

Thus, when community counselors in school settings learn of children being unfairly punished, they confront the school authorities. They also confront those authorities when children are denied the opportunity to learn in nurturing, exciting classroom environments.

When community counselors see their clients being treated without dignity by agency personnel, they confront those personnel. They also fight for their clients' rights to have access to services.

When community counselors see individuals denied their right to privacy in residential settings, they act to safeguard that right. At the same time, they seek recognition of clients' rights to a comfortable and stimulating environment.

Ideally, advocacy is prompted not by an immediate crisis but by a sensitivity to potential problems. In what may be called *preventive advocacy,* the community counselor recognizes a situation that might deprive individuals of their rights or of opportunities and acts to change the environment before individual clients are damaged. This arises most frequently when a population has been identified as having special needs that the environment could meet or as needing support in protecting their freedom. Acting on behalf of the group as a whole can prevent much damage to individuals.

Fortunately, community counselors do not need to bear the burden of advocacy alone. The development of *citizen advocacy* has meant that large numbers of people are available to work on behalf of others. Wolfensberger and Zauha (1973) have defined a citizen advocate as "a mature, competent citizen volunteer representing, as if they were his [or her] own, the interests of another citizen who is impaired in his [or her] instrumental competency (meaning the ability to solve practical problems of everyday living), or who has major expressive needs which are unmet and which are likely to remain unmet without special intervention (p. 11). As citizen advocacy has evolved, volunteer advocates have been utilized both in working with individuals and in broad-based class advocacy efforts.

Riessman (1985) has pointed out that the evolution of self-help movements from prepolitical to advocative often progresses through three stages. First, a sense of empowerment begins to emerge in the group. Second, the group turns to advocacy out of its understanding that external factors need to be addressed. Finally, groups and organizations begin to see the interconnections among issues and start forming coalitions. Class advocacy can be carried out most effectively if a variety of self-help and citizens' organizations work together in coalitions to address their mutual needs.

Coalition building   An example of coalition building can be found in the state of Washington, where organizations concerned with developmental disabilities have broadened their focus to speak up on behalf of all citizens with disabilities. In early 1983, representatives of several groups concerned with issues related to disability met together to explore the possibility of increasing their strength through unified action. As a result of this meeting, three separate organizations were formed.

The Washington Assembly for Citizens with Disabilities would act as a lobbying and political body. The Disabilities Political Action Committee would handle financial contributions to political campaigns and work on behalf of selected candidates for election. The Developmental Disabilities Research and Information Coalition would conduct research and disseminate information on issues affecting people with disabilities. These three organizations have continued to grow steadily, complementing one another's efforts on behalf of Washington's citizens with disabilities.

The Washington Assembly for Citizens with Disabilities (WACD) affects the political process by rating candidates and endorsing issues. The assembly also organizes community political activity for and against legislative issues regarding habilitation rights, services, and related issues.

The goals of WACD include the following:

1. Increase community support for developmental services.
2. Increase citizen participation in the political process to obtain and maintain developmental and support services.
3. Build a broad-based coalition to support adequate human services systems.
4. Improve the quality and quantity of services to citizens with disabilities by working for the continued development of a comprehensive service system that promotes: (a) the protection of individual interests in the areas of health and human and legal rights, (b) the presence of citizens with disabilities in the community, (c) community participation, (d) competency building, and (e) status enhancement.

WACD accomplishes these goals through activities such as voter registration and education, coalition building, the rating of legislators, candidate questionnaires, community organization, issue endorsements, operation of a hot line, lobbying, and statewide networking. The assembly comprises representatives from statewide groups dealing with every type of disability or handicap.

A key organizational mechanism of the assembly is the core group. A *core group* is a group of citizens responsible for organizing and maintaining a communications network for a specific region, which is used to share information and unite citizens for action in response to specific needs. Each core group endeavors to bring together parents, consumers, service providers, professionals, and local advocacy groups. These core groups provide a structure through which the power of individual communities can be fostered and tapped, as well as providing input to the assembly on important local issues. At the same time, the groups enable the assembly and other statewide organizations to mobilize local citizens for lobbying efforts.

The second component of the advocacy effort in Washington is the Disabilities Political Action Committee (D-PAC), which is focused specifically on the electoral process. D-PAC raises money for contributions to candidates, using these contributions to help elect legislators it endorses, those who support adequate funding and services for special education and human services. The organization also uses contributions and its endorsement to support the passage of ballot issues affecting habilitation rights and services.

The purpose of the Developmental Disabilities Research and Information Coalition is to provide information to the community, the legislature, administrative agencies, and others concerned with issues related to developmental disabilities. The coalition does not engage in political activity except to provide information. Its function is to provide a nonpartisan forum for generating and exchanging information on budgetary and other issues affecting special education and human services for people with disabilities. The coalition does this through research, analysis, dissemination of information to the legislature and citizenry, and publication of a newsletter.

Each of the statewide organizations representing people with disabilities in Washington thus plays a unique role in encouraging self-help and volunteerism, building an effective helping network, and safeguarding the rights of citizens with special needs. A small sampling of the legislation passed in Washington in the 1980s illustrates their combined impact (Washington Assembly for Citizens with Disabilities, 1987):

- A mandate that preschool programs must be made available for children with disabilities
- An expansion in learning assistance programs for students from kindergarten through ninth grade
- Maintenance of a special education office within the Office of the Superintendent of Public Instruction
- Increases in programs of family support and home aid
- Reinstatement of dental services for persons with disabilities
- A self-medication bill allowing people with minimal cognitive or physical skills who take medication to live in the community
- Funding for community residential placements

- Employment programs for previously unserved adults with developmental disabilities
- Habilitation rights legislation declaring that all persons have a right to habilitative services
- An amendment of state law making verbal or physical harassment of persons with physical, mental, or sensory disabilities a criminal offense
- Measures to ensure that persons who are deaf or hard of hearing will have certified interpreters when involved with the criminal justice system
- Provision of adaptive telecommunications devices at public expense
- Protection of client privacy when records are used for research purposes
- Establishment of the right of clients and their families to design and have funded less restrictive, alternative programs for themselves.

Legislation of the type supported by the Washington coalition is noteworthy for its sensitivity to human needs. At all governmental levels, policies that affect the helping network need to be responsive, well coordinated, and carefully planned.

Community-Based Planning

The effectiveness of the helping network in any community depends on the care with which it has been planned. Responsive and well-organized helping networks share several distinctive characteristics:

1. Both those who deliver and those who use services are active in planning and evaluating programs.

In traditional approaches to helping, an agency or institution plans what services are to be offered and then hires workers to perform specified roles in service delivery. Responsive helping networks are more likely to use community-based planning, with the creation and evaluation of new services an ongoing process as agency workers at all levels attempt to recognize community needs and to create or adapt programs to meet those needs. Community-based planning is thus a fluid process, with no clear beginning and no end. Often, when workers or community members recognize the need for a particular kind of program, they create spin-off agencies, using existing skills and resources in new programs or new locations.

Ongoing assessment of services by those who actually use an agency's services works most effectively when agencies are small. But small, localized agencies lack the power and the resources to influence communitywide planning. For this reason, other mechanisms are needed.

2. Agencies work together in cooperative helping networks.

In small agencies, workers and community members can feel a sense of ownership, a sense that the agency belongs to them. Small agencies also provide ample opportunities for workers and community members alike to participate in planning the agency's programs.

Yet, every community needs some kind of centralized planning. Resources are limited, and they must be allocated according to the community's priorities. But small, localized agencies can participate in planning that affects their own futures only if they join together in cooperative networks. Without cooperative networks, agencies find themselves simply competing against one another for limited funds. United, however, they can see gaps in the community's services, plan joint programs when appropriate, and share valuable resources. Most important, agencies working together have the power to influence the decision making of governmental bodies and established social planning agencies. Only then can the people who actually deliver services be a part of the communitywide planning process. In this way, too, planning, delivering, and utilizing services can be part of the same process, with community members involved in all phases.

3. The network has a coordinating organization that facilitates ongoing planning and includes workers and community members in the process.

If members of the helping network are to be adequately represented in the planning process, they must be able to rely on some ongoing, stable structure, an organization or group of people assigned to keep track of community needs and changes in the available resources. The advantages of such a body include the following: (a) network members can maintain ongoing relationships with other segments of the community, (b) planning can be continuous and developmental instead of being reactive and limited, and (c) support can be mobilized immediately whenever needed. An ongoing group is better able to recognize problems when they arise and see the positive potential in legislative changes. As long as it maintains effective communication, a coordinating group can call on all member agencies when necessary and keep them informed of changes in the community.

4. The network has a mechanism through which it can react to specific issues.

In addition to making long-range plans, the network should be prepared to take advantage of opportunities when they arise and deal intensively with specific issues. One way network members can prepare is by forming alliances or coalitions with other community groups. With this mechanism in place, groups can act en masse when a relevant issue or opportunity arises. Such action happens most efficiently when the groups or agencies communicate regularly. If a situation requires joint planning, separate organizations can be forged quickly into effective work units.

Another mechanism that can facilitate the network's response to specific issues is the creation of a task force or research group focusing on a particular topic. Small groups like task forces can study a community's needs and resources in relation to particular areas intensively. They can gain in-depth knowledge, create concrete plans, and share the results of their studies with other network members. This planning strategy is particularly efficient because it combines the strength of large numbers (the network) with the specialization possible in small groups (the task forces).

5. Conventional planning agencies are open to broad participation.

It is not enough that the work of community members and agency workers parallel the efforts of agencies traditionally involved in central planning. There must also be constant exchanges between expert planners and field workers, between social scientists and community members. Such exchange is most effective when the planning agencies themselves are open to participation by individuals representing a variety of community groups. Community input should be encouraged, not just in regard to direct service agencies but also in regard to agencies in the private and public sector that have the power to allocate funds. It is, after all, through financial decisions that a community implements its real priorities.

6. Governmental agencies, social planning agencies, direct service agencies, and community groups maintain an ongoing dialogue.

Planning is most effective when the participating individuals, groups, and agencies are interdependent and maintain a continuing exchange of ideas. At times, their dialogue may be confrontational instead of collaborative; it is hoped that in the long run, however, planners will find that they are able to resolve their philosophical differences in the interest of delivering efficient, relevant services.

When diverse agencies and institutions are able to work together, the resulting plan is more likely to be efficient. Through open dialogue, community needs can be analyzed and resources allocated realistically. Consequently, competition for scarce resources is lessened, since the most is made of each available dollar, property, and worker. Instead of duplicating services, agencies can develop programs that complement one another. Most important, the rights of consumers are given priority.

7. The rights of consumers, as well as the uniqueness of each agency, are protected at all stages of the planning process.

Community-based planning allows the planners to remain sensitive to the needs of individuals and to the will of the community. Planners working in isolation can inadvertently overlook the rights of individuals. When planning is done by a broad coalition, however, all segments of the community are more likely to be represented in decisions. Agencies are also more likely to retain the flexibility and informality they need to maintain their roots in the community. Thus, as the community changes, its helping network can change with it.

A community can move rapidly toward community-based planning with the participation of a broad coalition, as the experiences of the Community Congress of San Diego illustrate. The Community Congress had its origins in the alternative agencies that arose in the 1960s to work with alienated young people and the drug subculture. These street agencies used largely voluntary staffs to provide services such as drug counseling, crisis hot lines, draft counseling, and shelters for runaways. The agencies attempted to offer alternatives to traditional bureaucratic agencies, developing structures that emphasized participatory decision making and a sense of community. The agencies were clearly successful in reaching their young clients, many of whom became program volunteers.

Needing additional funding to expand their services, individual agencies found it difficult to gain access to resources. In 1969, six agencies organized the Drug Coalition to increase their chances of gaining recognition and funding. The Drug Coalition succeeded quickly in getting the attention of the city and county, leading to the creation of the Mayor'ss Council on Youth Opportunities and a county-administered drug education and hot-line program.

When the Drug Coalition expanded its focus and adopted the name Community Congress, its first venture was to get the United Way to recognize and fund more nontraditional agencies. The Congress gradually succeeded; by 1974, a number of Community Congress representatives had been appointed to United Way committees and open membership was adopted.

The Congress continued to grow, focusing much effort on increasing the total funding available for human services, reducing the competition among agencies for scarce resources, and opening city and county budget processes to broad public input. The Community Congress has stood the test of time, acting as a bulwark in the protection of urgently needed human services despite severe attacks on their funding base. The early 1980s, for instance, brought a funding crisis, with administrators trying to slash the county's human services budget in half. This crisis simply mirrored a nationwide trend toward reduced funding and toward criticism of mandated services. Yet the community-based agencies of San Diego had a history of cooperation that helped them avoid the competitiveness that led to the downfall of service delivery systems in other locales. Their strategy, as described by Takvorian and Haney (1981), involved:

1. Educating and informing the Board of Supervisors and county bureaucrats of the cost-effectiveness and high quality of services provided by community-based agencies.
2. Obtaining information relevant to the budget process.
3. Rapidly disseminating this information to the network.
4. Developing position papers.
5. Consistently dispersing information to the media.
6. Organizing regular and frequent meetings of service providers throughout the network and in each district.
7. Mobilizing mass attendance at key Board of Supervisors' meetings (p. 12)

Although the human services agencies could not maintain their funding at previous levels, they received considerably more than had originally been allocated them for the fiscal year 1981–82, and the viability of the network as a whole was maintained. As two members of the network have pointed out, "The bottom line is that networks who have the support of their communities can significantly influence the expenditure of public monies" (Takvorian & Haney, 1981, p. 14).

The Community Congress has changed with the times, evolving from a coalition representing alternative agencies to an organization capable of providing timely technical assistance to member agencies needing more sophisticated management. The organization's attention to the expansion of human service resources, while still important, has been combined with a focus on staff support, training, and consultation. The following list of some of the accomplishments of the Community Congress illustrates the scope of its efforts over the years (Community Congress of San Diego, 1986):

1971	Successfully advocated that public employment program trainees be assigned to community agencies.
1971–1972	Persuaded the United Way of San Diego County to open its membership to additional agencies.
1973	Provided agency staff with access to group health plan at reasonable rates.
1974	Advocated the use of new Federal Revenue Sharing funds to support local health and human services.
1975–1979	Provided management training to community agency staff members through the Training Trainers project.
1977	Provided twenty community-based organizations with administrative and organizational assistance.
1979	Provided technical assistance to reduce crime in eight San Diego neighborhoods through a consortium of agency members; trained workers in 30 community agencies to set up staff development programs; developed legal information pamphlets on issues affecting community agencies.
1980	Developed the San Diego County Foundation Directory to expand private giving to include community agencies.
1981	Trained 50 senior citizens as consumer advocates.
1982	Trained the San Diego County delegation to the California Senior Legislature.
1983	Obtained continuing Federal Revenue Sharing funding for local health and human services.
1983	Negotiated "at-cost" sales of computer equipment to local community agencies by the manufacturer.

1984	Provided staff support to the local Youth Services Network and San Diego County Human Care Providers Council.
1984	Assisted the National Network of Runaway and Youth Services in creating a telecommunications system.
1985	Successfully sought, in conjunction with local agencies, an additional $500,000 in resources to support local services.

Accomplishments in 1986 alone included convening conferences on such issues as the proposed federal budget, child care, and the rising cost of health care; publishing a bulletin to provide information on issues of interest to nonprofit agencies; securing community development funds in conjunction with the Black Federation, the Union of Pan-Asian Communities, and the Chicano Federation of San Diego County; obtaining funding to develop an alcohol abuse curriculum for workers staffing shelters for runaways and homeless youth; and completing a self-study of the role, function, and performance of the Community Congress itself.

The Community Congress's increasing attention to consultation and technical assistance may help direct community counselors toward the most useful contribution they can make to the helping network as a whole. Through consultation with other service providers, counselors can improve the quality and responsiveness of the help their clients receive.

Consultation

Consultation enables individuals and organizations to improve their effectiveness. Like counseling, consultation serves a dual purpose: helping consultees deal with immediate problems and improving their ability to solve future problems.

A widely accepted definition of *consultation* describes it as "a process of interaction between two professional persons—the consultant, who is a specialist, and the consultee, who invokes the consultant's help in regard to a current work problem with which he [or she] is having some difficulty and which he [or she] has decided is within the other's area of specialized competence." (Caplan, 1970, p. 19)

In practice, it is no longer necessarily true that only professionals engage in consultation. In reality, most members of the helping network find themselves acting sometimes as consultants and at other times as consultees: sometimes, they help their colleagues; sometimes, they ask for help. Which they do does not always depend on their formal roles or specializations; their practical knowledge of and competence in dealing with specific aspects of human behavior are far more relevant.

The process of consultation has several special characteristics:

1. *The consultee asks for help.* If a relationship between two people or between a consultant and an organization is to be termed consultative, participation must be voluntary. The consultee recognizes the existence of a real or potential work problem and requests assistance from someone he or she considers competent to offer it.

2. *The consultant has no power over the consultee's actions.* The relationship between the consultant and the consultee is cooperative. Just as the consultee chooses whether or not to participate in the process, he or she can choose whether to follow the consultant's recommendations or reject them. Though the two participants work together to solve immediate problems and to increase the consultee's skills, the person or persons who asked for help remains responsible for deciding what actions or solutions to implement.

3. *The consulting process is educational.* Often the consultee requests help to deal with an immediate situation. Yet, "the twin goals of consultation are to help the consultee improve his [or her] handlings or understanding of the current work difficulty and through this to increase his [or her] capacity to master future problems of a similar type" (Caplan, 1970, p. 29). The consultee may learn to work more effectively with a particular kind of client or a special kind of problem. Just as important, though, he or she may learn to be more proficient at solving problems and making decisions.

4. *Concentration is on the consultee as a worker.* To be effective, the consulting process must deal with the consultee's feelings, attitudes, and values. The relationship is similar to a counseling relationship, but the desired end result is different. The consultee's personality is dealt with primarily in terms of its effect on his or her work as a helper. The goal is to increase the consultee's effectiveness in this one specific aspect of living.

5. *The focus is on an external individual, group, or issue.* The long-range beneficiary of the consultation process is the individual or group to be helped by the consultee.

Although the consultee may learn a great deal through participation in the process, what he or she learns is intended to help another. Whether that other is a current client or a future one, the focus of a consultation is on that invisible third person who, though not present during the consultation, is nevertheless central to its content.

In general, then, the process of consultation involves two-way, equal communication between the consultant and the consultee, with the focus placed on a third party: the individual or group identified as the consultee's client. Consultation may focus on direct services or on organizational issues. In either instance, the consultant's role is advisory or collaborative; the responsibility for implementation belongs to the consultee.

Consultation with individuals A network of helpers may have more resources than is normally perceived. Instead of considering a small group of experts as potential consultants for a large group of potential consultees, helping professionals should recognize that every one of them has expertise to share and that every one of them might, at some time, need to ask someone else for assistance. What results is cross-consultation among cooperating equals, with the roles of consultant or consultee depending on the specific issue. Counselors routinely assist such diverse service providers as school personnel, police officers, correctional workers, and family service workers. Yet, in dealing with special situations, they must in turn seek assistance from these same professionals. Substance abuse counselors often act as consultants to educational institutions and as consultees of health care providers. These roles are reversed if the counselor needs assistance in setting up an educational program or the health care provider requires specialized information in regard to a patient's needs. Consultation is not hierarchical; it is a responsibility of all helping professionals to recognize when they need help from others and when they should give it and to maintain the links that can keep the network running smoothly.

Consultation often involves a dyadic collaboration, with the consultant assisting another helper with some aspect of service delivery. In most cases, the purpose of the consultation is to help the consultee gain greater skill or objectivity in working with types of problems he or she will face again in the future. Thus, the consultant might share specific information concerning the needs of certain client groups or the likely effects of specific behaviors. Rarely, however, does the consultant present solutions in a vacuum. The purpose of consulting is, rather, to improve the long-term effectiveness of individual helpers and their agencies. Whether the consultant is working with a coworker or with a colleague in another agency, he or she should facilitate the consultee's exploration of the problem, encourage him or her to actively search for alternatives, and collaborate with him or her in developing a concrete plan for resolving the problem.

A large group of potential consultees exists outside of formal human service agencies. Many people have jobs that place them in close contact with others or give them a degree of power over other people's lives. Access to consultation enables these members of the informal helping network to be more constructive and more sensitive to the needs of those whose lives they touch. It also enables them to handle many problems in the client's normal setting, without the need for direct services from an agency.

An employer who has just hired an ex-offender or a disabled person, for instance, may tend either to overemphasize the new employee's difference from others or to be unaware of real issues, such as the question of confidentiality. Consultation can help such an employer find a responsive middle road.

A teacher may encounter a student who has a unique learning problem or who behaves in an unusual manner. Talking with a consultant enables the teacher to devise, try out, and evaluate new approaches to the situation while becoming more aware of his or her own attitudes toward the child. A consultant's support may mean the difference between effectively teaching the child in a regular classroom or sending him or her to special education facilities.

Police officers, who are often the first to make contact with individuals or groups in crisis, can respond more appropriately if they have access to information about the psychological aspects of a situation and the most effective methods of communicating personal concern.

In these and other situations, the presence of a consultant can help community members deal with difficult problems in the settings in which they occur. If the practice of consultation spreads, many of these problems can actually be prevented.

Consultation with organizations   Because of their human relations skills, community counselors are often called upon to act as consultants within their own and other work settings, not only to help develop individual competencies but also to improve the climate of the organization as a whole. Through *organizational development,* they can help bring about planned change in whole systems.

The strategy for change in [organizational development] is to develop a process which will help the organization to diagnose its problems, plan ways to solve them, and implement these plans. . . . The strategy is to change the organization's culture from one of dealing with problems "as we always have done" to a culture that (1) takes full advantage of the human resources the organization has available, and (2) allows for a process to develop which will ensure that the organization can plan and implement needed change at all levels. (Burke & Schmidt, 1979, p. 209)

In addressing the ways in which organizations solve their problems, consultants can apply any combination of interventions, including (1) group process interventions, such as team building, laboratory training, or observation and feedback concerning group dynamics; (2) intergroup process interventions, including conflict resolution strategies, intergroup confrontations, and joint problem-solving sessions; (3) training programs designed to enhance organizational skills; (4) survey feedback, or the gathering, diagnosis, and dissemination of data about the organization; (5) action research, in which behavioral science technologies are applied to develop strategies for change; and (6) changes in the organizational structure based on consensus about the changes (Lewis & Lewis, 1983, p. 186). The key to defining an intervention as part of organizational development is not the specific strategy used but the democratic involvement of members of the organization who might be affected by potential changes.

Consultation with communities Community counselors also serve as consultants to improve the problem-solving capacities of community groups. Rothman (1979) has identified three basic orientations to the field of *community organization:* locality development, social planning, and social action. Distinguishing these three modalities can help community counselors clarify ways in which they can adapt procedures used in consultation with organizations to community settings.

In *locality development,* as in organizational development, various groups of people are assumed to share common interests that good communication can help them to identify. The role of the consultant is to facilitate that process, using such tactics as leading small problem-solving groups, planning and implementing intergroup meetings, or providing training in problem solving and communication. Seeing community self-help as a primary goal, the consultant concentrates on helping the community become the kind of environment in which people collaborate in identifying and resolving problems. A community counselor might use this approach to deal with the entire community or to improve the problem-solving capabilities of one segment of the community affected by the program's services. This process-oriented approach to the community would be used:

1. To encourage the development of self-help groups for service consumers.
2. To enhance community involvement in the work of the agency or institution.
3. To build more effective support systems for individual community members.
4. To generate creative solutions both to current problems and to long-range issues.
5. To enhance the problem-solving capacities of the community.
6. As a first step in readying a community group for social action. (Lewis & Lewis, 1983, p. 191)

Consultants taking a *social planning* approach to community organization assume that specific problems exist that can be solved rationally. Following this model, the consultant gathers data through research and makes substantive recommendations based on his or her analysis of the data. Community counselors use this approach when asked to assess a community's needs, to conduct empirical studies, or to make suggestions based on their knowledge of social or psychological systems. Such content-oriented consultation might be carried out:

1. When community groups have set clear goals for themselves and require only technical assistance.
2. When identifiable ecosystem changes might be important to the well-being of clients.
3. When agency plans will be affected by the results of local research.
4. When those sponsoring the planning process have the power, resources, and commitment needed to implement changes. (Lewis & Lewis, 1983, p. 191)

In *social action* approaches, a group within the community is assumed to be entitled to a more equitable share of available resources and power than it is currently receiving. The social action consultant sees him- or herself as accountable to this segment of the community, with the ultimate goal of the consultation to bring about a shift in power. The consultant's role is to facilitate the development of leaders within the group and to lend his or her expertise to the planning and implementation of political strategies. This approach might be used:

1. To increase community responsiveness to the needs of community members.
2. To enhance the feelings of potency and self-esteem among community members who might be unable to affect their environment as individuals.
3. To improve environmental influences impinging on human development.
4. To develop responsive local leaders.
5. To encourage the use of resources for services actually desired by consumers. (Lewis & Lewis, 1983, p. 192)

Whether the process of consultation is focused on individuals or organizations, its overall purpose is to make the help that is available to community members as sensitive and responsive as possible. Like community-based planning and class advocacy, consultation helps improve the effectiveness of a community's helping network.

Summary

Indirect client services are designed to make the environment more responsive to the rights and needs of specific populations. Frequently, clients who need specialized services possess some disability that might cause them to be stigmatized or devalued by the community at large. The act of becoming a client may actually exacerbate the problem by increasing the individual's feelings of dependence and powerlessness. When the community counselor works with clients who might be stigmatized, he or she endeavors to put the label or problem in perspective as only one part of the individual's total being, to end clients' self-devaluation, to bring excluded individuals into the mainstream of social interaction, to increase the power of the group to fight for needed social changes, and to increase the community's responsiveness to the needs and rights of the people involved. To accomplish these ends, the community counselor encourages self-help and voluntary efforts while working to make the community's helping network more responsive.

In self-help organizations, people dealing with common issues or problems make contact with one another, provide mutual support, and have the opportunity both to seek and to offer assistance. The fact that each member can act as a helper to others is key to the effectiveness of such groups. According to the "helper therapy" principle, giving help is even more beneficial to the individual than receiving it. Another key to the effectiveness of self-help organizations is their adherence to a common ideology. A good example of such an ideology can be found in the Twelve Steps and Twelve Traditions of Alcoholics Anonymous. The Twelve Traditions have helped AA to maintain its integrity as a self-help organization, while the Twelve Steps have provided guidelines to aid the recovery of individual members. Self-help groups also provide social support that can make up for gaps in the individual's natural support network. Because these organizations are so empowering, the self-help phenomenon has evolved into an important and rapidly growing movement.

Although many self-help efforts are focused on the ability of individual members to control their own lives, some have developed strong advocacy components as members have become aware of the external causes of their problems. A good example of the marriage between self-help and advocacy is the disability rights movement as it has been implemented by agencies such as the Center for Independent Living (CIL). CIL provides a number of direct services by and for disabled individuals, but the agency's staff members recognize that independent living depends as much on the environment as on the individual's skills and attitudes. For this reason, the agency has remained at the forefront of the disability rights effort, addressing such issues as community integration and accessibility in transportation and housing.

Self-help and voluntary groups form one part of the total network of caregivers in any community. For clients who sometimes need additional help, almost all communities possess a number of individuals, agencies, and institutions that together constitute a helping network. Community counselors try to improve the responsiveness of this helping network through such strategies as class advocacy, community-based planning, and consultation.

An example of class advocacy is provided by the disabilities coalition currently active in the state of Washington, where concern for developmentally disabled individuals evolved into a recognition of the common concerns of all disabled citizens. Accordingly, several statewide organizations concerned with issues related to disability are working to develop a broad consensus on these issues.

Clients' well-being also depends on the existence of a cohesive network of service agencies. Well-planned service networks involve service deliverers and consumers in planning and evaluation; coordinate the work of separate agencies; maintain an ongoing dialogue among government agencies, social planning agencies, direct service agencies, and community groups; and protect the rights of consumers. The Community Congress of San Diego is an example of a network that has helped to expand the financial resources available to all of its member agencies, while developing capabilities in training, consultation, and staff development.

Consultation among members of the helping network may, in the final analysis, be the best means community counselors can use to improve the effectiveness of the helping network in their own locales. Consultation serves a dual purpose: helping individuals and organizations deal with immediate problems and improving their ability to solve future problems. Community counselors frequently act as consultants to individuals, organizations, and communities, using a variety of methods to make the helping network more responsive to clients' needs.

Supplemental Activities

1. Understanding the process of stigmatization is difficult without actually experiencing it. Although you can never duplicate the experience of another individual or group, you can attempt, at least temporarily, to learn something about how social devaluation affects people. Choose one population, preferably one that you hope to work with professionally. Find a way to experience what a member of that population might face as a part of everyday living. Spend at least part of one day seeking services or relating to others as though you had a disability that you have not experienced before. Examine the differences between your usual interactions with others and the interactions you have when you are perceived as disabled.

2. Considering again the hypothetical agency or program that you have been creating, try to fill in the fourth facet: client advocacy. How would you go about making the community and the helping network more responsive to your clients' needs? What self-help options can you identify that might be available to this specific group?

Related Reading

BROWN, D., PRYZWANSKY, W. B., & SCHULTE, A. C. (1987). *Psychological consultation: Introduction to theory and practice.* Boston: Allyn & Bacon.

CAPLAN, G. (1970). *The theory and practice of mental health consultation.* New York: Basic Books.

GARTNER, A., & RIESSMAN, F. (Eds.). (1984). *The self-help revolution*. New York: Human Sciences Press.

GOFFMAN, E. (1963). *Stigma: Notes on the management of spoiled identity*. Englewood Cliffs, NJ: Prentice-Hall.

JEGER, A. M., & SLOTNICK, R. S. (1982a). Part 3: Consultation as indirect service. In A. M. Jeger & R. S. Slotnick (Eds.), *Community mental health and behavioral-ecology: A handbook of theory, research, and practice*. New York: Plenum.

JEGER, A. M., & SLOTNICK, R. S. (1982b). Part 5: Social support networks. In A. M. Jeger & R. S. Slotnick (Eds.), *Community mental health and behavioral-ecology: A handbook of theory, research, and practice*. New York: Plenum.

KETTERER, R. F. (1981). *Consultation and education in mental health*. Beverly Hills: Sage Publications.

KURPIUS, D. J. (1985). Consultation interventions: Success, failures and proposals. *Counseling Psychologist, 13*, 368–389.

PEARSON, R. E. (1986). Support groups [Special issue]. *Journal for Specialists in Group Work, 11*(2).

RAPPAPORT, J., SEIDMAN, E., TORO, P. A., McFADDEN, L. S., REISCHL, T. M., ROBERTS, L. J., SALEM, D. A., STEIN, C. H., & ZIMMERMAN, M. A. (1985). Collaborative research with a mutual help organization. *Social Policy, 15*(3), 12–24.

RIESSMAN, F. (1985). New dimensions in self-help. *Social Policy, 15*(3), 2–5.

STANFORD, G., & PERDUE, J. (1983). Support groups and health care. *Counseling and Human Development, 16*(2), 1–16.

WOLFENSBERGER, W. (1972). *Normalization*. Toronto: National Institute on Mental Retardation.

References

ALCOHOLICS ANONYMOUS. (1953). *Twelve steps and twelve traditions*. New York: AA World Services.

ALMOND, R. (1974). *The healing community: Dynamics of the therapeutic milieu*. New York: Aronson.

BORKMAN, T. (1984). Mutual self-help groups: Strengthening the selectively unsupportive personal and community networks of their members. In A. Gartner & F. Riessman (Eds.), *The self-help revolution* (pp. 205–216). New York: Human Sciences Press.

BURKE, W. W., & SCHMIDT, W. H. (1979). Primary target for change: The manager or the organization. In C. R. Bell & L. Nadler (Eds.), *The client-consultant handbook* (pp. 192–209). Houston: Gulf Publishing Company.

CAPLAN, G. (1970). *The theory and practice of mental health consultation*. New York: Basic Books.

CENTER FOR INDEPENDENT LIVING. (Undated brochure available from the Center for Independent Living; 2539 Telegraph Avenue; Berkeley, CA 94704.)

COMMUNITY CONGRESS OF SAN DIEGO. (1986). *Accomplishments.* (Available from the Community Congress of San Diego; 3052 Clairemont Drive, Suite H; San Diego, CA 92117–6805.)

CULL, J. G., & HARDY, R. E. (1974). *Volunteerism: An emerging profession.* Springfield, IL: Charles C Thomas.

DEVELOPMENTAL DISABILITIES PLANNING COUNCIL. (1981). *State plan.* Olympia, WA: State of Washington, Division of Developmental Disabilities.

GARTNER, A. (1982). Self-help/self-care: A cost effective health strategy. *Social Policy, 12*(4), 64.

GARTNER, A., & RIESSMAN, F. (Eds.). (1984). Introduction to A. Gartner & F. Riessman (Eds.), *The self-help revolution* (pp. 17–23). New York: Human Sciences Press.

GOFFMAN, E. (1963). *Stigma: Notes on the management of spoiled identity.* Englewood Cliffs, NJ: Prentice-Hall.

LEWIS, J. A., & LEWIS, M. D. (1983). *Management of human service programs.* Pacific Grove, CA: Brooks/Cole.

RIESSMAN, F. (1985). New dimensions in self-help. *Social Policy, 15*(3), 2–5.

ROTHMAN, J. (1979). Three models of community organization practice. In F. M. Cox, J. L. Erlich, J. Rothman, & J. E. Tropman (Eds.), *Strategies of community organization* (pp. 25–45). Itasca, IL: F. E. Peacock.

SKOVHOLT, T. M. (1974). The client as helper: A means to promote psychological growth. *Counseling Psychologist, 4,* 58–64.

STANFORD, G., & PERDUE, J. (1983). Support groups and health care. *Counseling and Human Development, 16*(2), 1–16.

STEELE, R. L. (1974). A manpower resource for community mental health centers. *Journal of Community Psychology, 2*(2), 104–107.

STENSRUD, R., & STENSRUD, K. (1981). Counseling may be hazardous to your health: How we teach people to feel powerless. *Personnel and Guidance Journal, 59,* 300–304.

TAKVORIAN, D., & HANEY, L. S. (1981). Strategies for surviving funding assaults. *C/O: Journal of Alternative Human Services, 6*(2), 7–14.

WASHINGTON ASSEMBLY FOR CITIZENS WITH DISABILITIES. (1987). *Assembly consensus agenda results.* (Available from the Washington Assembly for Citizens with Disabilities; P. O. Box 2577; Olympia, WA 98507)

WILSON, M. (1976). *The effective management of volunteer programs.* Boulder, CO: Volunteer Management Associates.

WINTER, M. (1986, Winter). Disabled community: 15 years on the move with CIL and independence. *Friends of CIL,* p. 1. (Available from the Center for Independent Living; 2539 Telegraph Avenue; Berkeley, CA 94704)

WOLFENSBERGER, W. (1972). *Normalization.* Toronto: National Institute on Mental Retardation.

WOLFENSBERGER, W., & ZAUHA, H. (1973). *Citizen advocacy and protective services for the impaired and handicapped.* Toronto: National Institute on Mental Retardation.

Adaptations of the Community Counseling Model

The four facets of the community counseling model are appropriate to any setting in which a counselor might work. Regardless of the nature of the specific agency or institution, effective programs should include both services to individuals and efforts to improve the environment. Regardless of the kinds of problems being addressed, community counseling's main emphasis is still on fostering the development of personal competency and preventing dysfunction.

The community counselor intervenes in a number of ways. The precise nature of these interventions—the actual content of the programs developed—depends on the setting in which the counselor works and the needs of his or her particular group of clients. Since community counseling represents an approach, rather than a job title, community counselors can be found almost anywhere, in any one of a multitude of agencies and institutions. To make the approach more concrete and understandable, however, we have selected several types of settings to use as examples, describing the specific kinds of programs that might be developed in each. We selected these settings as examples because they tend to employ many kinds of helpers with different specializations and training backgrounds. In no way is community counseling limited to the settings described here.

In the long run, each community counselor must find the most appropriate adaptation to fit his or her own setting.

Community Mental Health Agencies

Community mental health agencies are usually responsible for addressing the mental health concerns of a general population residing within specific geographical boundaries. Agencies serving such specifically defined communities have the opportunity to develop well-coordinated services and, at the same time, to recognize and assist the local population in remedying detrimental environmental conditions. Community mental health centers can provide multifaceted services whether they are small agencies dedicated to outpatient care or major centers offering comprehensive services to meet a variety of mental health needs. Table 7.1 presents an example of a multifaceted program that community counselors in such agencies might implement.

Direct Community Services

A community mental health agency's educational programs should be accessible to the entire community and may have two distinct thrusts: (1) educating community members about mental health and (2) providing experiences that foster community members' personal development and prevent the occurrence of serious problems.

Programs in which mental health itself is the subject matter should be aimed at clarifying what is currently known about the factors that promote health and effectiveness in everyday living. They should help participants understand the interaction between individuals and their environments and help to erase the stigma that is all too often placed on people who have needed intensive assistance with psychological problems in the past.

A community mental health agency's educational programs should teach the dynamics of mental health and mental illness while defining the kind of contribution that the agency is trying to make. This can help community members set their own

Table 7.1 Community Counseling in Community Mental Health Agencies

	Community services	Client services
Direct	Educational programs on the nature of mental health	Counseling and rehabilitation programs
		Crisis intervention
	Preventive educational programs teaching mental health–related life skills	Outreach programs for populations dealing with life transitions or other high-risk situations
Indirect	Helping the local community to organize to work for environmental changes	Advocacy for groups such as people with chronic mental health problems
	Action on policies affecting community mental health	Consultation within the helping network
		Promotion of self-help programs
		Linkage with other helping systems

goals and become more actively involved in planning and evaluating the services being offered.

An agency's educational programs should also help community members develop skills and awareness that can aid them in their own development as effective human beings trying to create healthful environments for themselves. Community mental health agencies deal with relatively large, heterogeneous populations and have a mandate to try to meet all of their mental health needs. Particularly appropriate to such agencies are programs that help community members and the community as a whole become more self-sufficient in dealing with personal and interpersonal needs as they arise. Such programs might include:

1. Training programs that teach helping skills to community members. Such programs, offered on an open basis to individuals who wish to become more skillful helpers, can make effective help more readily available to community members when they need it and may prevent serious impairment. Such programs can also boost the sense of community within a locality, since, through them, mutual help becomes everyone's responsibility instead of the special province of professionals.

2. Group experiences that help community members develop better interpersonal relationships. Workshops or

ongoing groups can help community members deal with one another more effectively; such groups should be focused on development and education instead of on the remediation of existing problems.

3. Skill-building programs that help individuals live more effectively and deal with issues more competently. Many community members can be reached through educational programs presented in a large-group format or through a mass medium.

4. Education for everyday living. Programs may be most effective if they help individuals develop competence in meeting the issues they face everyday. Competence-building programs may be focused on specific areas such as family relationships or other issues that community members see as important.

Direct Client Services

Client counseling programs aimed at individuals who need or want more active intervention in their lives must be highly accessible. The concept of mental health must be interpreted broadly, so that agencies can offer assistance with any everyday problems.

When dealing with troubled individuals, community counselors strive to recognize and build on the strengths of their clients and do all they can to prevent the need for inpatient treatment. If an individual's problems interfere with his or her self-sufficiency or require intensive treatment, however, the counselor must work toward rehabilitation in accordance with the client's own goals. The community counselor has a particular responsibility to help former inpatients live and work effectively in the mainstream of the community. Thus, services to clients should include (1) assistance with any human needs that are interfering with an individual's growth and well-being; (2) individual, group, or family counseling; and (3) rehabilitation and reintegration into the community.

Counselors in community mental health settings can also recognize and address situations that put individuals at risk for mental health problems. Mental health centers have pioneered in creating outreach programs for people affected by such crisis-provoking situations as the loss of a family member, marital disruption, financial problems, health concerns, and life transitions. These programs have, in many cases, succeeded in providing temporary assistance and support, enabling individuals to deal more competently with the problems they were facing.

Indirect Community Services

Because of their close association with the people of their community, counselors in community mental health centers are particularly well positioned to recognize factors in the environment that are interfering with human development. They are also in a position to be aware of the strengths and resources available within the community.

When the mental health agency is an integral part of the community, staff members can assist community members in organizing to support their own goals. Citizens can, with the agency as a central coordinator and facilitator, organize to (1) plan services that can best meet the needs they themselves have defined; (2) confront political and economic forces to ensure that policies are responsive to community needs and that decision making is open to citizen participation; and (3) act to meet immediate needs such as adequate housing, sanitation, transportation, employment, and medical care.

Although mental health workers can support and encourage this process, leadership must come from the community itself. Community counselors' leadership can be important, however, in bringing about changes in the mental health system. Community counselors may find themselves acting as advocates for the general consumers of mental health services, fighting for the provision of health care in place of incarceration, for alternatives to institutionalization, and for policies based on respect for human dignity.

Indirect Client Services

Counselors working in comprehensive community mental health agencies are also in a good position to forge links with the total human services network. Dealing with the mental health needs of a local population, and treating clients as whole human beings, means working with a broad range of agencies and services.

Counselors in community mental health settings provide links between their clients and any services those clients may need. Good mental health requires that practical needs be met, and a client may need any one of a number of services to meet those practical needs. The counselor can serve as a first contact and coordinator, ensuring that the maze of services and facilities is reasonably clear and accessible to the consumer.

Because the mental health of an individual depends, to a great degree, on his or her interaction with the other people who make up part of his or her environment, the counselor, in working with any one individual, also works with that individual's family and associates—in fact, with any community members who might be contributing to the client's problem or be part of the potential solution. In working with the client's environment, the community counselor may act not solely as a link but also as an advocate.

Finally, the community counselor may act as a consultant, helping members of the helping network work more effectively with the people whose lives they touch.

Career Development Agencies

Many agencies have as their primary task helping clients through job placement, vocational rehabilitation, or general career development. Their programs are considered successful when their clients find work that is appropriate to their abilities, their interests, and their goals.

Yet, such agencies go far beyond their traditional image as places where individuals are merely "fitted" with—or perhaps trained for—new jobs. Effective career development agencies emphasize (1) helping individuals formulate and act on career goals and strategies, (2) helping clients develop the skills they need to enter and succeed in the work world, (3) working with employers to increase the job opportunities and support available to clients, and (4) working to shape policies that affect career development opportunities for clients and for the community at large.

The work of the community counselor in such an agency must, in fact, be multifaceted. Possible adaptation of the community counseling model for career development and vocational rehabilitation agencies is shown in Table 7.2.

Direct Community Services

Agencies focused on helping clients make career decisions should offer developmental programs that allow individuals to explore their values, goals, and occupational options before they face the crisis of unemployment. Group workshops are helpful and can provide much of the training that might otherwise have to be repeated in one-to-one counseling relationships. Participation can be open to any community members who might be interested, regardless of their current job status. Through structured workshops, individuals can examine their current work situations and lifestyles, explore their values and goals, and develop skills in problem solving and decision making.

Table 7.2 Community Counseling in Career Development Agencies

	Community services	Client services
Direct	Workshops and educational programs on career planning and work-related skills	Counseling, evaluation, and placement services Programs for workers with special needs
Indirect	Support of efforts to promote job safety and the humanization of workplaces Action against discriminatory hiring practices	Consultation with employers Linkage of clients with other services Advocacy for workers with special needs

Direct Client Services

A high priority must of course be placed on meeting the immediate goals of people needing training, employment, or rehabilitation. Counselors will always be involved in individual counseling, helping clients to evaluate their own interests and abilities, to consider the alternatives open to them, and to plan strategies for furthering their careers.

Direct services to individuals and groups should also take into account the strong personal impact that unemployment has on anyone affected by it. Brenner (1973), for example, has found long-standing correlations between economic changes and hospital admissions for emotional disturbances. Individuals seem to find sudden unemployment most stressful when they cannot point to broad economic trends as the reason for their problem. "The more an individual feels that he [or she] is among a minority of the economically disadvantaged, or the closest he [or she] comes to feeling singled out by economic loss, the more likely he [or she] is to see the economic failure as a personal failure, one due to his [or her] own incompetence" (Brenner, 1973, p. 236).

When economic downturns do affect a community, counselors working in career-related agencies can help prevent adverse effects.

When a social stressor cannot be prevented, the role of mental health professionals lies in mitigating the adverse effects of social stress. Monitoring the economic changes in a region should . . . allow the development of primary prevention programs. . . . These programs would aim at preparing the population

> to deal with the psychological ramifications of an economic downturn. . . . Techniques such as anticipatory guidance . . . could be used to persuade the about to be unemployed that their situation is not of their own doing. . . . They should not view themselves, nor be seen by family and friends, as failures. (Monahan & Vaux, 1980, pp. 22–23)

Counselors can be most effective in their direct work with clients if they combine this service with others, preventing work-related problems by addressing relevant issues before employment crises occur.

Indirect Community Services

The workplace is an environment that affects every actual or potential client of vocational agencies. Accordingly, such agencies endeavor to make the work world more responsive to the needs of all community members.

A primary concern must be the hiring, training, and promotion practices of businesses in the community. Combating sexism and racism in employment practices is an obvious and necessary part of any attempt to improve the work environment. Counselors should also be aware of unnecessary obstacles that may be placed in the paths of job seekers, such as screening tests that are culturally biased or that measure aptitudes not relevant to the job, or the denial of opportunities to ex-offenders, former psychiatric patients, or individuals with disabilities.

Counselors must extend their awareness not only to the hiring process but to what happens to clients once they have begun working. Counselors may not have the power to change the work environments of large corporations and bureaucracies. They can, however, lend their active support to groups seeking to improve industrial safety, to expand workers' roles in making decisions that affect them, and to make workplaces more suitable for human beings.

Indirect Client Services

Community counselors may act as advocates either for workers in general or for individual clients. Where vocational matters are concerned, client advocacy is most likely to be needed in instances of employment discrimination or other unfair practices.

In agencies focused on career development, as in any other setting, the counselor's concern is with the client as a whole person. Career development cannot be separated from human development, nor one's work from the rest of one's life. The counselor whose primary mandate is in the sphere of employment must, like any other community counselor, be aware of the interaction between the individual and the environment. In the employment counseling setting, the counselor should be particularly aware of those aspects of the individual's immediate surroundings that affect vocational decisions and the likelihood of job success. Because vocational development cannot be isolated from other factors, the community counselor often acts as a link, helping clients find assistance with matters not directly related to employment that may, nonetheless, affect their career development. In many instances, the community counselor may act as a consultant, helping others serve clients more effectively. Just as often, he or she may consult others to better understand the social, psychological, or physical factors affecting vocational development.

Specialized Agencies

A specialized agency is one that has been created to deal with a specific population or concern. Such agencies may focus on the members of a specific group (for example, women, adolescents, or the elderly) or on a specific problem (for example, substance abuse or family violence). Such agencies recognize that their individual clients may need a variety of direct services. Primarily, however, these agencies deal with those aspects of the environment that most directly affect the people they serve. The kinds of services that a specialized agency might implement are shown in Table 7.3 on page 220.

Direct Community Services

In specialized agencies, community services often take the form of courses or workshops that provide knowledge or skills that the particular populations they serve have identified as important. Women's centers, for instance, often provide courses on issues such as women's health concerns, assertiveness, self-defense, or career development. Agencies for the elderly may provide education related to health concerns, retirement planning, or social security and other benefits—perhaps even training for second careers. Youth agencies typically provide courses related to drug and alcohol use, sexuality, decision making, and life planning. These agencies should have close ties to the people they serve, involving them actively in setting priorities for educational programs and other services.

Community counselors in some specialized agencies deal with a specific area of concern on an everyday basis. This gives

Table 7.3   Community Counseling in Specialized Agencies

	Community services	*Client services*
Direct	Preventive educational programs for the community at large	Accessible counseling services utilizing volunteers and peer counselors when possible
	Training and skill-building programs for members of the population being served	Outreach programs for clients with special needs
		Rehabilitation services focused on independent living
Indirect	Efforts to change legal, economic, political policies affecting the targeted problem or population	Advocacy for the population being served
		Consultation with other helpers concerning the special needs and interests of the population being served
	Identification of aspects of the social environment that affect the prevalence or severity of the targeted problem	Linkage with other agencies and individuals in the helping network
		Linkage with self-help groups

them a special sensitivity to the issues related to that concern. If they work with individuals affected by a particular disability, for instance, they are very much aware of both the effect of the disability and the strengths of their clients. Knowing how small the differences may be between their own clients and the rest of the community, community counselors at specialized agencies are able to place problems or disabilities in perspective. By providing educational programs for the community at large, they can both help prevent the problem with which their agency is concerned and increase public awareness of the difficulties that those affected by the problem face.

Workers in drug or alcohol abuse treatment settings, for instance, often provide educational programs to the community at large, offering lectures and discussions to students at all educational levels, parent groups, and civic or church-related organizations. Such programs can play an important role in the community if they avoid scare tactics and concentrate instead on presenting accurate, up-to-date information on dealing with drug or alcohol use as a decision based on personal values; on correcting misinformation; on involving community members in the planning of preventive strategies; and on eliminating stereotyped images of substance dependent individuals.

Breaking through stereotypes is also important when providing information about physical or mental disabilities. Educational programs should help participants understand that people with disabilities are individuals with the same needs, desires, and rights of other citizens. Although educational programs can deal with the causes and effects of particular disabilities, and with the special needs of disabled individuals, programs should emphasize the community's responsibility for integrating all of its members into normal community life. Such programs can inform the public while enlarging the pool of volunteers ready to devote time and energy to building necessary bridges.

Direct Client Services

Agencies focused on the needs of a specific population can be particularly responsive to those needs.

Agencies serving specific populations often include among their services some kind of mechanism for helping people in crisis. One reason for this is that an agency with close ties to the community may be the first place to which an individual will turn in a time of severe stress. A second reason is that such an agency is uniquely aware of—and usually thus better prepared for—the kinds of crises most likely to occur among members of the population it serves. Thus, many youth agencies offer short-term housing and assistance to runaways. Women's centers have developed crisis intervention services for women who have been raped or battered. Many counseling centers serving gay men and lesbians have developed AIDS information hot lines.

Because they recognize the types of situations that tend to put their clients at risk, such agencies can also prevent crises by providing supportive group and individual interventions to help people weather life transitions and high-stress situations. Knowing what types of situations place their clientele in jeopardy, counselors in specialized agencies can provide timely and appropriate outreach. Ongoing counseling services need to be highly accessible, with peer counseling by members of the population being served provided whenever possible.

Specialized agencies dealing with a specific problem or disability also provide rehabilitation programs to help each individual become self-sufficient and live independently. Effective rehabilitation involves the whole person—in many cases, a whole family—and the immediate environment. The process may include services like the following:

1. Individual counseling on personal or career issues.
2. Group counseling that includes interpersonal, support, and skill-building components.
3. Family counseling.
4. Locating appropriate medical or legal services.
5. Help in ensuring that physical needs are met.
6. Locating appropriate financial resources and benefits.
7. Providing for equipment needed to enable the client to remain financially and personally self-reliant.
8. Assistance in selecting and beginning training or educational programs.
9. Placement in training programs or jobs.
10. Assistance in developing necessary support systems.
11. Assistance in finding avenues for recreation and positive social interaction.

The process of rehabilitation must be adapted to each individual's particular goals and needs.

The focus of a particular agency will, of course, affect the kinds of programs its counselors design. In an agency dealing with substance abuse, particular attention will be paid to training clients how to prevent relapses. An agency focused on individuals with physical disabilities will concentrate on helping clients maintain the greatest possible mobility and independence. An agency assisting people with developmental disabilities might emphasize normalization and personal care. These services vary greatly, as do the problems individuals and agencies face. What the programs have in common is that they attempt to deal with whole individuals, helping them make the most of their strengths and live as fully and as independently as possible.

Indirect Community Services

Working to change social policies is at the core of community counselors' work in specialized agencies. Through such efforts, counselors address whatever environmental factors affect the agency's clientele. Community counselors in youth agencies might focus on school policies or on the job and recreational opportunities available to young people in the local community; counselors in women's centers fight discriminatory practices and support women's rights to make personal choices without governmental interference; counselors working with the elderly may take a stand to help bring about solutions to urgent economic and health care problems. Agency workers may thus play a part both in broad-based efforts for social change and in efforts to deal with immediate, local issues. Further, community counseling agencies can be places in which local groups come together, learn to organize, and begin to actively seek solutions to common problems.

Indirect Client Services

Counselors should see themselves as advocates not only for the populations with which they work but also for individual clients. In the final analysis, public policy can make a difference only when individuals are aware of their rights and can act to safeguard them. Counselors often see individual clients denied rights to education, to needed services, or to equal employment opportunities. Community counselors can act on their clients' behalf if counselors are aware of clients' rights and willing to confront inequities when they occur.

Working with the whole person means that community counselors must be able to link clients with other needed services. They must therefore maintain close ties with other agencies. By staying aware of all the helping resources available in the community, counselors can help clients contact the most appropriate agencies and facilities for their needs.

Because community counselors in specialized agencies develop expertise in dealing with a specific area of human concern, they are often called upon to act as consultants to other helpers. By sharing their knowledge of the specific problems and special needs of the populations they serve, they help to make the human services network more responsive to those populations.

The goal of specialized agencies is to enhance the strength and resources of the clients they serve while also making the environment more conducive to their personal growth. A major factor in the client's struggle for independence involves independence from professional helpers themselves. Accordingly, part of the counselor's job should be to encourage the formation of self-help groups that allow individuals with common problems to help one another and, at the same time, themselves. Such groups allow individuals to receive the assistance they need, to grow as human beings through the process of assisting others, and to develop relationships with successful and productive people.

Community Counseling in Business and Industry

Counseling programs for employees in their work settings have become more and more widespread, with the number of consultants involved in such programs increasing rapidly. Counseling programs in industrial settings, normally termed *employee assistance programs* (EAPs), focus on helping troubled workers to return to their former levels of productivity. It is, in fact, because of their positive effects on employee performance that corporations fund and support employee assistance programs.

In the past, employee assistance programs have tended to emphasize treatment, rather than prevention.

> EAPs tend to be treatment-oriented. By stressing referral to professional assistance, an EAP is focusing on activity designed to get the employee's performance back to an acceptable level. While there certainly is nothing wrong with improving the employee's performance, this approach neglects to initiate any activity to reduce or eliminate factors causing or contributing to the problem. The employee's "problem" (e.g., stress, marital, family, drug abuse) may actually be a symptom of the real problem or combination of problems, such as a boring job, improper placement . . . insufficient or too much job responsibility, undue pressure to achieve results, or lack of recognition for superior performance. (Hollmann, 1981, pp. 37–41)

Service providers could improve the effectiveness of employee assistance programs if they would concentrate on both enhancing employees' coping skills and reducing the stressors in the work environment. A multifaceted approach to employee assistance programming is illustrated in Table 7.4.

Table 7.4   Community Counseling in Business and Industry

	Community services	*Client services*
Direct	Stress management programs Health promotion programs Life skills training	Assessment, short-term counseling, and referral of individual employees Outreach programs for employees in transition
Indirect	Efforts to reduce stressors in the workplace Efforts to improve the organizational climate	Consultation and training for supervisors Linkage with the local helping network Promotion of employee participation in self-help programs

Direct Community Services

Programs based on community education models are well suited to business and industry. Such programs may focus specifically on stress management. Murphy (1982), for example, reported on the successful delivery of programs teaching stress-reducing techniques such as biofeedback, muscle relaxation, and meditation. But any program that might normally be presented as a workshop or seminar, or in a self-instructional format, can be presented at the work site, making it accessible to people who might not otherwise attend skill-building programs. Examples of programs provided to workers during lunchtime or after work include workshops on communication skills, parenting, alcohol and drug information, time management, assertiveness training, and preparing for retirement—some only indirectly related to job performance.

An employee assistance program can also form part of a company's total approach to employee health and wellness. "Increasingly, corporations are seeing themselves in the role of health care service providers for their employees" (Manuso, 1981, p. 137). When this corporate responsibility takes the form of health promotion, instead of just treatment and rehabilitation, the employee assistance program can complement fitness programs in improving the physical and psychological well-being of employees.

Direct Client Services

Counseling services constitute a major part of the employee assistance effort in any company. Normally, counseling provided at the work site is limited to short-term assistance in problem solving, decision making, or coping with situational stressors. If more assistance is needed, employees are referred to community agencies. The EAP thus serves as "a method for disentangling employee problems from routine personnel concerns" (Sonnenstuhl & O'Donnell, 1980, p. 35).

In counseling, an employee may focus on alcohol or drug abuse, family conflicts, stress, interpersonal difficulties, or legal or financial crises. Help offered in the employment context can be particularly timely. As long as they know their use of the service will be held in confidence, employees are more likely to seek assistance through an accessible service provided free of charge by their employers than through an agency that they assume is meant for people with serious problems.

Counselors sensitive to organizational factors can also reach out to employees facing job-related transitions or crises. A transition may involve joining the organization, promotion, relocation, retirement, a change in the organization's structure, or the threat of job loss. Regardless of the nature of the transition, employees may need help exerting control and taking responsibility for themselves. They may also need stronger support systems. In their workshops for employees in transition, Leibowitz and Schlossberg (1982) try to ensure that employees receive three types of support: (1) support from other participants experiencing the same type of transition, (2) support from the workshop facilitators, and (3) support from employees who have successfully dealt with similar transitions in the past. Of course, the nature of the transition and the characteristics of the employees must dictate the type of counseling strategy utilized. In general, however, effective outreach strategies share several common characteristics. They:

1. Demonstrate the organization's commitment to assist in the transition.
2. Use whatever sources of support are available, including peers, counselors, and models of successful coping.
3. Give affected employees maximum opportunities to help themselves and one another.
4. Provide information concerning the characteristics of the new role or situation.
5. Assist employees in self-assessment, goal setting, and strategy formulation. (Lewis & Lewis, 1986, p. 179)

Indirect Community Services

The organization of a company may itself contribute to the development of stress-related problems among employees. Among the most common stressors on the job are role conflict, role ambiguity, work overload, responsibility for the activities of other people, career development problems, and physical factors (Ivancevich & Matteson, 1980). The general organizational climate may also affect employees' well-being. Of particular importance is the degree of social support available to employees in the work setting. Even in the presence of severe stress, social support in the workplace can have a buffering effect. "If social support is to be effective in reducing stress, preventing health problems, and increasing workers' ability to adapt to the irreducible stresses at work, all people must be able to obtain support from the persons with whom they routinely work—superiors, subordinates, and co-workers or colleagues" (House, 1981, p. 120).

Employee assistance counselors, like other community counselors, can attempt to make the environment as a whole less stressful and more conducive to the health of employees.

> Employee assistance counselors can have a major impact on organizational efforts to enhance social support systems and decrease environmental stressors. Because they see the victims of stress every day, they tend to be among the first to recognize problem areas. Moreover, they have the kinds of human relations skills that are needed to bring about positive changes in the work environment. . . . Efforts to change the way an organization addresses its problems can take a number of forms, including intervening in group processes, developing conflict resolution strategies, conducting training programs, gathering and sharing diagnostic data about the work environment, and suggesting changes in the organizational structure. All of these activities should be seen as part of the effective EAP consultant's role. (Lewis & Lewis, 1986, pp. 148–149)

Indirect Client Services

A counseling program in the work setting can offer an alternative to disciplinary measures, but only if supervisors know how to use it. A major focus of indirect service delivery is supervisory training. Counselors in virtually all employee assistance programs provide training for managers and line supervisors, teaching them to recognize incipient employee problems, to confront issues directly while facilitating communication, and to make appropriate referrals. An effective supervisory training program makes the organization more responsive to the needs of employees facing either personal or work-related problems.

The counselor also provides a link between troubled employees and the local helping network. When an individual needs social, psychological, medical, or other services, the counselor indentifies and contacts the appropriate service system, and even acts as a personal advocate when needed.

The counselor can obviously be a more effective link if he or she is familiar with all of the options for help available in the community. A high priority should be placed on finding options that cause the least disruption in the client's life and offer the greatest opportunity for the client to help him- or herself. Lewis & Lewis (1986), have suggested the following guidelines:

1. Locate and use self-help options available in the community. . . .
2. Develop a personal knowledge of local resources. . . .
3. Develop a method for evaluating local services. . . .
4. Offer objective choices to each client. . . .
5. Provide ongoing linkage between the client and the helping network. (pp. 82–85)

The counselor who is familiar with the issues affecting individual employees as well as knowledgeable about the company and the local community can provide the kind of consultation needed to ensure that systems work for troubled employees, not against them.

Educational Settings

Counselors who work in educational institutions rather than agencies can still be considered community counselors. School counselors, in fact, are responsible to two separate but interlinked communities: that of the school itself and that of the neighborhood or district in which the school is located.

We have defined community as a system of interdependent persons, groups, and organizations that meets the individual's primary needs, affects the individual's daily life, and acts as intermediary between the individual and the society as a whole. The school or college, then, functions as a community. Accordingly, counselors have a responsibility to deal with the school environment as it affects the people who work and study there. Because the school also belongs to a larger community, counselors must deal with that community, too; in particular, they must form ties with its helping resources and provide assistance to community members who are also parents.

In an educational setting, perhaps more than in any other kind of agency or institution, community counselors can create programs that promote human growth and development instead of concentrating on the remediation of existing problems. The very environment of the school community offers a counselor the possibility of concentrating on no other goal but creating the best possible setting for learning and growth. The community counselor's task is to make that potential a reality, both by providing dynamic, nurturing programs for students and community members and by improving the environment in ways conducive to learning.

As in other settings, community counselors create and implement the following services:

1. Direct community services that provide developmental learning experiences for students and community members.
2. Direct clients services that provide special experiences, such as individual and group counseling, for students or community members.
3. Indirect community services aimed at improving the learning environment within the school as a whole.

4. Indirect client services aimed at making both the school and the community more responsive to the needs of individual students who might be at risk for dysfunction.

All four facets of community counseling can be adapted to meet the special needs of elementary and secondary schools and institutions of higher education.

Elementary and Secondary Schools

Elementary and secondary schools touch the lives of all of our citizens. Free, compulsory public education means that most individuals in our culture have experienced schooling at some time in their lives. It also means that the school is a central, recognized institution in virtually every community.

The central role educational settings play in our culture gives community counselors in elementary and secondary schools a unique opportunity to affect their world. It also presents the difficult challenge of meeting diverse needs in a variety of ways. Counselors can begin to meet that challenge by taking a multifaceted approach to the task of school counseling. Table 7.5 shows the kind of program such an approach might yield.

Table 7.5 Community Counseling in Elementary and Secondary Schools

	Community services	Client services
Direct	Educational programs for students on issues such as career development, interpersonal skills, value clarification, problem solving, and health and family issues	Individual and group counseling
		Peer counseling
		Outreach to children in high-risk situations
	Community and parent education	
Indirect	Action on social policies affecting children and youth	Consultation with school personnel and members of the community's helping network
	Efforts to improve the school's learning environment	Linkage with community agencies
		Child advocacy

Direct community services   Direct community services are intended to provide opportunities to grow and learn to a broad range of individuals, not just to those who need special services. In schools, such programs can be offered to the community at large. Schools possess a unique combination of human and physical resources that, if allowed, the community can use to meet the educational needs of adult citizens. Schools can provide leadership in planning innovative educational programs, can respond to the requests of community members themselves, and can place special emphasis on creating learning situations for adults likely to, in turn, affect the lives of children.

During the school day, students must have the chance to develop personally as well as academically. Schools that treat students as whole people offer a curriculum that allows students to learn about themselves and their relationships with others. In some instances, community counselors may create and implement special programs available to any student who wishes to participate. More often, however, efforts to promote personal awareness and the development of skills are integrated into the general curriculum. Community counselors can use a number of strategies, including the following:

1. Going into classrooms themselves, both to teach and to demonstrate skills to teachers.
2. Helping teachers select appropriate materials and plan and implement new programs.
3. Providing assistance in working new subject areas into the curriculum.
4. Using resources from the community to enhance the school's educational programs.
5. Encouraging and supporting teachers in their attempts to create new learning experiences adapted to the needs of their students.
6. Helping groups of students develop educational programs in accordance with their own goals.

These kinds of strategies are introducing students to many aspects of the human condition—aspects that previously often went unmentioned. School counselors are involved in programs related to AIDS education (Brutvan & Mejta, 1987), alcohol-abuse prevention (Spoth & Rosenthal, 1980), social problem solving (Alpert & Rosenfield, 1981), assertiveness (Jean-Grant, 1980), premarital education (Martin, Gawinski, Medler, & Eddy, 1981), democratic values (Hayes, 1982), moral development (Kohlberg, 1981; Mosher, 1980), and affective education (Dinkmeyer & Dinkmeyer, 1980). Topics such as career development, personal and interpersonal understanding, value clarification, decision making, and intergroup relationships are now as much a part of many schools' curricula as any subject matter or academic discipline.

Educating parents is also central to community counselors' work in elementary and secondary schools. Although many schools serve as centers for adult education, offering community members a variety of learning experiences, major emphasis should be placed on education that promotes effective parenting. Community counselors in many schools participate in planning and implementing courses or study groups designed to help parents function effectively, thereby having long-range effects on the students themselves.

Working in groups gives parents a chance to share their feelings, frustrations, and successes with one another and to support one another in what can be a difficult process for many. Counselors should concentrate on developing programs open to any parent who wishes to participate, not just specialized programs for the parents of children with problems.

Unstructured, or loosely structured, group programs can be helpful, regardless of the specific topics being discussed. Several structured programs have been developed, however, that offer tested guidelines for implementing classes for parents. Many counselors offer evening programs for parents based on such structured approaches as STEP (Systematic Training for Effective Parenting), a nine-session program developed by Dinkmeyer and McKay (1976); STEP/Teen (Dinkmeyer & McKay, 1983); and Parent Effectiveness Training (Gordon, 1971). In developing educational programs for parents, as in developing programs for children, counselors and teachers can use guidelines prepared by others or create curricula to meet specific local needs.

Direct client services   For many children and adolescents, group experiences in the classroom will provide all of the personal assistance they want or need in the school setting. As they grow up, however, young people often encounter situations in which they need extra help and support. The option of participating in one-to-one or small group counseling should therefore be open to all young people, instead of being limited to those who have somehow been labeled problem students. Counseling should be a process through which the client can learn about him- or herself through self-examination, learn about the environment and its effects, set realistic goals, try out and evaluate new ways of behaving, and solve immediate problems while learning long-range problem-solving skills. This kind of process is particularly important to children and adolescents as they strive to find their personal identities and learn to relate with others. As they struggle for independence and individuality, they must develop their own value systems and goals. In the process, they must also contend with the immediate, practical pressures of family, school, and peer group.

Students have the right to expect that someone in the school setting will spend time helping them through these important aspects of their personal growth. They have a right to expect quick, informal access to a counselor, at least for short-term assistance with situational problems.

School counselors should, of course, set a high priority on being readily available to provide individual counseling and support when it is needed. Effective counseling tends, however, to create a still greater demand for the service. As this occurs, counselors need to look beyond themselves for resources to meet this demand. They can make counseling more readily available by training others as helpers. In particular, training students as peer counselors brings double benefits: not only are more helpers available but the counseling becomes more psychologically accessible to students. For some young people, going to another student for help is preferable to seeking assistance from an adult. Shared experiences and mutual concerns make turning to peer counselors for help easier for many students.

Whether the helpers being trained are students or community members, the training process itself is essentially the same. Potential helpers—usually working together in small groups—are generally given the opportunity to:

1. Discuss the kinds of issues they are likely to encounter.
2. Discuss their role as helpers.
3. Observe demonstrations of the helping process.
4. Evaluate the interaction they observe, according to clearly defined criteria.
5. Practice the helping process repeatedly, under supervision.
6. Receive feedback on their helping skills.
7. Give feedback to other group members on their helping skills.
8. Evaluate their own strengths and weaknesses as helpers.

After the initial training period, active helpers should have the opportunity for ongoing training and supervision, particularly as their participation in the actual helping process brings up new questions and concerns. If programs are to be effective and far-reaching, school counselors must be both accessible helpers and trainers and supervisors of others.

The school setting provides a prime opportunity for outreach to young people. Counselors recognizing situations that put children at risk for problems can intervene to offer support and help in solving problems. Family pressures, for instance, may make children vulnerable at certain times of their lives, making short-term, group interventions appropriate. Groups for children whose parents have recently divorced (Pedro-Carroll & Cowen, 1985; Stolberg & Garrison, 1985) and for children of alcoholics (Brown & Sunshine, 1982; Lewis, 1987; Morehouse, 1986) are examples of such interventions.

Indirect community services Counselors in school settings are intensely involved in meeting the needs of children and adolescents. This involvement makes them highly conscious of the degree to which the community provides—or fails to provide—a nourishing, responsive environment for young people. For this reason, it is often appropriate for school counselors to confront detrimental public policies and to participate in creating healthful alternatives. Counselors have often been active, for instance, in bringing about changes in police or court policies regarding youth, in sensitizing community agencies to the needs of children and families, in creating social or recreational programs for the young people of a community, and in encouraging local businesses to create meaningful job opportunities for students.

More immediately, however, the environment of the school itself must be made more responsive to the needs of the students it was created to serve. If, as is ideal, local educational leaders are open to change, the counselor can act as an internal consultant, encouraging the development of democratic decision-making mechanisms and improving communication among students, teachers, administrators, and community members. The counselor can play an important role in formulating policies and procedures to make the school a more responsive institution.

Unfortunately, schools as institutions are not always easy to change; sometimes, change can be brought about only through political action. Counselors, because of their unique role in the school setting, have several attributes that, if they recognize them, they can use as a power base:

1. A global perspective relative to a targeted individual or a group of individuals with an understanding of the targets' many environments.

2. A role definition and set of functions that are flexible, allowing counselors to readily adapt as circumstances require.
3. The opportunity to readily interact with targeted individuals and members of all significant referent groups.
4. Access to confidential information regarding targeted populations.
5. A role of gatekeeper as evidenced in information dispensation, placement, and referral functions. (Erpenbach & Perrone, 1985, pp. 4–5)

According to Erpenbach and Perrone, counselors can use their power on behalf of students if they recognize their power base, accept the responsibilities that go with exercising power, and use their power as a beginning point for gaining wider support. Positive changes that could not be accomplished by counselors alone can be brought about through the concerted efforts of counselors, teachers, parents, and other school and community members. A collective power base can begin to develop if counselors take the leadership in bringing members of various groups together to work on projects related to their common concerns.

The school environment can become more responsive and more stimulating when power is distributed widely and when many individuals and groups play an active part in decision making. The counselor can be key to initiating these kinds of processes.

Indirect client services   The school counselor is a key link between the school and local community agencies. Often, individual children need services that are more specialized than those a school can offer. Such services may be medical, legal, social, psychological, or vocational. In any case, the counselor can help locate the appropriate agency and then follow through by maintaining close communication with the agency to which the referral has been made. Such ongoing liaison is important because it allows the student's school program and the outside help to be complementary, with all of the child's helpers working along the same lines. The counselor is well positioned to coordinate this effort, working closely with school administrators and teachers, parents, and the community agency.

Community counselors are frequently called on to act as consultants, both within the school and in the local community. Counselors employed in schools are often considered knowledgeable about the needs of children and adolescents. For this reason, they are frequently asked to assist in developing community programs or services for youths or in training workers who are likely to have close contact with young people. Many school counselors, for instance, maintain close ties with local police officers who work primarily with youths.

Just as important is the counselor's role as a consultant to people within the school itself. Counselors must work closely with administrators, teachers, and other school personnel to make school practices and policies responsive to the needs of all children and to ensure that the special needs of individual students are met. Consultation is, of course, voluntary, so consultants to teachers must respond to the teachers' priorities. Teachers tend to ask for help in dealing with individual children, immediate problems, or special situations. Often, however, this can lead to opportunities to help the teacher create a more effective learning environment for all his or her students. Through consultation, teachers can be helped to examine their current practices, generate new ideas, consider their alternatives, and select and evaluate new plans for action. Consultants cannot solve their consultees' problems. They can, however, help teachers examine the values, goals, and behaviors that they bring to their relationships with young people.

In consultation, the consultee is assumed to be willing to learn and to change. The counselor cannot always wait for such willingness, however. Often, an individual child or group of children will need an advocate to initiate change. Children are often powerless to bring about changes in their own environments; they then need advocates who can either pave the way for the creation of beneficial services or halt policies or practices that may be detrimental to their development. Counselors in school settings have a dual responsibility: to help young people develop into healthy, independent, mature adults and to work toward an environment that nurtures growth and creativity.

Colleges and Universities

In higher education, two long-standing traditions are gradually being eliminated.

The first tradition is that of considering the university an island in the midst of a community, isolated from the life of the town or city surrounding the campus. This tradition is crumbling, both as college personnel and students reach out to the world around them and as community members' interest in higher education and its role in community life grows. That significant movement has been made toward integrating institutions of higher learning into their local communities is evidenced by the growth of community colleges, whose very name suggests a new role and a new mandate for higher education.

The second tradition involves treating the college counseling center as another isolated island—this one in the midst of the college or university campus. This tradition, too, is crumbling as college counselors search for new ways to reach out to the populations they seek to serve and make a real difference in the whole campus community.

Counselors at colleges or universities must now be true community counselors. They must treat the college campus as an environment that affects every student and staff member. They must also bridge the gap between the institution and the surrounding community. These tasks can be very complex, particularly in large institutions. The form that community counseling might take at a college or university is illustrated in Table 7.6.

Direct community services   An important area of community outreach on campuses involves helping groups of community members to examine their vocational and educational goals and make decisions regarding their career plans. Many individuals who would not seek assistance from a community agency might be comfortable participating in a program connected with a local college or university, especially if considering the possibility of further education for themselves. Instead of simply recruiting new students, therefore, college counselors can help community members examine the place of education in their lives and make decisions based on their values, their strengths, and concrete knowledge of the options open to them.

Table 7.6   Community Counseling in Colleges and Universities

	Community services	*Client services*
Direct	Educational programs for the community at large	Outreach counseling
		Supportive services for specific groups of students
	Preventive, skill-building programs on issues such as stress management, career development, loneliness, and young adult transitions	Peer counseling
Indirect	Efforts to improve campus life	Consultation with faculty and staff
	Facilitation of conflicts between the campus and neighborhood	Efforts to make the insitution more responsive to the changing student population

Programs like this have been particularly effective in opening new doors to women, to individuals seeking midcareer changes, to retirees searching for new vocations or avocations, and to people in need of job retraining.

Brief courses or workshops can also be used to provide other kinds of educational experiences to community members. College counselors can actively try to assess local educational needs or respond to needs identified by community groups. When a community need or objective has been identified, the counselor can examine the resources of the college or university to determine how assistance can best be offered.

Most educational programs are, of course, designed to meet the needs of students. Making meaningful programs accessible to all interested students means moving away from dependence on traditional one-to-one counseling and using a variety of techniques to encourage individuals to help themselves. Great strides have been made at the college level in the creation of programs that use a group format to teach life skills and interpersonal effectiveness. Groups have become especially common for helping university students develop skills in decision making and career planning, with many centers offering workshops in self-assessment, decision making, goal setting, information gathering, and interviewing techniques.

Community counselors in higher education settings also work to develop workshops or seminars that focus on problems common among their clients. For instance, both Frew (1980) and Meeks (1980) have discussed the use of minicourses to deal with issues related to loneliness, both as pressing concerns on a college campus and as universal life themes. Barrow (1981) reported using intensive, structured workshops to deal with three general topics: (1) stress management and relaxation, (2) managing test anxiety, and (3) ways to feel more comfortable with others.

Self-instructional methods that can be used independently also seem particularly appropriate for helping college and university students deal with vocational and personal issues. Increasing numbers of students are likely to be exposed to such methods as interactive computer programs that facilitate decision making (Katz, 1980), taped self-help messages accessible by telephone (Thurman, Baron, & Klein, 1979), and methods using television and other mass media (Warrington & Method-Walker, 1981).

Direct client services   No matter how many preventive programs may be offered, many students will need or want individual counseling, and some will experience crises that call for immediate, intensive intervention. In the past, when counseling centers were isolated from the mainstream of college and community life, only a small percentage of students was ever reached. Outreach programs and crisis intervention make counseling services more accessible and more likely to be used by a greater number of people before they develop chronic problems.

Counselors in many colleges and universities now set up satellite counseling offices to provide services closer to the mainstream of campus life. Counseling is seen as a normal part of college living when counselors themselves are part of the scene in dormitories, classroom buildings, student recreational centers, and other high-traffic locations. Their presence conveys the message that participating in counseling is natural.

This message is underscored when counselors train others to act as helpers. Professional counselors cannot meet the total demand for services alone; they can, however, train others to provide effective help and thus expand the range of services offered. College campuses have provided much of the impetus for the peer counseling movement, with students in many institutions taking advantage of the chance to help others.

In addition to peer helpers, counselors at colleges and universities often train other members of the campus community, such as residence hall supervisors, health service workers, student personnel workers, and faculty members, teaching them to recognize potential problems and make appropriate referrals to the counseling center.

Indirect community services   Indirect community services are designed to make the environment more responsive to the needs of all community members. In the college setting, such programs address both the community in which the institution is located and the environment of the campus itself.

One important aim of environmental programs is to ensure that the college or university itself is a resource rather than a deficit for the community. Particularly when large, sprawling universities are located in crowded urban areas, the growth of the institution and the well-being of the community at large may occasionally conflict. Disagreements may arise around such issues as land use, traffic, construction, or the destruction of parks or homes to make room for campus development. Sometimes, severe conflict can be avoided by involving citizens in making decisions that affect their environment and, therefore, their lives. Community members will always be dissatisfied at some level unless they feel that the institution belongs, at least in part, to them and that policy makers will face the problems of the locality.

Community counselors trying to help college students develop competency and effectiveness cannot overlook the powerful effects of the institutional environment. That environment can promote human development or interfere with it, can support the institution's stated goals or run counter to them. Particularly when students are in full-time residence, the climate of the institution may have more influence on their development than any other factor in their college experience. The college is their community, the place where their needs are met, where they interact with others, and where they express their competence and individuality.

Institutions of higher education—particularly very large ones—can be impersonal and depersonalizing. They can allow students to go through their college years feeling both isolated and powerless. Counselors, of all people, must recognize and act on their responsibility for building a sense of community and finding ways to make use of the vast human resources that the campus has to offer.

Indirect client services In many colleges and universities, faculty members as well as students may feel isolated. Counselors can take the initiative in breaking through the barriers that separate people, if for no other reason than to bring to the surface the helping skills that many members of the college community possess.

In colleges and universities, even more than in elementary or secondary schools, academic and nonacademic aspects of the educational process have traditionally been separate and distinct. Consultation between counselors and instructors has been rare. But individual development does not occur in separate and distinct segments; students' academic and personal growth are inseparable. Faculty members, as well as other workers in the college setting, constantly interact with students. That interaction can be helpful to students as whole persons if faculty and staff are encouraged to view themselves as potential helpers. Consultation with faculty members can make them part of the college's helping network, able to recognize situations that require specialized assistance and to relate more effectively with all students. Promotion of this kind of attitude can make the campus setting more responsive to the special needs of individual students as these needs surface.

Counselors can also help to prevent many individual problems by recognizing and pointing out the need to make the campus environment more responsive to the needs of particular groups of students. Many colleges and universities are organized to meet the needs of a student population that is homogeneous in terms of age, culture, and academic background. But students are changing, and many campuses have failed to keep pace with the changes. Every institution must adapt its curriculum, student services, housing, and activities to make college life more welcoming to the rapidly changing student body.

Institutions of higher education are often very complex communities. It is difficult for those in power to respond to the needs of all the students and the community. The counselor can be a link, acting to facilitate communication among diverse groups and individuals.

Summary

The four facets of the community counseling model can be suitably adapted to a variety of agencies and institutions. In any setting, services should include both services to individuals and efforts to improve the environment; in any setting, the prevention of dysfunction should be a priority. The nature of a community counselor's interventions depends on the nature of the setting and the clientele, but the basic model remains the same. In this chapter, we have examined examples of how the model might be applied in several kinds of settings.

In community mental health agencies, direct services entail providing educational programs to community members to enhance skills and competencies related to mental health and reaching out to client groups at risk for psychological problems. Indirect services include advocacy on policies affecting mental health, consultation within the helping network, and the promotion of self-help options for clients.

In career development agencies, community counselors focus specifically on vocational issues using a multifaceted approach. Workshops and counseling programs address career planning and job placement; indirect efforts address concerns such as job safety, humanization of the workplace, and discriminatory hiring practices.

Specialized agencies also take a multifaceted approach to specific issues. Specialized agencies focus either on the members of a specific population or on a specific problem. In such agencies, indirect services address those aspects of the environment that most directly affect the people they serve, while direct services are aimed at building clients' resources. Special efforts are made to strengthen the client group by utilizing peer counseling and self-help whenever possible.

Counseling in business and industry—a rapidly growing specialization—can also be community counseling if multifaceted services are provided. Counselors in employee assistance programs can help prevent employee problems by providing stress management, health promotion, and life skills training programs and by attempting to reduce stressors in the workplace.

Because we define a community as a system of interdependent persons, groups, and organizations that meets the individual's primary needs, affects the individual's daily life, and acts as intermediary between the individual and the society as a whole, we consider schools and colleges to be communities. School and college counselors are, in fact, responsible to two communities: the school itself and the neighborhood in which it is located. In schools and colleges, as in agencies, community counselors focus on prevention and provide services that enhance the learning environment while strengthening the personal resources of students, parents, and community members.

Supplemental Activities

1. Now that you know how community counseling concepts are applied, you will find visiting another community agency helpful. Using the community counseling model as a guide, try to evaluate the methods used by this agency. Are the activities that constitute the agency's programs likely to be sufficient to meet the agency's goals?
2. Reexamine your own hypothetical program. Are the methods you have designed for reaching your goals appropriate to those goals? Having seen several examples of community counseling applications, do you see additions you should make to your program?

Related Reading

AUBREY, R. F. (1988). Excellence, school reform, and counselors. In J. Carlson & J. Lewis (Eds.), *Counseling the adolescent: Individual, family, and school interventions* (pp. 189–204). Denver: Love.

BLOOM, B. L. (1984). *Community mental health: A general introduction.* Pacific Grove, CA: Brooks/Cole.

ERPENBACH, W. J., & PERRONE, P. A. (1988). School counselors: Using power and influence to better meet student needs. In J. Carlson & J. Lewis (Eds.), *Counseling the adolescent: Individual, family, and school interventions* (pp. 259–274). Denver: Love.

HAYES, R. L., & AUBREY, R. F. (1988). Part 4: Expanding

career options for counselors. In R. L. Hayes & R. F. Aubrey (Eds.), *New directions for counseling and human development* (pp. 223–285). Denver: Love.

HERR, E. L., & CRAMER, S. H. (1984). *Career guidance and counseling throughout the life span: Systematic approach.* Boston: Little, Brown.

LEWIS, M. D., HAYES, R. L., & LEWIS, J. A. (Eds.). (1986). *An introduction to the counseling profession.* Itasca, IL: F. E. Peacock.

LEWIS, J. A., & LEWIS, M. D. (1986). *Counseling programs for employees in the workplace.* Pacific Grove, CA: Brooks/Cole.

PERRY, L. (1982). Special populations: The demands of diversity. In E. L. Herr & N. M. Pinson (Eds.), *Foundations for policy in guidance and counseling* (pp. 50–69). Alexandria, VA: American Association for Counseling and Development.

RICHARD, B. K., & BRADLEY, L. J. (1986). *Community agency counseling.* Alexandria, VA: American Association for Counseling and Development.

SHAW, M. C., & GOODYEAR, R. K. (Eds.). (1984a). Primary prevention in schools [Special issue]. *Personnel and Guidance Journal, 62.*

SHAW, M. C., & GOODYEAR, R. K. (Eds.). (1984b). Primary prevention on campus and in the community [Special issue]. *Personnel and Guidance Journal, 62.*

References

ALPERT, J. L., & ROSENFIELD, S. (1981). Consultation and the introduction of problem-solving groups in schools. *Personnel and Guidance Journal, 60,* 37–40.

BARROW, J. C. (1981). Educational programming in stress management. *Journal of College Student Personnel, 22,* 17–22.

BRENNER, M. H. (1973). *Mental illness and the economy.* Cambridge: Harvard University Press.

BROWN, K. A., & SUNSHINE, J. (1982). Group treatment of children from alcoholic families. *Social Work with Groups, 5*(1), 65–72.

BRUTVAN, E., & MEJTA, C. (1987, August 27). *AIDS education.* Paper presented at the Illinois Institute on Drugs and Alcohol, Peoria.

DINKMEYER, D., & DINKMEYER, D., JR. (1980). An alternative: Affective education. *Humanist Educator, 19,* 51–58.

DINKMEYER, D., & McKAY, G. (1976). *STEP: Systematic training for effective parenting.* Circle Pines, MN: American Guidance Service.

DINKMEYER, D., & McKAY, G. (1983). *STEP/Teen.* Circle Pines, MN: American Guidance Service.

ERPENBACH, W. J., & PERRONE, P. A. (1985). School counselors: Using power and influence to better meet student needs. *Counseling and Human Development, 17*(8), 1–10.

FREW, J. E. (1980). A group model with a loneliness theme for the first year college student. *Journal of College Student Personnel, 21,* 459–460.

GORDON, T. (1971). *A new model for humanizing families and schools.* Pasadena, CA: Effectiveness Training Associates.

HAYES, R. L. (1982). Democratic schools for a democratic society. *Humanist Educator, 20,* 101–108.

HOLLMANN, R. W. (1981). Beyond contemporary employee assistance programs. *Personnel Administrator, 11,* 213–218.

HOUSE, J. S. (1981). *Work stress and social support.* Reading, MA: Addison-Wesley.

IVANCEVICH, J. M., & MATTESON, M. T. (1980). *Stress and work: A managerial perspective.* Glenview, IL: Scott, Foresman.

JEAN-GRANT, D. S. (1980). Assertiveness training: A program for high school students. *School Counselor, 27,* 230–237.

KATZ, M. R. (1980). SIGI: An interactive aid to career decision making. *Journal of College Student Personnel, 21,* 34–40.

KOHLBERG, L. (1981). *Essays on moral development.* New York: Harper & Row.

LEIBOWITZ, A. B., & SCHLOSSBERG, N. K. (1982). Critical career transitions; A model for designing career services. *Training and Development Journal, 36*(2), 12–19.

LEWIS, J. A. (1987). Children of alcoholics. *Counseling and Human Development, 19*(9), 1–9.

LEWIS, J. A., & LEWIS, M.D. (1986). *Counseling programs for employees in the workplace.* Pacific Grove, CA: Brooks/Cole.

MANUSO, J. S. F. (1981). Psychological services and health enhancement: A corporate model. In A. Broskowski, E. Marks, & S. H. Budman (Eds.), *Linking health and mental health* (pp.137–158). Beverly Hills: Sage Publications.

MARTIN, D., GAWINSKI, B., MEDLER, B., & EDDY, J. (1981). A group premarital counseling workshop for high school couples. *School Counselor, 28,* 223–226.

MEEKS, C. (1980). On loneliness seminar. *Journal of College Student Personnel, 21,* 470–471.

MONAHAN, J., & VAUX, A. (1980). The macroenvironment and community mental health. *Community Mental Health Journal, 16,* 14–26.

MOREHOUSE, E. R. (1986). Counseling adolescent children of alcoholics in groups. In R. J. Ackerman (Ed.), *Growing in the shadow.* Holmes Beach, FL: Learning Publications.

MOSHER, R. L. (1980). *Moral education: A first generation of research.* New York: Praeger.

MURPHY, L. R. (1982). Worksite stress management programs. *EAP Digest, 2*(3), 22–25.

PEDRO-CARROLL, J. L., & COWEN, E. L. (1985). The Children of Divorce Intervention Program: An investigation of the efficacy of a school-based prevention program. *Journal of Consulting and Clinical Psychology, 53,* 603–611.

SONNENSTUHL, W. J., & O'DONNELL, J. E. (1980). EAPs: The why's and how's of planning them. *Personnel Administrator, 25,* 35–38.

SPOTH, R., & ROSENTHAL, D. (1980). Wanted: A developmentally oriented alcohol prevention program. *Personnel and Guidance Journal, 59,* 212–216.

STOLBERG, A. L., & GARRISON, K. M. (1985). Evaluating a primary prevention program for children of divorce. *American Journal of Community Psychology, 13,* 111–124.

THURMAN, C. W., BARON, A., & KLEIN, R. L. (1979). Self-help tapes in a telephone counseling service: A three-year analysis. *Journal of College Student Personnel, 20,* 546–550.

WARRINGTON, D. L., & METHOD-WALKER, Y. (1981). Career scope. *Journal of College Student Personnel, 22,* 169.

Managing the
Community
Counseling Program

Effective community counseling programs depend on thoughtful planning, deliberate organization, rigorous evaluation, and responsive leadership. In human service settings, management of a program involves developing a plan to achieve a desired outcome, organizing the people and resources needed to carry out the plan, encouraging the human service workers who will perform the component tasks, and evaluating the results. Clearly, community counselors must be aware of and competent in these managerial functions if they are to control the direction their programs take. Like other human service workers, they are "forced to choose either to participate actively in the administration of their own programs or to leave leadership in the hands of others who may have little understanding of the helping process. Many are being forced to manage their programs or lose them altogether" (Lewis & Lewis, 1983, p. 2).

Because community counseling programs are innovative and multifaceted, their management is challenging. Because such programs are based on clear philosophical assumptions, their direction must be controlled by people who understand their goals. Community counselors have little choice but to gain expertise in the tasks of management: planning, budgeting, organizing, supervising, and evaluating.

Planning

Community counselors base their work on the assumption that they should identify and choose among many kinds of services in the interests of meeting goals related to mental health. As Krumboltz and Peltier (1977) have pointed out, "The interview is only one tool in our kit. We need to begin looking at ourselves as change agents, concerned with discovering and applying the best means to help the largest number of people effectively, efficiently, and inexpensively" (p. 58). For community counselors, this means developing multifaceted programs. These programs, or sets of related services, are designed to respond to community needs. The goals of each program must therefore be based on the results of careful needs assessment.

Needs Assessment

The planning process in any human service setting must begin with a careful evaluation of the needs and desires of community members. Through this needs assessment, the community counselor attempts to determine what problems members of the community are facing, what resources are available to solve the problems, and what services could help to fill the gaps in the current delivery system.

Although the main objective in this process is to identify problems or unmet goals, the perceptions of community members concerning the seriousness of any situation must also be taken into account.

> Many conditions in society are not perceived as social problems. Only a few conditions become social (or community) problems for which policy is developed. For conditions to become recognized as problems, there must be a process of perceived, collective definition in which a given condition is selected and identified as a social problem. (Barton, 1978, p. 38)

Thus, counselors cannot identify problems in isolation. They must also assess the perceptions and values of the communities they seek to serve. If a need is defined as "the lack of a positive condition or the presence of a negative condition which affects

the health, social, or economic well-being of the community"
(Barton, 1978, p. 40), the community itself must define whether
each situation or condition is negative or positive.

A comprehensive needs assessment can use any one or a
combination of tools or instruments, including the following:

1. *Surveys:* Community members may be asked,
through questionnaires or interviews, for information related to their characteristics or needs. Such surveys can
be administered to all members of a target population or
to a sample of community members. Community counselors might utilize this method to develop new programs,
to update needs assessment data, or to reevaluate current
services.

2. *Community meetings:* The perceptions of community members can also be assessed through community
forums. Meetings serve two purposes: they reveal local
priorities, and they increase community involvement in the
service system. Such meetings may be formal hearings or
informal get-togethers. Often, meetings can suggest strategies that might not come to mind using other assessment
methods.

3. *Social indicators:* The community counselor can use
existing quantitative information on aspects of the community that might indirectly relate to service needs. Social
indicators might include demographic characteristics,
health and education statistics, socioeconomic variables,
employment patterns, family patterns, and other data.
Statistics such as the delinquency rate, suicide rate, school
dropout rate, divorce figures, or other data on problems can
help to shed light on possible service priorities.

4. *Surveys of local agencies:* Surveys can be used to
determine what services are currently being offered in the
community. Questionnaires dealing with services and
client profiles can help in identifying service gaps and
avoiding needless duplication.

5. *Interviews with key informants:* Local leaders or
informal caregivers might be able to provide information
concerning unmet service needs or community opinion.
This information can provide the basis for developing other
assessment tools, such as questionnaires.

Needs assessment tools provide the means for identifying
the priorities on which the program's goals and objectives will
be based.

> Assessment provides one important informational input to a much broader planning process that leads to (a) the selection of and priority setting among problems and target populations to be addressed; (b) the selection and operationalization of specific community program activities; and (c) the evaluation of these program activities. (Siegel, Attkisson, & Carson, 1978, p. 221)

Once initial needs assessment has been completed, community counselors can turn their attention to setting program goals.

Goal Setting

Setting clear goals may be the single most important task in managing a community counseling program. Program goals determine precisely what services will be provided: those that meet program goals will be included; activities that do not relate to the objectives that have been set will be eliminated. Providing a coherent set of services thus depends on the existence of clear goals, reached through a consensus among policy makers, service deliverers, and consumers.

The goals of a community counseling program should accord with the outcomes that are desired for the community or for clients. They should be systematically related to objectives that are measurable, realistic, and acceptable to all groups affected by the success or failure of the program. The desired outcomes provide the basis for all subsequent decisions concerning the nature of services to be delivered.

Decision Making

The difference between community counselors and human service workers having a narrower focus on services is that community counselors avoid what Odiorne (1974) called the "activity trap." When human service professionals become caught in the activity trap, their activity becomes an end in itself. "Having spent years mastering one class of activities, called a profession, [they] persist in practicing those activities, as learned, even when the objectives practically cry out for some other kind of behavior" (Odiorne, 1974, p. 7).

The community counseling approach, in contrast, depends on a number of different activities, all leading toward accomplishment of the program's goals. In making decisions concerning program development, for example, community counselors canvass a wide range of alternatives for service delivery, weigh the negative and positive implications of each, and finally make choices based on a reasonable search of available data. The key to this decision-making process is openness, with counselors considering innovative activities as freely as they consider familiar services, such as one-to-one counseling.

The following questions should be asked about each alternative.

1. Does this kind of service fit our program goals?
2. What resources are available for delivering this service?
3. Are community members and consumers interested in this service?
4. Do the potential benefits of this service outweigh the projected costs?
5. How can we measure the effectiveness of this service?

Once services have been selected, a plan for implementation and evaluation can be developed.

Planning for Implementation

Once the set of services to be delivered has been selected, planners can plan delivery. For each service, counselors must perform a series of specific activities to get the program into motion. Young (1978) has suggested that the following questions be answered at this point.

1. What are the major activities necessary to implement the methods selected?
2. Who will be responsible for performing each activity?
3. What are the starting and completion dates for major activities?
4. What are the basic resources needed to perform each activity? (p. 16)

A time line can be utilized to ensure that plans are carried out on schedule. At the same time that this initial plan is developed, methods for evaluation should also be devised. This careful planning process enables managers to carry out other management tasks, from budgeting through evaluation, more efficiently.

Budgeting

Developing a budget means translating plans into financial terms. Community counselors must be involved in, or at least understand, the budgeting process, since it brings plans into reality.

> A budget is a "plan of action." It represents the organization's blueprint for the coming months, or years, expressed in monetary terms. This means the organization must know what its goals are before it can prepare a budget. . . . All too often, the process is reversed and it is in the process of preparing the budget that the goals are determined. (Gross & Jablonsky, 1979, p. 359)

The budget is, and should always remain, the servant of the agency's previously determined goals and objectives, especially when resources are severely limited.

> During a period of growth, the absence of any clear understanding of purposes, plans, and resources may not threaten the survival of the organization—at least not immediately. Resources are growing. There is no need to deny support to anyone. . . . Next year there will be an additional increment of resources, which can be used to expand those activities that proved worthwhile without having to eliminate the ones that failed. (Behn, 1980, pp. 616–617)

When resources are dwindling, rather than expanding, the budget must be based on a clear understanding of the agency's mission.

The traditional budgeting process has always been based on the assumption of growing resources. Human service agencies have most commonly used a *line-item budget,* with expenditures categorized by function, such as personnel, consultant costs, supplies, travel, telecommunications, capital outlay, and so on. Normally, a budget request is made each year, with estimations of the necessary resources based on a slight increment over the current year's budget. In this process, expenditures, rather than specific programs, are usually emphasized. Accountability is based more on limiting expenditures than on accomplishing program goals, and current levels of spending are often accepted as a "given" to which the agency is entitled.

Reforms in the budgeting process have tied the budget more consciously to programs, however. *Program budgeting* involves categorizing expenditures by program area, rather than by line item, and holds programs accountable for accomplishing their goals. *Zero-based budgeting,* a related budgetary reform, requires each program to justify its existence in order to obtain funding. Decision makers judge each program according to its success in meeting agency goals, and existing programs compete equally with new sets of services. These budget reforms use cost-benefit or cost-effectiveness analysis to relate costs to program accomplishments.

Using complex rational analyses may be beyond the funds and technical expertise available to small community counseling programs. The idea of relating budgets to program priorities can be adapted, however, even without highly sophisticated analyses. A yearly budget may be developed using the line-item approach in conjunction with the plans for implementation developed as part of the planning process. Budget makers can determine the costs of each of the activities to be carried out, using these figures to make an accurate estimate of the costs of a program. These costs can then be integrated into the line-item budget of the agency or institution. If the plans have been reasonably detailed, the creation of a budget involves simply translating activities into dollar amounts.

The creation of an annual budget depends on estimates of both expenditures and expected revenues. Community counseling programs receive revenues most frequently through appropriations, grants and contracts, fees, contributions, or a combination of sources.

Appropriations, money allocated by the legislative branch of government, directly affect the support of mandated public services. Often, programs are affected indirectly, through contracts received from public agencies that depend on appropriations each year. Dependence on legislative appropriations means that an agency is subject to variations in funding due to economic stress or political changes. Planners at such agencies need to develop a high degree of sensitivity to economic and political forces to be able to make accurate forecasts.

Grants and *contracts* can be either from private foundations or from public funders. A grant is awarded to the agency receiving it to enable it to meet certain goals and objectives. A contract usually specifies the activities to be carried out in meeting goals and objectives even before a recipient is chosen. Whether funding is in the form of a grant or a contract, the funds are allocated to specific projects that meet the priorities of the funding source. Thus, if a proposal is made to a funding agency or foundation, the project will not be considered unless it meets the priorities and guidelines set by the funder. Proposals that meet the funding guidelines are usually considered on the basis of the completeness of the needs assessment, the clarity and attainability of the project's objectives, the suitability of the plan of action, the appropriateness of the budget, the stringency of the evaluation plan, and the track record of the agency seeking funds. An agency that uses effective planning processes can put those same procedures to good use in applying for earmarked funding.

Community counseling programs may also charge *fees,* either directly to clients or through third parties, such as insurance companies, Medicare, or public agencies. It is important for counselors in programs depending on fees to recognize that a fee structure tends to encourage direct, rehabilitative services and to discourage the kinds of indirect, preventive programs that form the heart of the community counseling concept. Fees tend to be paid for direct services to individuals, so counselors must seek other methods of support for innovative modes of service.

Contributions also add significantly to the operating budgets of most agencies. Such contributions may sometimes be restricted to use for specific purposes, in which case agencies need to educate contributors concerning the kinds of programs that can best meet clients' needs. People making contributions to programs may be unfamiliar with innovative approaches to human services, so public relations efforts need to make the public aware of communitywide organizational or educational efforts.

An agency's revenues can come from any of these sources. Getting funding from a variety of sources, however, can help to sustain an agency's autonomy. Eliminating one source of funding should not throw a program into crisis.

Regardless of the kind of funding involved, community counselors need to be careful to keep their primary mission clearly in mind. When funds become available, it is tempting to take on new projects, even if they do not fit the agency's overall goals and objectives. Yet continual implementation of projects that are tangential to the agency's mission or clients' assessed needs can move an organization away from its programmatic thrust.

Organizing

The way a program or agency is organized should also be based on its mission and approach to helping. When planning has been completed, an organizational structure is needed to facilitate the performance of the activities constituting the plan. There are tremendous variations in organizational design, and the kind of structure that is built can have major implications for the work of the community counselor. The organizational design indicates how activities are divided among individuals or groups, who makes decisions, how specialized roles and jobs should be, how activities are to be coordinated, and how communication is to take place.

Many agencies are structured along traditional, bureaucratic lines because their organizational designers are unaware of the alternatives that are possible. A traditional bureaucracy is based on a hierarchical chain of command. Each member of the organization has a clear, specialized function to perform; each individual reports to one direct supervisor; and each manager is responsible for the activities of his or her subordinates. In a bureaucracy, routine is important. Each employee depends on written regulations and procedures to provide guidelines for action.

If a human service agency is organized along bureaucratic lines, the tasks to be performed tend to be specialized, with one employee or department doing individual counseling, another doing community outreach, another performing managerial tasks, another doing consultation, and still another conducting groups. Members of the organization tend to become highly involved in their own specialty, and only executive-level managers have a picture of the workings of the whole agency.

Organizational structures based on human relations approaches are in direct contrast to the traditional hierarchy. In these more organic structures, freedom of action and widespread participation in decision making are encouraged. Instead of departmentalizing by function, designers tend to divide activities according to purpose or the population being served, so that each individual works as part of a team to determine what activities can best serve common goals. Control and power are shared, rather than centralized, and motivation is based on responsibility and participation, rather than just on economic rewards.

Human service agencies organized following human relations approaches tend to use task forces or teams to work out the problems of helping particular populations. Both agency employees and consumers are involved in policy making, and staff members participate in planning and evaluating their programs. Work is divided along project lines, rather than along lines of specialization. Individual service deliverers maintain an awareness of all of the needs of a client group, rather than identifying solely with a professional specialization. This approach to organization is more in keeping with the community counseling model, since it brings about consistency in the way both clients and employees are treated. Yet managing an organic agency is a difficult task, and people have to be encouraged and trained to adapt to a structure that is less familiar to them.

Many organizational designers find it useful to consider using parts of each approach. No one type of design is always appropriate. "Contingency theorists" (Burns & Stalker, 1961; Lawrence & Lorsch, 1967; Woodward, 1965) have indicated that the most effective type of structure for a specific organization depends on the contingencies that organization faces. Mechanistic, or traditional, forms of organization are appropriate when conditions are stable and efficiency is a high priority. Organic, less formal methods are needed when the organization must be ready to deal with rapid change or solve new problems. If the environment is in a state of rapid change, the organization has to have many points of contact with the external world, a good flow of information, and the flexibility to adapt quickly.

In human service settings, contingency theories offer a conceptualization that helps in determining the most appropriate form of organization. If counselors view themselves primarily as specialists who offer consistency in their services to a large number of clients, they can consider using a mechanistic organizational structure, which emphasizes stability. Yet this approach would be less useful for counselors attempting to deliver multifaceted services based on the needs and goals of the community. Counselors dealing with stable environments and steady funding can use hierarchical forms of decision making. This approach, however, would be too slow and unwieldy for dealing with sudden changes in the populations being served, funding patterns, or community priorities.

At best, human service settings are complex and difficult to manage. Many programs belong to not-for-profit organizations, which means that they tend to have intangible objectives and that rewards, punishments, and funding are not completely under internal control (Newman & Wallender, 1978). Even more difficult is the factor of professional commitment. Most human service agencies employ a number of professional helpers, whose training makes close supervision unnecessary but whose commitment to their professional identity may override their concern for the agency's goals. When professionals adhere to their traditional role, they sometimes fail to change with shifting consumer needs. Yet it is inappropriate and wasteful to attempt to force professional helpers into placing organizational priorities above what they interpret client needs to be. Kouzes and Mico (1979) have identified three domains in human service organizations: the policy domain, the management domain, and the service domain. Each of these domains has different goals and interests. No method of organization can work unless those with a stake in the agency's success can find some commonality in their goals and commitments.

Supervision

Community counseling programs depend on the cooperative efforts of a number of people, including service deliverers, support personnel, community members, and other participants in the helping network. The community counselor who wishes to improve the quality of service delivery must, at times, act as a leader, influencing others in the interest of achieving goals. The most direct and common form of leadership required of community counselors is supervision of less experienced service deliverers. The form that such supervision takes depends on the supervisor's leadership style, the supervisee's motivation, and the nature of the supervisory relationship.

Leadership Style

Many approaches to the study of leadership involve making distinctions between opposing forms of relating to others. McGregor (1960) described one of the most commonly used distinctions: Theory X and Theory Y leadership styles. McGregor's Theory X leader is one who assumes that people lack interest in work, lack intrinsic motivation, and try to avoid responsibility. The Theory Y manager assumes that people desire responsibility and enjoy having the opportunity to work, to create, and to work toward organizational objectives. The different assumptions of the two types of leaders result in different approaches to supervision. The Theory X leader supervises closely, controls carefully, and uses reward and punishment to keep employees in line. The Theory Y manager is more likely to delegate decision making and responsibility, and to encourage natural creativity.

Many students of leadership style believe that there are no pure types. Instead, leadership behavior may form a continuum, with the authoritarian, boss-centered, Theory X leader at one pole and the employee-centered, process-oriented, Theory Y leader at the other. The "managerial grid" of Blake and Mouton (1978) uses a two-axis model distinguishing between "concern for people" and "concern for production." An individual leader may have a high degree of concern for one factor, for both, or for neither. The most effective manager is considered to be the team management leader, who combines a high degree of concern for production with a high degree of concern for people. The two concerns are seen as complementary, with concern for people potentially enhancing their productivity.

Hersey and Blanchard (1982) also use a two-axis model but add the component of appropriateness to the situation. Hersey and Blanchard acknowledge in their "situational" model that different leadership styles may be appropriate in dissimilar situations. They distinguish between leaders who are oriented toward the relationship they have with their followers and leaders who are more oriented toward the task that has to be accomplished. The appropriateness of each kind of leadership behavior depends on the maturity level of the follower. Thus, a supervisor should use a task-oriented approach with people who have not yet developed expertise and internal motivation, a task-and-relationship-oriented approach with supervisees who need help in performing the job, and a relationship-oriented approach with people who lack motivation, while delegating responsibility to supervisees who are willing and able to accomplish their tasks without assistance.

As Hersey and Blanchard have made clear, the nature of the supervisor is only one of the components of the supervisory process. The motivation of the supervisee must also be considered in developing an appropriate leadership style.

Motivation

Supervising human service workers, like counseling clients, requires an understanding of the complex needs that affect individual behavior. The needs and drives that determine how actively an individual will work toward job-related goals have been examined from a number of perspectives.

Many managers, for instance, find it useful to think of motivation in terms of Maslow's hierarchy of needs (Maslow, 1954). Maslow's hierarchy includes, from lowest to highest: (1) physiological needs; (2) needs for safety and security; (3) needs for belonging, love, and social interaction; (4) esteem and status needs; and (5) self-actualization needs. The individual becomes motivated to satisfy higher needs only when the lower needs have been met. The relevance of this construct to work-related motivation becomes clear when one considers that lower needs are limited in the degree to which they can serve as motivators. When economic security has been achieved, workers can best be motivated through attention to the higher needs. At some point, workers can be motivated only if their jobs give them the opportunity to work toward self-actualization.

Herzberg (1975) also distinguished between different sets of motivating needs. Herzberg terms *maintenance factors* those aspects of the work environment that relate to job dissatisfaction. *Motivator factors* relate to the job itself and can bring about job satisfaction and motivation. Qualities like salary, job security, and working conditions can affect job dissatisfaction but cannot serve as motivators. The opportunity to demonstrate competence, to accomplish things, and to grow and develop serve as motivators for hard work and dedication.

Another motivator is the degree of fit between the person and the task to be accomplished. Individuals vary in the things that motivate them. Thus, some individuals are motivated by the need for achievement (McClelland, 1965), while others are more interested in having a chance to express themselves in the work setting (Johnson & Stinson, 1980). The effectiveness of the supervisory process depends on the goodness of fit between the supervisor's leadership style, the supervisee's motivation, and the work to be accomplished.

The Supervisory Relationship

Most community counselors act as supervisors at least on occasion, whether they are directing the work of volunteers, paraprofessionals, or less experienced professionals. Such supervision normally involves the following elements:

1. Providing encouragement and support for the supervisee.
2. Building motivation.
3. Increasing the mutuality of individual and organizational goals.
4. Enhancing the supervisee's competence in service delivery (Lewis & Lewis, 1983, p. 135).

All of these responsibilities contribute toward meeting the general goal of helping supervisees help clients more effectively.

The supervisory relationship itself must vary, not only from one supervisee to another but also from one time to another in working with the same person. The supervisory process changes because its nature depends on the supervisee's needs and developmental level, as well as on the supervisor's methods. More mature and competent supervisees need different approaches than beginners who are unsure of their own skills. As an individual grows in competence and self-esteem, he or she is likely to grow in independence as well.

Boyd (1978) described three stages in the supervision of counselors: (1) the initial stage, during which a working relationship is established; (2) an intermediate stage, during which the supervisee's competence is appraised and performance goals are set; and (3) a terminal stage, when the now-competent supervisee learns to work autonomously. As supervision proceeds through different stages, the nature of the supervisory relationship also changes. Littrell, Lee-Borden, and Lorenz (1979) have pointed out that the early stages require a high degree of activity by the supervisor, who acts as a counselor or teacher and directs the process. Later, the supervisee takes increasing responsibility for setting goals, while the supervisor acts as a consultant. In the final stage, "self-supervison," supervisory activity is no longer needed.

When community counselors act as supervisors, they need to take into account the maturity level of their supervisees. This can, at times, be difficult, since a supervisee may be highly mature and competent in delivering familiar services but unsure and inexpert in using innovative methods. Effective supervision requires sensitivity to the difficulty that service deliverers may face in adapting their work to changing client needs. Supervisor and supervisee can work together to determine what services should be provided and how much supervision and training the counselor needs in order to provide them. Most human service workers are motivated by higher needs, and seek self-actualization and feelings of accomplishment through their work. Good supervision builds on this factor and provides the kind of supportiveness that people need if they are going to use themselves as instruments for helping others.

Evaluation

Evaluating community counseling programs facilitates the decision-making process, providing useful data based on which counselors can plan new projects or adjust current services. Attkisson and Broskowski (1978) have defined program evaluation as being:

1. A process of making reasonable judgments about program effort, effectiveness, efficiency, and adequacy.
2. Based on systematic data collection and analysis.
3. Designed for use in program management, external accountability, and future planning.
4. Focused especially on accessibility, acceptability, awareness, availability, comprehensiveness, continuity, integration, and cost of services. (p. 24)

Although evaluation uses many of the same methods and techniques as research, its central purpose is to be put to practical use in program planning. Evaluation forms part of the cycle of management, from planning, to implementation, to evaluation, and then to replanning. Thus, evaluation helps in managerial decision making, brings about improvement in current programs, makes services accountable, and can even increase public support. It can accomplish these purposes, of course, only if the results are widely disseminated to policy makers, managers, service deliverers, consumers, and the public at large.

Comprehensive program evaluation looks at both process and outcome. The objective of *process evaluation* is to determine whether or not services are actually being carried out in accordance with plans. The objective of *outcome evaluation* is to assess whether or not services have had the expected impact on the target population.

Process Evaluation

Process evaluation assesses whether or not members of target populations were served in the numbers expected and whether or not the services provided were in accordance with the quality and quantity expected. The process evaluation depends on the existence of clear, measurable program objectives. Process evaluators begin by specifying clear, quantifiable objectives and developing management information systems that provide the data required for evaluation. When programs are being planned, the decision makers should specify the kind of information that will be needed for process evaluation. Then, appropriate data can be gathered routinely, through direct observation and service records, and from service providers and program participants. The information system should include demographic information about the community, data on clients, information about services and staff, and information about the resources that are available. Services can then be monitored, so that the progress being made toward meeting objectives can be easily assessed at any time.

Professional evaluators cannot carry out these procedures alone. They obviously require the active involvement of all human service workers, since appropriate objectives must be set and data must be gathered continually. If service providers are involved from the beginning, they can play a useful role in making sure that the objectives are appropriate and that monitoring procedures are workable. Service consumers, too, can be very helpful in planning and evaluation, since they are often well aware of any problems in the service delivery system.

Outcome Evaluation

Outcome evaluation assesses the impact of services, measuring the degree to which clients and the community have been affected by the program. Community outcomes might be measured by changes in the incidence of a targeted problem, while changes in clients are normally evaluated in terms of their level of functioning before and after receiving services.

The real goals of community counseling programs, which tend to emphasize prevention, are difficult to assess, since only a combination of many programs can lead to measurable differences in the prevalence of dysfunction in a community.

> Prevention research is faced with two separate problems. The first is to determine the effects on behavior of specific intervention programs. The second is to link proximal objectives such as effective behavior change (if the program was successful) with the ultimate reduction in rates for the end-state goals in question. . . . When the data are in on how separate risk factors can be modified, we would be in a better position to mount intervention programs that combine a number of interventions which would be likely to impact on the distal goal. (Heller, Price, & Sher, 1980, p. 292)

Thus, evaluating preventive programs might best be done by evaluating the effectiveness of interventions in bringing about client changes that can reasonably be expected to affect risk factors and, ultimately, the incidence of a disorder. For instance, programs that demonstrate effectiveness in enhancing developmental levels and competency can be assumed to affect real-world functioning (Sprinthall, 1981). A combination of many evaluation studies, measuring a number of client competencies, can reveal the types of interventions that have the greatest preventive potential.

At the programmatic level, outcome evaluation, like process evaluation, depends on the existence of clear objectives. Routine measurement of outcomes can be used to provide ongoing assessments of the impact of services. Criteria and standards can be developed to make any real objectives measurable. For many objectives, standardized instruments for assessing client functioning are available. In addition, measures of client satisfaction can be used, not as a sole measure of program effectiveness but in combination with other measures.

Of course, routine measurement of outcomes does not indicate whether or not the program or service was responsible for the change in the client. Community counselors can also expect to use experimental or quasi-experimental designs to gain more useful information about the efficacy of specific programs.

The most important aspect of any evaluation—whether of process or of outcome—is the need to measure objectives that accord with the real goals of service providers and consumers. It is always necessary to search for ways of measuring the real goals of those with a stake in a program's effectiveness, rather than to settle for objectives that are easily measured but less central to the agency's mission. As Carver (1979) has pointed out, "A crude measure of the right concept is far more effective in directing organizational activity than a precise measure of the wrong one" (p. 6).

Unique Managerial Challenges

The special nature of community counseling brings unique managerial challenges. Each aspect of the model has implications for the management of community counseling programs.

Community counseling programs use a number of services to reach their goals. As community needs change, the focus of services also changes, and service deliverers must adapt their efforts accordingly. The multifaceted nature of community counseling programs places a major burden on planning and evaluation. Goals and objectives must be clear so that the services selected are the ones that are most appropriate. At the same time, service providers must continually retrain themselves to act innovatively as needed. This requires broad participation in planning, as well as highly supportive supervision. Professionals cannot be asked to deal with constant risk and change unless they have been closely involved in the decision making at every possible point and unless they receive encouragement in their efforts to develop new skills. Community counseling programs virtually require a participatory approach to management.

The community counseling model is also based on the assumption that resources in the community should be discovered and heavily used. In accord with this emphasis on self-help and volunteerism, programs should be planned by task forces comprising both service deliverers and consumers. Efforts need to be made to provide effective supervision for volunteers and paraprofessionals, as well as for professionals, and to make all of these groups part of the planning, implementing, and evaluating processes.

Because community counselors deliver highly innovative services, they need to maintain vigilance concerning the central missions of their programs. Often, funding methods and reward structures support traditional methods. Managing community counseling programs often requires developing bases that support innovation and working doubly hard at evaluation and accountability.

Summary

Effective community counseling programs require effective management, and counselors should expect to perform a number of managerial tasks. The tasks of management in human service settings include planning, budgeting, organizing, supervising, and evaluating.

Effective planning begins with careful assessment of the needs and desires of community members. Using surveys, meetings, social indicators, and interviews, community counselors can begin to lay the groundwork for setting appropriate goals. Once goals and objectives have been set, decisions can be made concerning the most appropriate services or activities to be used in meeting the identified needs.

The program budget translates plans into reality by allocating financial resources for specific activities. Although the traditional budgeting process has been based on the line-item budget, reforms have tied the budget more consciously to program accomplishments. Even without using highly sophisticated analyses, budget makers can create a budget around the activities selected in the planning process.

Community counselors should be careful to keep the agency's central mission in mind, both in seeking funds and in establishing an organizational structure. Many agencies are structured along traditional, hierarchical lines, with each member of the organization specializing in a particular function. An alternative is to organize agencies or programs more organically, encouraging widespread participation in decision making. Departmentalization can be designed either by function or by the population being served. The design that is chosen has major implications for the kinds of services that are provided.

Since community counseling programs depend on the cooperative efforts of many people, supervision is particularly important. Supervision—whether of professionals, paraprofessionals, or volunteers—involves providing encouragement, building motivation, and enhancing competence in service delivery. The form that supervision takes depends on the supervisor's leadership style, the supervisee's motivation, and the nature of the supervisory relationship.

Finally, the cycle of management also includes evaluation. Comprehensive program evaluations aid in decision making by assessing the success of services delivered. Process evaluation attempts to measure whether or not services were provided in the amount and of the quality expected. Outcome evaluation assesses the impact of the services on clients and the community.

Although all human service programs depend for their effectiveness on good planning, budgeting, organizing, supervising, and evaluating, community counseling programs present unique challenges. Because programs are multifaceted, community based, and innovative, they require widespread involvement in decision making and vigilance concerning their central missions.

Supplemental Activities

1. Try to describe the behavior of the best manager you have known (preferably someone in an administrative capacity in a place where you yourself have worked). What was it about this manager that made him or her effective? Would the approaches he or she used in that setting be effective in a community counseling program, or would they have to be adapted?
2. Suppose that you had an immediate opportunity to implement the community counseling program that you have been designing. What skills do you have now that would help you manage your agency? What skills would you need to develop? Lay out a plan of action that would help you to develop your managerial effectiveness.

Related Reading

CONYNE, R. K. (1987). Section 3: Quality assurance. *Primary preventive counseling: Empowering people and systems.* Muncie, IN: Accelerated Development.

COWEN, E. L. (1982). Research in primary prevention in mental health [Special issue]. *American Journal of Community Psychology, 10,* 239–367.

COWEN, E. L., & GESTEN, E. L. (1980). Evaluating community programs: Tough and tender perspectives. In M. S. Gibbs, J. R. Lachenmeyer, & J. Sigal (Eds.), *Community psychology: Theoretical and empirical approaches* (pp. 363–394). New York: Gardner Press.

EGAN, G. (1985). *Change agent skills in helping and human service settings.* Pacific Grove, CA: Brooks/Cole.

GOLDMAN, L. (1986). Research and evaluation. In M. D. Lewis, R. L. Hayes, & J. A. Lewis (Eds.), *An introduction to the counseling profession* (pp. 278–300). Itasca, IL: F. E. Peacock.

LACHENMEYER, C. (1980). A complete evaluation design for community mental health programs. In M. S. Gibbs, J. R. Lachenmeyer, & J. Sigal (Eds.), *Community psychology: Theoretical and empirical approaches* (pp. 339–362). New York: Gardner Press.

LEWIS, J. A., & LEWIS, M. D. (1983). *Management of human service programs.* Pacific Grove, CA: Brooks/Cole.

LORION, R. P. (1983). Evaluating preventive interventions: Guidelines for the serious social change agent. In R. D. Felner, L. A. Jason, J. N. Moritsugu, & S. S. Farber (Eds.), *Preventive psychology: Theory, research, and practice* (pp. 251–268). New York: Pergamon Press.

NATIONAL INSTITUTE ON DRUG ABUSE. (1981). *Preventive planning workbook* (DHHS Publication No. ADM 81–1062). Washington, DC: U.S. Government Printing Office.

PRICE, R. H., KETTERER, R. F., BADER, B. C., & MONAHAN, J. (Eds.). (1980). *Prevention in mental health: Research, policy, and practice.* Beverly Hills: Sage Publications.

References

ATTKISSON, C. C., & BROSKOWSKI, A. (1978). Evaluation and the emerging human service concept. In C. C. Attkisson, W. A. Hargreaves, M. J. Horowitz, & J. E. Sorensen (Eds.), *Evaluation of human service programs* (pp. 3–26). New York: Academic Press.

BARTON, A. K. (1978). A problem, policy, program model for planning community mental health services. *Journal of Community Psychology, 6,* 37–41.

BEHN, R. (1980). Leadership for cut-back management. *Public Administration Review, 40,* 613–620.

BLAKE, R. R., & MOUTON, J. S. (1978). *The new managerial grid.* Houston: Gulf Publishing Company.

BOYD, J. D. (1978). Integrative approaches to counselor supervision. In J. D. Boyd (Ed.), *Counselor Supervision* (pp. 133–168). Muncie, IN: Accelerated Development.

BURNS, T., & STALKER, G. M. (1961). *The management of innovation.* London: Tavistock.

CARVER, J. (1979, September 8). *Mental health administration: A management perversion.* Address to the Association of Mental Health Administrators Annual Meeting.

GROSS, M. J., & JABLONSKY, S. F. (1979). *Principles of accounting and financial reporting for nonprofit organizations.* New York: Wiley.

HELLER, K., PRICE, R. H., & SHER, K. J. (1980). Research and evaluation in primary prevention: Issues and guidelines. In R. H. Price, R. F. Ketterer, B. C. Bader, & J. Monahan (Eds.), *Prevention in mental health: Research, policy, and practice* (pp. 285–313). Beverly Hills: Sage Publications.

HERSEY, P., & BLANCHARD, K. H. (1982). *Management of organizational behavior: Utilizing human resources* (4th ed.). Englewood Cliffs, NJ: Prentice-Hall.

HERZBERG, F. (1975). One more time: How do you motivate employees? In Harvard Business Review, *On management* (pp. 361–376). New York: Harper & Row.

JOHNSON, T. W., & STINSON, J. (1980). Person-task fit and leadership strategies. In P. Hersen

& J. Stinson (Eds.), *Perspectives in leader effectiveness.* Athens: Ohio University, Center for Leadership Studies.

KOUZES, J. M., & MICO, P. R. (1979). Domain theory: An introduction to organizational behavior in human service organizations. *Journal of Applied Behavioral Sciences, 15*(4), 449–469.

KRUMBOLTZ, J. D., & PELTIER, B. (1977). What identifies a counseling psychologist: Methods or results? *Counseling Psychologist, 7*(2), 57–60.

LAWRENCE, R. R., & LORSCH, J. J. (1967). *Organization and environment.* Cambridge: Harvard University Press.

LEWIS, J. A., & LEWIS, M. D. (1983). *Management of human service programs.* Pacific Grove, CA: Brooks/Cole.

LITTRELL, J. M., LEE-BORDEN, N., & LORENZ, J. (1979). A developmental framework for counseling supervision. *Counselor Education and Supervision, 19*, 129–136.

MASLOW, A. H. (1954). *Motivation and personality.* New York: Harper & Row.

MCCLELLAND, D. (1965). Achievement motivation can be developed. *Harvard Business Review, 43*, 6–8, 10, 12, 14, 16, 20, 22, 24.

MCGREGOR, D. M. (1960). *The human side of enterprise.* New York: McGraw-Hill.

NEWMAN, W. H., & WALLENDER, H. U. (1978). Managing nonprofit enterprises. *Academy of Management Review, 3*(1), 24–31.

ODIORNE, G. S. (1974). *Management and the activity trap.* New York: Harper & Row.

SIEGEL, L. M., ATTKISSON, C. C., & CARSON, L. G. (1978). Need identification and program planning in the community context. In C. C. Attkisson, W. A. Hargreaves, M. J. Horowitz, & J. E. Sorensen (Eds.), *Evaluation of human service programs* (pp. 215–252). New York: Academic Press.

SPRINTHALL, N. A. (1981). A neomodel for research in the service of guidance and counseling. *Personnel & Guidance Journal, 59*, 487–494.

WOODWARD, J. (1965). *Industrial organization: Theory and practice.* London: Oxford University Press.

YOUNG, K. M. (1978). *The basic steps of planning.* Charlottesville, WV: Community Collaborators.

Author Index

Subject Index